"Daddy, I want to be a policeman when I grow up."

When Edward F. Droge, Jr. heard his young son say that, he knew it was time to quit the force.

For Edward F. Droge, Jr. had wanted to be a policeman when he was a kid, too. And he had made it. He had done just about everything a policeman could do, won the citations and the awards, become a plainclothesman, and now when he looked in the mirror the last thing he wanted was for his little boy to become what he had become.

Droge did quit, and made it to California before the long arm of the Knapp Commission pulled him back to New York to work as undercover agent for them. He did that last job and then quit for good.

Edward F. Droge, Jr. knows better than any other man just what makes a good cop, and the pressures that turn him into a bad one. Now he tells all.

Other SIGNET Books You'll Enjoy

☐ **KRUMNAGEL by Peter Ustinov.** KRUMNAGEL asks the all-important question: Can an honest, law-loving, crime-hating police chief overcome the forces of weak-kneed liberalism and stuffy courts of law that want to stop him from using his gun as it was meant to be used—that is to say, every time he feels the urge? "Devastatingly funny!"—*Publishers' Weekly.* "Krumnagel is the antihero of the year!"—*Harper's* (#Y5238—$1.25)

☐ **FUZZ by Ed McBain.** A homemade bomb, a couple of fun-loving youngsters and an ingenious extortion scheme add up to big excitement. Now a major motion picture from United Artists, starring Burt Reynolds, Racquel Welch, and Yul Brynner. (#T5151—75¢)

☐ **HAIL, HAIL, THE GANG'S ALL HERE by Ed McBain.** In this 87th Precinct Mystery all of Ed McBain's detectives come together for the first time and they're all kept hopping. Some of the stories are violent, some touching, some ironic, but all are marked by the masterful McBain touch ... the "gang" has never been better. (#T5063—75¢)

☐ **THE FAMILY by Leslie Waller.** A marvelous blend of high finance, illicit romance and the Mafia makes THE FAMILY compelling reading. (#Y4024—$1.25)

☐ **SAM THE PLUMBER by Henry Zeiger.** The explosive real-life saga of Mafia chieftain, Simone Rizzo—taken from thirteen volumes of verbatim conversation overheard by an FBI "bug." (#Q4290—95¢)

THE NEW AMERICAN LIBRARY, INC.,
P.O. Box 999, Bergenfield, New Jersey 07621

Please send me the SIGNET BOOKS I have checked above. I am enclosing $_____(check or money order—no currency or C.O.D.'s). Please include the list price plus 25¢ a copy to cover handling and mailing costs. (Prices and numbers are subject to change without notice.)

Name_____

Address_____

City_____State_____Zip Code_____
Allow at least 3 weeks for delivery

The Patrolman:
A Cop's Story

by

EDWARD F. DROGE, Jr.

A SIGNET BOOK
NEW AMERICAN LIBRARY
TIMES MIRROR

Copyright © 1973 by Edward F. Droge, Jr.

All rights reserved.

SIGNET TRADEMARK REG. U.S. PAT. OFF. AND FOREIGN COUNTRIES
REGISTERED TRADEMARK—MARCA REGISTRADA
HECHO EN CHICAGO, U.S.A.

SIGNET, SIGNET CLASSICS, SIGNETTE, MENTOR AND PLUME BOOKS
are published by The New American Library, Inc.,
1301 Avenue of the Americas, New York, New York 10019

FIRST PRINTING, JULY, 1973

1 2 3 4 5 6 7 8 9

PRINTED IN THE UNITED STATES OF AMERICA

In Memoriam

TO MY BELOVED FATHER

EDWARD F. DROGE, SR.

12/14/08—2/3/73

WOULD THAT I CAN BE

BUT HALF THE FATHER

TO MY CHILDREN

THAT HE WAS TO HIS

For my wife, Joanne, and my three children, Christopher, Cheryl, and Kim, who deserve so much more than a simple dedication.

A note of special thanks and dedication from the author to the following (in alphabetical order), without whom this book wouldn't be.

All the great people in the Homeport who understood, especially John, Eddie, Tom, and George.

Fred and Diane for literally making their home my home and for countless other favors.

Marcia Higgins of W.M.A. for finding Michael Seidman for me.

Michael Seidman and the people of New American Library for taking a chance on me and my ability to write.

My parents, my in-laws, and the rest of my family for standing behind me when I needed them.

My wife, Joanne, for taking a course in hieroglyphics, necessary to decipher my scribbling, and for her excellence in typing the entire manuscript.

Pete C., Pete D., and Pete V., fine police officers, but, most notably, good friends before and after October 22, 1971.

The fine men of the New York City Police Department, especially those of the 80th precinct.

Walter and his family for enduring any pains they may have suffered as a result of my testimony.

CHAPTER 1

"... Think about it. If you decide that you want to listen to the tape, call me at the Beverly Hilton this afternoon, room 2320."

"OK," I said and he hung up. I stared out the window into the blur of the multicolored, sunlit garden, but saw nothing. I held the phone to my ear but wasn't conscious of the drone from the dial tone. I sat down.

Lou Daniels. It had to be the deal with Lou Daniels. If it wasn't, they were bluffing. All the others were regular contracts. Gamblers and hoods who have been paying the police for years. They wouldn't set up a cop. It had to be Lou Daniels. Dammit. God damn it.

I pushed the button on the phone down, released it, and nervously dialed the operator.

"May I help you?"

"Yes, operator. I'd like to call area code 212 ... 566-8661, collect, please."

"Your name, sir?"

"Edward Droge."

"Thank you, sir. One moment, please."

It had to be Lou Daniels. But I hope it's not. Oh, God, do I hope it's not.

"Knapp Commission."

"I have a collect call for anyone from a Mr. Edward Droge in California. Will you accept the charges?"

"Yes, operator."

"Hello, this is Ed Droge. Is Mr. Armstrong there?"

"Just a minute, please. He's been expecting your call."

She put her hand over the phone and, muffled, called: "Mike. It's Droge on 61."

"Hello."

"Mr. Armstrong, I've just spoken with a Mr. Foley out here and he tells me you would like to talk to me. What's this all about?"

"Did he tell you he's got a tape he'd like you to hear?"

"Yes."

"Well, that's what it's all about. That tape is one of many recordings we have of your conversations with a man named Daniels."

Oh my God.

"Are you still there, Droge?"

"Yeah, I'm here."

"You know a man named Louis Daniels?"

"Yes, I locked him up last year. Listen, what's this all about?"

"I think you know what it's all about, Ed. I think you better go listen to that tape and then call me back. Then, maybe we can talk about what I've got in mind."

"Collect?"

He paused and then: "OK, collect."

The Beverly Hilton is a towering building, located at Wilshire and Sunset, in the heart of Beverly Hills. It took about twenty minutes to get there from Hollywood. I parked in the guests' parking compound and walked briskly up the arched roadway entrance and into the lobby. He was to be wearing a brown suit. I didn't see him. Ten minutes passed and ...

"Ed?" came a voice from behind.

Turning, I saw a well-dressed, Irish-looking man in his thirties, holding an oversized attaché case. "Mr. Foley?"

"Yes. Come on, let's go upstairs."

We took the elevator to the twenty-third floor, stepped out onto a plush red carpet, walked the length of the corridor, and entered 2320.

"Have a seat, Ed," he said as he lifted a tape recorder from the floor near the bed to a table by my chair. "What did Mike Armstrong have to say?"

"He just told me that it would be to my benefit to listen to this tape."

"Did he tell you what's on it?"

"No," I lied.

"This is one of the tapes of a few telephone conversations you had with a man you arrested named Louis Daniels. The reason we want you to hear it is ... well, why don't you listen to it first and then we can talk about it." By this time he had taken a reel of tape from his pocket and set it up in the recorder. He pushed the "play" button and for a while there was nothing. Lou Daniels's arrest flashed into my mind.

"Looking for a bust tonight, Ed?" quizzed a weasel-like countenance, covered by an overly long-brimmed "Clyde."

"What have you got, Roger?" I asked the usually reliable informant. The night was biting and I contemplated the warmth of the station house. An arrest would enable me to elude the winter of 1970 for at least a few hours.

"Right around the corner in 1314," he replied. " 'Big Lou' Daniels."

The name rang a bell. "Wasn't he just busted last month ... for sale?"

"Yeah, Shula grabbed him, but he's right back at it again. Too much money in it to stop. And besides, what's the big deal? Lately you're out the next day, if not sooner, anyhow." He laughed. If it were not so sad, I might have laughed too. In an Amos and Andy dialect, he concluded: "We the poor underprivileged people—you know that."

Roger proceeded to tell me the whole setup: what the place looked like, how much stuff he thought Daniels had, and most importantly, where he might stash it. I instructed him to make a buy and be sure to drop a bag of the junk to the floor.

I waited around the corner a few minutes after Roger disappeared into the building, getting the strategy straight with my partner that night, a lethargic old "hairbag" (oldtimer) who could not be aroused by Raquel Welch, let alone a drug collar in Bedford-Stuyvesant. Like many a cop, he wasted away, avoiding activity, just waiting for his twenty years to be up so he could draw half pay. It was well understood if there were any arrests to be made that night, they would all be mine.

I pushed the tenement door in slowly, surprised that it

did not squeak, and was met with a nauseating stench. A dark, winding staircase began climbing immediately and disappeared in the direction of voices. Roger's and "Big Lou's," I assumed.

Slowly, softly, I inched up the stairs, listening intensely, trying to deduce if the sale had been consummated. No matter. "Old Faithful," behind me, coughed loudly and the talking at the top halted abruptly. I clattered up the steps as fast as I could, only to see a startled, goateed dealer drop a deck to the floor and run into his apartment, slamming the door behind. Roger fled to the safety of the roof.

"Open up," I demanded, wishing my regular partner had not taken the night off. "You're under arrest," I shouted to the door, picking up the bag of dope.

No response.

Three steps back, I charged the door, shoulder forward, crashing with an explosive thump. It didn't even budge. I rushed again. And again. No good. My partner, seated on the banister, watched bemused.

"You could give me a hand!" I said.

Before he could reply, a sliding Yale bolt urged me to slap my back to the wall alongside the apartment and draw my revolver. The old-timer scurried for cover.

The goateed pusher, brown skinned, loud clothes on a medium frame, appeared, a wry look on his face. "Can I help you?" A toilet filled in the background.

"Get your coat, wiseass.... You're under arrest."

"For what?"

"220.05 of the Penal Law, pal, possession of heroin." Before he had a chance to argue, I held up the bag he had dropped. "Here's one you forgot to flush."

Now the whirring of the tape recorder was interrupted by a telephone ringing, a pause, a click, then a voice.

"Lou?"

"Yeah, who's this?"

"Donald," came the reply. It was me. I was to be called Donald through the entire transaction.

"Oh yeah, what's happenin', Donald? Listen, I could only get two hundred ..."

I didn't really listen to the rest. It played and Mr. Foley

listened, but I had heard enough. The tape ended with an arrangement to meet at eight o'clock one morning the next week.

Daniels had been arrested many times before I collared him. In fact, he had been busted for sale of narcotics the month before. But still the judge set a minimal bail. He left the courthouse before I did.

The case came up repeatedly and, as happens with almost all arrests in New York City, was adjourned repeatedly. A police officer could not seriously expect to finish up with any of his arrests until he went back to court unnecessarily at least three times. Adjournment after adjournment. Frustration after frustration. Multiplied by the forty or fifty arrests I had made that year, I was annoyed and impatient. I was leaving the department soon and when, eight months after the arrest, the case was due for the court calendar again, I seriously contemplated not going back. When Daniels offered me three hundred dollars not to show up, I decided to take it.

Foley pushed the "stop" button and stared poker-faced at me before asking: "What do you think?"

"It sure sounds like me, doesn't it?"

"It is you, Ed."

"Well, suppose it is. I'm not saying it is but just suppose it is. That's just a conversation between two guys named Lou and, what was it, Donald. Ain't no way in the world you can prove that it was me."

"On the contrary, Ed. As I said before, this is just one of many tapes. You had quite a few telephone conversations with Lou Daniels. Not only that but the payoff was witnessed by six federal agents and Daniels was wired. I don't think you stand too much of a chance."

"On the contrary, Mr. Foley. You seem to forget one, most important fact."

"What's that?"

"I'm in California. Over three thousand miles from New York. Do you think the good governor would want to be bothered signing extradition papers for me, or the district attorney would want to go through the time and the expense of getting me back."

"To tell the truth, I don't know, Ed. That's something that you're going to have to decide. Think about it. Call

Mike and see what he's got in mind. Right now the only people who know about this incident are you and the commission members. Neither the Police Department nor the district attorney's office has even the slightest inkling. Of course, if you decide not to cooperate, they will know and then you'll find out just how badly they want you back. It's up to you. You've got a good head on your shoulders. Use it. Don't make a mistake you'll be sorry for the rest of your life."

"Thanks for the advice, Mr. Foley, but that's exactly what I don't want to do. It took over a year of explanations and preparations to be able to come here to go to school. I'm enrolled in the University of Southern California and there is nothing I want more than to get a law degree. Doing what Mike Armstrong will suggest might be that mistake."

"It's all up to you, Ed. The way I see it is that it's unfortunate that you got caught at all but you're lucky that it was the commission who caught you. Had it been the Police Department, you wouldn't be here talking to me right now. You'd be in jail. At least now you've got a chance."

"You seem certain that I'm guilty."

"Aren't you?"

I opened the door, started walking out quickly, planning to slam it behind me, then turned. "Thanks again for the advice, Mr. Foley. Maybe I'll see you again someday." I turned again and walked slowly into the corridor closing the door quietly behind me. On the way down in the elevator I stared at the floor.

"I don't want you to go, daddy," my cherub-faced, five-year-old daughter, Cheryl, whimpered as tears rolled uncontrollably from her eyes. Christopher, six, and Kim, four, more or less agreed, but they did not show their emotions as much as their sister. A pleasant female voice had just directed pink pass holders to board American's 747 flight to Los Angeles at gate 2.

"I have to, honey, but I'll be back," I promised simply, kissing her on salty lips. My eyes filled up unexpectedly, but I was able to add, "Now you kids be good for mommy while I'm gone," kiss them all once again, then my wife, and turn toward the gate before anyone noticed the tears forming.

Sitting, staring through the fogged plane window, I knew that someday we would all be happier because of my decision to continue college and earn a law degree, but realized more and more how difficult it was for the kids to comprehend. All they could understand was that their father was going far away and would be gone for a long time. They did not care why.

But it was very important to me. I had to get that degree. Four and one-half years in the New York City Police Department, spent mainly in the Negro slum areas of Brooklyn, had made me disappointed in my role as a patrolman. And in myself. It's ironic because as far back as I can remember I had wanted to be a police officer and it was not until I became one that I realized how naïve I had been. I thought I would like to share in the respect a policeman receives and was awakened to the fact that very little respect exists on the sidewalks of Bedford-Stuyvesant. I wanted to be proud of the uniform I wore, shine my shoes spotless and be able to cut butter with the crease in my trousers, but found that impossible to accomplish while crawling on darkened rooftops, investigating roach-infested buildings, or rolling on the rain-soaked pavement, fighting for my life. But most of all, I was disgusted the day I realized that, of all things, the New York City Police Department had transformed me from a basically honest, law-abiding individual to a thief.

Before joining the department I had never taken anything in my life, never been in any trouble whatsoever, but I learned quickly that the rule rather than the exception on the job was to take goods, services, and money illegitimately and mechanically. It started with free meals and worked its way up to payoffs from gamblers and drug dealers. That was bad but it was worse that it was classified by a majority of thirty thousand patrolmen as the thing to do and, in some respects, society condoned it also. And God knows I was only involved on the surface—there were a vast number of men a lot deeper than I.

In less than five years, I had developed into a robot, searching and taking, hardened, without feelings, functioning only physically as a human being. I was taking money as routinely as a bus driver accepting a fare. Not a lot of money. It would not make me wealthy. Pin money, spent superficially. And that made it all the worse; there was no dire need. It was just there. Mostly, the people offered and everybody took. I took too, but never stopped and really thought about it; I never foresaw the effects. I was being destroyed. I felt I had planed myself with the scum I was arresting. I had become cruel and ruthless, slithering in the gutter, awaiting my next "score." It was not just me. It was all around me. The system was such that it engulfed everyone. It did not discriminate. My wife knew. All policemen's wives must know. You cannot keep the reaction away from your home. The light dawned the day my son said: "You're a policeman, daddy? I want to be one too." The thought of my son becoming what I had become sickened me. And yet, when I was his age, I, too, looked forward to being a policeman. I was saddened by the life I was leading. I was grief-stricken the day I realized that the longer I stayed in the department, the deeper I would get into a corrupt world, and that is the day I knew I had to leave.

A heart-to-heart talk with my wife, Joanne, was in order and for weeks we discussed our problem. I disclosed things I had hidden for years. I told her how debased I felt as a result of conformance with an inlaid system of tradition in the Police Department. She understood. She understood not only that I would have to shift to a new career, but also that to accomplish that task and live comfortably, it was necessary to fulfill my desire to earn a degree. I did not stop there. I told her I must get out and get out now. I told her that in order to maintain respectable marks and possibly win a scholarship to law school, I must attend full-time. It would mean selling the house to get enough money to finance the plan, but I was convinced that it would be worth it in the end. I was completely prepared for her rejection of this idea but, again, she understood.

My next decision was where to go to school. I had attended Saint Francis College, in the Borough Hall section of Brooklyn, for a year after high school but felt that a sidewalk campus was not conducive to good grades.

Sick of New York City, I needed the base of a tree to lean on when studying for an exam. I had also attended New York City Community College, a part of the City University structure, for two semesters at night when working for the telephone company and was convinced, especially after the institution of a program called "Open Enrollment"—no requirements for admission—that the caliber of education in a free city school would not lead to a scholarship to law school. So I sent away for brochures from twenty-three colleges and universities across the country. As each day's mail poured forth a plethora of information about the various schools, I carefully examined every aspect important to me and my goal. I was most impressed with the University of Southern California, with 90 percent of the faculty holding doctorates, and was sure that it was right for me. I applied and was accepted. The days on the job grew bearable, now that I knew I would soon be gone. It was financially impossible and impractical to attempt moving my entire family across the nation so, reluctantly, we decided that I would go alone initially and, as soon as possible, send for my family, although my wife and I both knew that it would not be possible at all. My mother-in-law agreed to share her home with her daughter and grandchildren. Because they would not have to pay rent, the little profit made from the sale of the house and most of our furniture would support them for two years. If I could find an inexpensive place to live in Los Angeles, there would also be enough money for two years tuition. I would need two and one-half years for my undergraduate degree, so I was six months short, but confident that by that time something would turn up. I just had to win a scholarship to law school. My intense desire to escape a life of crime forced me to part from my family.

As my departure date got closer, I grew increasingly skeptical that I was doing the right thing. I was torn between peace of mind, a profound love of my family, and a course necessary to insure them comfort in life. My daughter's comments had struck me in the heart, and unless I had walked away at just the time I did, I would have surely reversed my decision. The scream of the engines, speed of the scenery, and gentle tilt of the cabin made me forget, for a while.

I got off the elevator, weaved my way through the lobby out to my car, and drove home. I was living with a family in Hollywood where I exchanged menial household chores for free room and board. The money I would save from that arrangement would make it possible for me to stay as long as necessary to get my degree.

It was two o'clock when I arrived.

I went up to my room, sat on the bed, and put my hand on the telephone. I picked up the receiver, dialed the operator, and went through the same procedure that I had previously, until I was talking to Mike Armstrong, the chief counsel of the Knapp Commission.

The commission was formed about a year and a half earlier to investigate allegations of widespread police corruption. It got its name from the chairman, Whitman Knapp, a righteous former assistant district attorney, now cashing in on his Wall Street law firm. Mike Armstrong, Yale College, Harvard Law School educated, a former assistant United States attorney, now, also, enjoying a partnership in a well-established New York law firm, was appointed chief counsel. He made all his reports to Knapp but, in actuality, he ran the show.

"Did you listen to the tape?"

"Yes, sir, I did."

"What do you think?"

"Just what have you got in mind, Mr. Armstrong. Let's stop playing games. What is it you want from me?"

"Well, first, Ed, I would like to talk to you in person. Right now, no one knows anything about the incident between you and Lou Daniels. If you listen to what I have to say and agree to cooperate with us, maybe we can work something out. If you refuse, I'll turn everything over to the district attorney's office and let him decide what he wants to do. We've got you dead, Ed. You'll be in jail for a long time."

"That's a matter of opinion. First of all, I needn't tell you that in this country, all men are innocent until proven guilty. Secondly, I'm out here in California. Thirdly, I've got my whole life in front of me out here. I've gone through a lot to be in the position I'm in now and, in a few years, I could be well on my way to a new career in law. And you're asking me to give it all up to come back there and help you catch other cops with their hands in the till. You've got to be kidding."

"You miss the point, Ed. Granted, you're innocent until proven guilty, but there's no way in the world you're going to beat this case. Granted, also, that you have your whole life in front of you, but just think of what happens if you don't come back. Even if the D. A. doesn't extradite, do you seriously think you'll be admitted to a bar in this country with an indictment hanging over your head in New York. Think, also, about your family, Ed."

"Exactly. That's exactly what I'm thinking about. . . . Listen, if I come back, what happens? I mean, why should I go back if there's a chance of me being arrested."

"There are ways, legitimate ways, that, if employed, could mean you won't get arrested."

"But how do I know for sure?"

"You don't. That's a chance you've got to take. I'll promise you one thing, though. If you come back here and work with us and I'm convinced that you're giving us 100 percent, I'll do everything in my power to help you."

"Like what?"

"Well, I can't promise you that the district attorney will grant you immunity, but I will tell you that he is very apt to listen to our suggestions. Nothing's impossible, Ed. There's an outside chance that you might just be able to get out of this mess and go back to California to school."

"Is this conversation being recorded?" I asked.

"No." He told me later that it was.

There was a long pause and then he asked: "Have you registered yet?"

"Yes. Yesterday."

"It's a very important decision, Ed. Weigh it carefully."

"I intend to. Listen, if I decide to come back, will you pay the air fare?"

"We can't, Ed. The funds are too low."

"Let me sleep on it. I'll call you tomorrow sometime."

"All right. After one, New York time."

"I'm calling collect."

"OK."

I hung up.

I sat on the bed, staring blankly for about an hour, then buried my head in the pillow and cried for the first time since I was ten years old. I didn't move more than a few inches all day and all night. For the first time in my life I thought seriously of committing suicide. I could picture myself jumping from a rooftop and actually experienced the weightlessness as I tumbled through the air and the crunch of my bones, knocking the life from me, as I crashed to the ground. I pictured, also, slicing my wrists with a razor blade and standing at the sink, staring at the blood as it gushed from my veins and washed down the drain, bringing my life with it. These and the other alternatives I contemplated through the night. I slept not at all.

At nine the next morning, I showered, dressed, and rode off to the University of Southern California to withdraw. I returned at six, packed my clothes, and was at the airport by nine-thirty. The plane was to leave at ten-thirty and get me to New York around six-thirty. I had called Mike Armstrong and told him I'd be in his office at eight to see what he wanted me to do. My last illegal act in the Police Department had induced me to return to the life I had so eagerly escaped.

CHAPTER 2

Bay Ridge is a small, all-White community on the southern tip of Brooklyn, nestled at the base of the Verrazano-Narrows Bridge. The streets are lined with trees, wide, clean, teeming with kids and relatively crime free. In between visits to Coney Island in the summer, the boys play stickball and slapball and, in the winter, sewer-to-sewer football and hockey. It is almost impossible to walk five blocks in any one direction without passing a church along the way.

I was born in Bay Ridge, the youngest child in a middle income family of six, with one brother and two sisters. I went to school there, got married there, and fathered my children there.

I had no relatives on the force and rarely came in contact with men of the 64th precinct, but I looked forward to becoming a policeman for as long as I can remember. I was taught to always respect the police and help them in any way that I could. I was struck by the aura of responsibility that surrounded them. I was never mistreated by a policeman and trusted them implicitly. Not once were they called to my home, but I knew that if they were needed, they were only moments away at all times." When talking to one I always addressed him as "sir." I marveled at the way they were able to keep their shoes shined and uniforms neat and shuddered at the fact that their guns were really loaded. I was proud of the policemen of the 64th precinct.

In 1964, at eighteen, I married and, because my

mother, father, and brother all worked for the New York Telephone Company, I followed suit with a $63.50 a week clerical job. It was only a matter of time, though, until the test came up. Then, one hot day in August, 1966 ...

"Hi, hon! I'm home."

Joanne, a little slower than usual, came in from the kitchen and met me in the living room of our small, four-room apartment. "This came for you today," she said as she held up an envelope. The top, left-hand corner read "Civil Service Commission." I grabbed it, ripped it open, and hurriedly examined the IBM card inside.

The wait was over. I had made it.

"Number 78. I wrote a 97 and I'm number 78 on the list. And with no veteran's preference." I was ecstatic. "Not bad, huh, hon?"

She forced a smile, but I knew. She would never stand in my way or try to prevent me from becoming a police officer, but, deep down, she really didn't want it. She was afraid. Afraid for my life, for hers and the kids'. Sure, there was a certain security: a twenty-year pension, a five-week vacation, an ever-increasing salary, which would double what I was taking home from the telephone company. But there was always the fear of death and the risks were ever present and dangerously high, especially if I were assigned to Bedford-Stuyvesant or Harlem, which was very likely. And the hours: 8 A.M. to 4 P.M. one week; midnight to 8 A.M. the next; 4 P.M. to midnight the next; then back to the eight to four. It wouldn't just be hard on me, but her, too. Having to have dinner at two when I'm working four to twelve, and at ten when I'm on midnights. And being alone at night; nobody likes that. And the impossibility of socializing normally with our friends because of my hours and my crazy days off. No, she really didn't want it, but she knew how badly I did, and she would never stand in my way.

"I'm so happy for you," she said as she hugged me and squeezed with all her might.

"I'm happy, too, hon. I'm happy for all of us."

Of course, I wasn't assured of making it quite yet. I had only passed the first part, a written test comprised of one hundred multiple choice questions, but there was still the physical. Five-nine, one-fifty, with twenty-twenty vision, at least I didn't have to worry about an automatic failure. It was the strength tests I wasn't sure about. Even though they weren't too demanding, I wasn't too strong. Your proficiency in each of five events was graded and the passing mark was based on the total accumulation of points.

First was an obstacle course: the faster you ran it, the higher your score; second was a weight lift with each arm, a minimum of twenty to score at all; third was a chinning bar; fourth, a sit-up with weights behind your neck; and fifth, a broad jump. The first and the last events proved to be my forte and I passed with a comfortable margin.

Never having been in any trouble as a youth—I used to give the extra money back when overpaid by a supermarket check-out—I passed the character investigation with flying colors.

Then, in the first week of May, 1967, I was notified to report to the Police Academy for my final medical. I passed, but my heart jumped into my mouth when the captain in charge of the group that day made the announcement that the class would be appointed May 15. I wasn't going to be twenty-one until May 18. Normally that's just tough luck and you wait for the next class to be appointed, which might be months, or even years, but, for the first time in the history of the department—so a detective at the chief clerk's office told me the day I was sworn in—an allowance was made and I was appointed three days later on my twenty-first birthday. Oddly enough, in the future I would again be a part of another "first" in the New York City Police Department.

The Police Academy Recruits Training School is located in a modern, eight-story building, on the Lower East Side of Manhattan. Aside from classrooms and a gymnasium, it also houses a firing range, the police museum, the computer banks, the medical laboratory, the evidence laboratory, and the ballistics laboratory. The hours for recruits were 7:15 A.M. to 3:15 P.M., and usually, but I never bet on it, Monday through Friday. Each day was broken into four hours of academic work, three hours of either gym or firearm training, and one hour for lunch.

A scientific method was used to determine who was in what group, or company. Representatives of each borough were formed into clusters and the tallest men went into one company and the rest went into another. For this reason I was placed in Company 17 of the class of 1967, or simply 67-17. Such scientific methods are prevalent in decision making throughout the department.

The first few days in the academy were used for orientation in our new surroundings. Included were a quick tour of the building, complete with provocative "war stories" from the gray-haired guide, an even quicker round of handshakes with the academy staff and an all-too-quick introduction to the policeman's Bible, the rules and procedures, henceforth known as the R & P. Approximately twelve inches by twelve inches and four inches thick, the book bursts with the "dos and don'ts" that govern a patrolman's every move. The main problem is the upkeep. Since nobody upstairs can ever decide for sure which is the right way to do any particular thing, or not do it, changes and amendments are issued almost every day and each year over 75 percent of the book is affected. Each patrolman is given his very own R & P to love, honor, and obey, till death do them part. Suspension, leave, resignation, or dismissal will also force you to part, however.

One day during the first week, all the recruits—in my case 250—squeezed themselves into the equipment bureau, the department's retail store on the ground floor of 400 Broome Street, Manhattan, the annex to Police Headquarters, to buy "rookie gray" uniforms. Altogether, with the blue uniforms, the grays, and all the leather, a new recruit spends over five hundred dollars. The department gives you nothing; you buy it. They even charge you fifteen cents for the safety pin necessary to keep your shield pinned to your shirt. You have your choice of where you buy your blues, but the grays must be bought at the equipment bureau.

The leather and other paraphernalia are the same for both uniforms and consist of two belts, one for your pants and one for your gun; a holster; handcuffs and case; a twelve-round ammunition pouch; a whistle and holder; a luminous belt; rain gear consisting of a coat, hat cover, and leggings; leather gloves and white cotton dress gloves; a blue cap; a cap device with your shield number on it; a black tie and tie clip; a memo-book holder; a day billy; and a nightstick. You have a choice of either a Smith and Wesson or a Colt .38 caliber, six-shot service revolver with a four-inch barrel. After probation, nine months then, one year now, you may buy any off-duty gun you desire as long as it is approved by the equipment bureau. You are not required to buy one, but most men do because you must have a gun with you twenty-four hours a day and concealing a service revolver is neither easy nor comfortable.

As if there weren't enough gear, most recruits went running out to the gun shops surrounding the academy and equipment bureau to buy such extras as jacks of all shapes and sizes, fancy holsters, Pancho Villa ammunition holders, sets of chains known as "come alongs," that, when wrapped around the wrists and squeezed, induce arrestees to "come along" peacefully, miniature shields for family and friends, and extra giant economy-sized nightsticks, guaranteed not to break when slammed over a prisoner's head. The demand for new whistles went skyrocketing right after somebody, rumor had it as one of the gun shop owners, realized that the white coating on the whistles the department had authorized for years was highly inflammable.

The gray uniform itself is composed of a chino-material shirt and pants and a heavy three-quarter-length jacket with a zip-out lining. All uniform pants are equipped with two extra pockets in the rear for flashlight and billy, a nine-inch, hard-rubber club. Just about the only time you'll see an officer with a billy instead of a jack (a lead club, covered with leather) in his back pocket is when he is in the gray uniform, attached to the academy. Once assigned to the street, the immeasurable superiority of the jack as a weapon induces the patrolman to throw the billy on the bottom of his locker, where it remains forever.

The blue uniform is a bit more sophisticated and must be awarded, literally, the seal of approval from the equipment bureau before you are allowed to wear it. It consists of a summer jacket, or blouse, a winter blouse, called a choker, and an overweight overcoat that causes severe shoulder pains the beginning of every winter. In addition there are summer pants, winter pants, and powder blue shirts, a blessing over the dark blue ones with brass buttons that had to be removed before and replaced after every washing. A leather car coat is optional.

In addition, each man is required to equip himself with a watch, a flashlight, and black shoes and socks.

Civilian clothes were worn to the academy until the class received the necessary training to be able to handle a gun, and because the gray uniforms fit like a sack of potatoes, none of the men were too anxious to wear them, anyhow. In the crush at the equipment bureau, the patrolman who sold me my pants convinced me that I should buy a bigger size to make room for the memo book, flashlight, and billy, so I wound up with a 36, though my waist was 32.

The major part of the next few days was spent on "How to Report Sick." The routine flu case at home is not as important as the broken leg while skiing out of state, for if any member is missing for more than twenty-four hours, he is automatically suspended and must report to the police commissioner before he is restored. If after five days he is still unaccounted for, his resignation is assumed and all benefits are forfeited. Reporting sick is simply a matter of a phone call most of the time, but the instructor wanted to make sure we knew who to call and what to do if a call was impossible.

I had always wondered who it was that put up and took down the police stanchions at parades. I found out on my first weekend when I received barrier detail. It wasn't bad, though, because you report in old clothes in the morning, set up the barriers along the parade route, take a couple of hours off for a movie while the parade is on, and report back in the afternoon to remove them. You earn a day's pay.

With the uniforms and sick reports out of the way, the second week started with a definition of the Police Department: a quasi-military organization whose duties and responsibilities are to protect life and property, detect and arrest offenders, prevent crime, enforce laws and ordinances and provisions of the Administrative Code within Police Department jurisdiction, preserve the public peace, regulate and direct traffic, guard the public health, preserve order at elections, provide police attendance at fires, arrest all street mendicants and beggars, inspect all places of public amusement and licensed businesses, suppress riots, mobs, and insurrections, disperse unlawful assemblages, and remove all nuisances in public. After the first five, the catchall is the last.

Next, because many of the men, myself included, were never in the army, came the order of rank in the department. Of course, the police commissioner, a civilian, is on top and under him are his deputy commissioners. These are the first deputy commissioner, and the deputy commissioners of legal matters, press relations, trials, community relations, licenses, and administration. Under these gentlemen begin the uniformed force. The highest member in uniform, wearing four stars, is the chief inspector. With three stars are the chiefs of detectives, patrol, personnel, and inspectional services. Two stars signify an assistant chief inspector and one a deputy chief inspector. An inspector wears an eagle, a deputy inspector a gold oak leaf, a captain two bars, a lieutenant one bar, and, of course, a sergeant three chevrons.

The five boroughs of New York City are broken down into seven patrol boroughs; Queens, Richmond, Bronx, Manhattan North, Manhattan South, Brooklyn North, and Brooklyn South. Each borough is broken into divisions and each division into precincts. A precinct is then subdivided into sectors for radio motor patrol and posts for footmen.

Among the many textbooks required at the academy, the major ones are: *The Penal Law, The Code of Criminal Procedure, The Administrative Code, The Traffic Regulations of New York City, The Vehicle and Traffic Laws of New York State,* and the *First Aid Handbook.* In the following weeks, our studies were concentrated on the organization of the department, a broad introduction to criminal law, a few penal law definitions, how and when to use the memo book, an introduction to the law of arrest, the lawful use of force, the United States Constitution, and person aided and accident cases.

It was kind of fun adjusting to the semimilitary way of life, with "Yes, sirs" and "No, sirs" and, after three weeks, when we started wearing our grays, saluting and getting used to the uniform. I made some good friends in the company and, although we all came from different walks of life before the job, we were all basically the same "green" rookies. One guy was a truck driver, another a baker, another had something to do with computers; there was a mechanic, a plumber's assistant, a clerk, a salesman. Only two men in the company had college degrees. One was a quiet, good-humored journalist and the other a fat man whose lack of common sense made him the "class cluck." Most of the men were neat and clean and made a sincere effort to look professional. One guy, however, looked as if he slept in his clothes and most definitely didn't give it much thought. Whenever I felt a little sloppy, I would always look over at him and automatically feel better. I was a bit naïve about corruption and graft but not much more than most of my new friends. Never once did we talk about it and, sadly enough, never once was it brought up by the instructors. I didn't join the Police Department to take free meals or money. I wanted to be an officer the way I had always envisioned an officer should be, the way you read about and the way they're depicted on television and in the movies. I wanted to be a friend of the people. I wanted to protect them from crime, buy a lost child an ice cream, be counted on and trusted. I was as proud as hell to be a member of "New York's Finest."

I was just starting to get the "big picture" and feel the weight of the innumerable responsibilities involved with being a patrolman, when word came down we were to be temporarily assigned. Because of the racial unrest the city had experienced in years gone by, the administrators initiated a policy of "dumping" as many uniformed bodies as possible in the street for the summer, regardless of training. So instead of the customary four and one-half months in the Police Academy, I was in a short four weeks before being sent into the street. Realizing how little I knew and how important my function, I was a bit apprehensive.

We had had two quick lessons on "The Care and Safeguard of Your Firearm" and, academically, we hadn't even touched on any of the major crimes: burglary, robbery, rape, drugs, larceny, assault, homicide, menacing. I didn't know my arson from my elbow. Well, at least I knew how to go sick.

On June 15, 1967, I was assigned to the 90th precinct.

CHAPTER 3

"Droge—Monday and Tuesday," the sergeant bellowed. Thirteen other probationary patrolmen were also assigned to the 90 (pronounced nine-O) and we were all crowded around in the back room of the station house as the sergeant, who made no bones about his disappointment in having been put in charge of us, called out our regular days off. It had already been established that our hours would be 6 P.M. to 2 A.M. All but one man were dressed in blue. The uniform of the day was shirt and tie, summer blouse optional, so most of us had run out the day before and bought lightweight pants, called tropicals, to beat wearing the grays. Aside from improvised cap devices without numbers and no 90 numerals on our collars, we looked just like the regular men. Nobody wanted to look like a rookie and the gray uniform was a dead giveaway. The poor guy who had dressed in gray was depressed the whole tour. Having finished with the days off, the sergeant told us to gather around and spoke with a voice hoarse from years of barking commands.

"Listen, you guys, I know you're new and most of you probably don't know whether you're coming or going, so I want you to stick close to the more experienced men. We'll try to have you working with a man permanently assigned to the 90 every tour." It was just six o'clock and some of the regular men were filtering into the room. They were working a 4 P.M. to midnight tour with a six o'clock post change to pick us up. At midnight we'd be assigned to the men on the late tour for two hours. "If that's impossible, we'll have to put two of you together, but at no time are you to work alone. If you come in one night and find that's the case, report to the desk officer and he'll find something for you to do in here. Now when you're out there on the street, look smart and be alert. Williamsburg isn't exactly the best neighborhood around, nor is it the worst, but some nights you'll be so busy you'll hardly have time for a smoke. The precinct is one-third Blacks, one-third Puerto Ricans, and one-third 'Beards.' We're bounded on the west by the Navy Yard, the south by Myrtle Avenue, the north by Broadway, and to the east where Broadway and Myrtle intersect. So take it easy for a while and watch how the regular men handle different things, but don't walk around with your thumb up your ass. You'll learn. It'll take time, but you'll learn. Any questions?"

"Yes, sir," one of the "probies" spoke up, "how about meals?"

"Oh yeah. You guys on foot posts, I'll be around later to scratch your books. I'll tell you what meal to take then. If you're in a car, you eat when your partner eats. After tonight, your mealtime will be on the roll call. Another thing, while I'm thinking of it, don't let the 'Beards' bother you. They're a very curious people, but they're peaceful. Sometimes they can be a real pain in the balls, but after a while you'll get used to them. Any more questions? Does everybody understand their assignments? Is there anybody on the floor whose name I haven't called? OK, take your posts."

We all filed out of the back room, past the desk, and out into the street. I was assigned to a foot post on Bedford Avenue with an eight-year veteran, Jack Ruffino. On the way to post, he explained that the "Beards" the sergeant had referred to were the Hasidic Jews in the neighborhood and that the post we were assigned to was right by one of their temples, so we were sure to have company for the night. No sooner had he said that than I found out what he meant. A little Hasidic boy, no more than twelve years old, walked up from behind and went stride for stride with us down to our post. He struck up a conversation immediately.

"So how come you don't have numbers on your hat?

And where's the 90 that's supposed to be on your collar? What're you, a rookie?"

I could see what the sergeant meant about curious. And I thought nobody would notice I was missing those things. I just humored him for about a half an hour until he got tired of the one-sided conversation and walked away. During the night about eight other little boys also came over and asked almost the same questions. To the man, they all wanted to know if I was a rookie. Jack got a big kick out of it and in between visits, as we walked our post, he kept telling me I'd get used to it. The tour went fast and by the end of the night, if nothing else, I had learned how to twirl my nightstick like Officer Joe Bolton on TV.

Aside from the obvious—preventing crime and preserving the peace—I was so unsure of what my functions were supposed to be, how I was to accomplish them, and what I could or could not do legally, that I was almost completely dependent on the more experienced patrolmen to show me the ropes. Though I would have liked to consider myself a leader, police business is such a grave matter that I was compelled to become a follower in order to avoid serious mistakes. Unfortunately, as I learned the ropes of good police work, I also learned that free meals and cigarettes were some of the small rewards most officers expected as a matter of course. I wasn't so naïve as to be shocked at getting a free meal, but rather quietly embarrassed. Initially, whenever I was with other officers I would accept free meals, but never when I was alone. I didn't mind paying; in fact, I often insisted.

Six weeks after appointment, two weeks on the street in the 90, I took my first bribe. Mind you, I had never taken anything dishonestly in my entire life. On a foot post with a patrolman permanently assigned to the 90, I witnessed a car mount the sidewalk, crash into the Brooklyn Navy Yard fence, and, smoking, continue on. A few blocks away, the vehicle stalled, apparently disabled. I ran toward it while the other patrolman commandeered a car and arrived at the scene at the same time I did. He was very calm and I was very excited. He told me I would have to take it easy if I were to last twenty years for the pension. He was not that much older than I, but on the job longer, and he acted as if he knew exactly what to do, whereas I had only a vague idea. The driver of the car was intoxicated, but sober enough to offer ten dollars to forget the whole thing. My partner took it and I just watched. My face was flushed. It's the old story—if I had known then what I know now, I would have spoken up. But I didn't and I walked away from the scene with the other patrolman. A while later, he gave me five dollars. He didn't say anything; he didn't have to—I knew what it was for. There was nobody around; no one would ever know; he acted like it was the thing to do; so I took it. I didn't stop and seriously think of the consequences at that time. I firmly believe this incident to be the key to my future actions. Had I been better trained and familiar with what I should legally do on the street, had I been instructed thoroughly on the *problem* of corruption and how to combat it, had I been with a patrolman with a similar background, I would never have taken that money.

The first five dollars had paved the way for further involvement—all of it relatively minor, but still a beginning. I learned it was a good idea to be around a break-in when the owner showed—so you wouldn't miss out if he wanted to "throw" you something for helping him check out the premises. I learned that food processing plants were very generous with their goods to uniformed officers and so, too, were bartenders with their drinks. For four months, I watched, listened, and participated. No one was ever caught doing anything wrong by either superior officers or civilians. For that matter, most of the smaller offenses, such as accepting free meals and groceries, were often prompted by the local merchants. There didn't seem to be much wrong with it and nobody appeared too concerned. Senior patrolmen's conversations and attitudes indicated a loose atmosphere of corruption and various reasons for participation: take whenever you can; you might as well, everybody else is; compensate for what you don't get in your paycheck; if the people insist, what can you do? These might all be categorized as personal and relative opinions, but the overriding reason that I now discern as the most prominent, though hardly stated, was the *tradition*. They had been broken in the same way they broke me in. The constant corrupt activity with so few, remote instances of detection or serious punitive action allayed a large part of the fear.

The first time I rode in a radio car as a policeman was the first time I rode in a radio car. It's basically the same as any other Ford, Chevy, or Plymouth except that it's equipped with a police-band radio, a flashing red light, and a siren. There's no power steering or air-conditioning and in the summer it must be ten degrees hotter inside than it is outside. In the beginning the radio messages sound garbled and it is quite easy to miss an assignment when you're called. But gradually the ear becomes attuned and then it is hard to understand why you couldn't catch everything before. The Ten Code is used, which means that every signal is prefixed by a ten and suffixed by a number denoting the meaning. For example: 10-1 means call the station house, 10-2 means report to the station house, 10-3 means call the radio dispatcher by land line, and everybody knows 10-4 means acknowledge. Perhaps the most important code for any police officer is 10-13—assist patrolman. When that signal is transmitted over the air, every patrolman in the vicinity rushes to the scene to help his brother officer. Most of the time the calls are unfounded, but you go anyhow because there will always be that once when it's not. You go as fast as you can because you know if it were you in trouble, you would want help as soon as possible. Every second counts and could mean the difference between life and death.

I was assigned to a radio car one night with a real ladies' man who couldn't stop talking about his conquests while we cruised our sector casually.

"So we're laying on the couch and she says to me: 'Whatever you want, Frank. Whatever will please you the most. Anything.' So I pull down my zipper, take out my dick, and . . ."

The radio blasted an interruption.

"10-13. Assist patrolman. 10-13. Nostrand and Park in the 90. Repeat. A signal 10-13, assist patrolman, at Nostrand and Park in the 90. What units to respond, K? [over.]"

"Nine-O Charley on the way."

"Nine-O David on the way."

"Seven-nine John on the way."

"Nine-O Frank on the way," I said.

"10-4, units. Nostrand and Park. That's all we've got. First unit on the scene advise Central as to the condition, K."

"Give me the light, Ed," my partner yelled as he flicked the siren switch to "constant." I hit the light toggle and we were on our way. The surge of the car pushed my body backward until my spine smashed against the seat and my neck against the headrest. The tires screeched the first block until they grabbed the pavement firmly. We made a sharp left that sent me hurtling into the door, and when we straightened out, I threw my right foot up on the dash to brace myself for the rest of the ride. Park and Nostrand was right in the middle of the Negro third of the precinct.

As dangerous as it is, there's something quite exhilarating about whipping through the streets of New York in a police car with turret light flashing and siren wailing. On each corner it was my job to check my side for traffic and on every one I shouted, "All clear. Go." We were still two blocks away when the radio blared again.

"Nine-O David to Central, K. Advise all units that there are bottle throwers on the rooftops. This unit is on the scene with Nine-O Adam. That's Nostrand between Park and Myrtle." The sound of glass breaking was distinct in the background throughout his report. "Advise all units to enter the area with helmets on, K."

"How many perpetrators, David?"

"It's hard to tell, Central, but they're all over the roofs. There's a housing project here and bottles are flying everywhere, K."

"10-4, David. Attention all units in the 14th division. Nine-O David is on the scene at Park and Nostrand and advises all units respond with helmets. There are bottle throwers on the roofs, K."

"Nine-O David to Central, K."

"Go ahead, David."

"Nine-O Charley is on the scene also and we're going up to flush them out, K."

"10-4, David. Use caution, K."

"10-4, Central."

We screamed into the block at the same time as a 79th

precinct car, narrowly avoiding a collision. About six other cars were already on the scene. Broken glass was everywhere and people were running through the streets, yelling. It wasn't such a good idea to have all the radio cars bunched up the way they were because they made a perfect target for the bottle throwers on the roof. No sooner had we arrived than a soda bottle smashed down on the hood of the radio car and splintered into hundreds of pieces. These guys meant business.

"The helmets are in the trunk," my partner yelled before rolling out the door and dashing to the rear. I jumped out and met him back there. The only two helmets in the trunk were from World War II: an American and a German. The German one was closer to me so I grabbed it and put it on. Just then the barrage increased and bottles were smashing, cracking, and breaking everywhere. I drew my revolver and crouched behind the radio car. You can't shoot what you can't see and it was too dark to see anyone on the top of any of the roofs but I strained my eyes, just the same. The streetlamps were out and the only lights on the block were intermittent red-and-white rays from the turrets of the radio cars, flashing off the buildings. You couldn't see the bottles until they were almost on top of you.

An inhuman scream filled the air and I looked quickly behind me. One of the other patrolmen, crouched behind his car, was clutching his face with both hands and yelling in pain. Blood was spurting from between his fingers. His partner guided him into the car, jumped behind the wheel, and, with lights and siren, zigzagged his way out of the block, rushing to the hospital.

My partner was crouched alongside me, scanning upward as fruitlessly as I. With gritted teeth he thought out loud: "These fuckin' niggers."

Throughout grammar school, high school, college, and the telephone company, many of my good friends were Black. I played ball in grammar school with the only Negro in the neighborhood. In high school and college, one of my best friends was a Negro. In the telephone company, half of my good friends were Negroes. One of them was a special friend and our families often exchanged visits to each other's house. I had never thought of the

The Patrolman: A Cop's Story

Blacks as any different than anybody else, but at that moment, hiding behind the car like an animal, unable to strike back, I couldn't help feeling exactly like my partner.

Suddenly it was quiet. As abruptly as it had begun, it had ended. The only sounds were those of police officers running from car to car, stomping on broken glass. From one of the roofs, the men from 90 David and Charley called down that there was nobody in sight. They had fled. Without provocation, for no apparent reason at all, a bunch of animals had succeeded in terrorizing the neighborhood. Why, I wondered. Why? I never found out.

After milling around for a while, exchanging bitter remarks with the other officers on the scene about the Black scum who were responsible for the disruption, my partner and I resumed patrol. All was silent for a while, then ...

"Hey, Frank, where do you suppose they got all those bottles, anyway?"

"They probably saved them up for months."

There was quiet for a few more moments and suddenly it dawned on me that the housing project we had just come from was the home of my good friend from the telephone company and I felt a little queasy. I didn't mention it to Frank.

"Did you notice, Ed?"

"Did I notice what?"

"Those bottles ... they were no deposit. I bet if they were deposit bottles, they wouldn't have thrown them away."

We both laughed and the rest of the night passed quickly. I tried to forget but could not.

On July 12, another probationary patrolman and I were assigned to a foot post covering Bedford Avenue and Rodney Street. We were shooting the breeze on the corner when a Black girl, about fourteen years old, came running up to us. She was nearly hysterical.

"Quick. Come quick, he's killing her."

"Calm down," I said. "Who's killing who?"

"My father. He's beating my mother and he said he's going to shoot her."

"Where do you live?" my partner asked.

"Right down the block here. Oh, please come quick before it's too late."

"OK," I said as the three of us began trotting down Rodney Street, "take it easy. Does your father have a gun?"

"Yes, a shotgun and a pistol."

"Do you know where he keeps them?"

"No."

In a few seconds we had reached the house, a three-story brownstone with a huge stoop leading from street level to the second floor. The girl climbed the stoop first and we followed closely behind. I had withdrawn my revolver and let my arm hang straight down, pointing it at the floor, ready to use it if I had to. We were met just inside the door by a woman in her forties with a black curly wig askew on her head. Most of her face and the top of her arms were badly bruised, her lip and her wrist were bleeding, and she was crying.

"He's downstairs in the living room. He went to get a gun. He says he's gonna shoot me."

"How do we get down there?" my partner asked.

"Over there," she said as she turned and pointed behind her to a door underneath a stairway.

"How about the front door?" I asked. "Is that open?"

"Yes, it's always open."

Without a word, my partner peeled off toward the door on the second floor and I raced down the stoop to the front entrance. A screen door was ajar and I pushed the main door in, ever so slowly. There were no lights on in the hall and I could hardly make out my partner as he reached the bottom of the stairs and stationed himself to the left of a huge archway, draped with curtains. I crept gently to the right of it. I took my hat off and peered into the dark room. I saw a massive bulk of a man, sitting on a couch facing us, with what looked like a shotgun in his hands. To the left was another archway, also draped, that led to a bedroom.

"I know you're out there, mother-fucker, and I'm gonna blow your fuckin' head right off," he yelled.

"It's the police, mister, throw down the gun," my partner demanded. With that he turned and walked down the hall, planning to position himself at the other archway. The relatively new leather of his uniform squeaked as he did so.

"I ain't throwin' down my gun. This is my house and you ain't got no right to be here. Now get the fuck out."

"We were called here by your wife. Put the gun down and let's talk," I said.

"I told you I ain't puttin' no mother-fuckin' gun down. Now if you want to talk, you do it right where you are."

At that instant my partner knocked into something and the figure on the couch swiveled the gun toward the other archway. Without thinking, I sprang through the curtains, yelled as loud as I could, and dived headfirst toward him. I knocked the gun from his hands and my partner ran in to assist me. There was little or no struggle as we cuffed him behind his back. I put the light on and gasped a bit when I saw that he had only one leg. He was about forty-five and his arms were extremely well developed, probably from years of traveling about with crutches. In the ensuing search, I came up with the pistol his daughter had told me about and, with less than a month in the street, I had made my first arrest.

Every permanently assigned patrolman I talked with congratulated me on a fine arrest. Most urged me to "write it up" for departmental recognition. "Who knows?" one guy said. "You might even win the gun." He was referring to the off-duty pistol awarded to the probationary patrolman with the best arrest while on probation. There were also similar awards for the best shot, the man with the highest academic marks (which I wound up missing by less than one point), and the highest mark in a physical achievement test. I wrote up a scratch copy of the arrest, including all pertinent details, and submitted it to one of the clerical men in the precinct. It is his job to type up a request for departmental recognition, but tradition dictates you "toss him a pound" (five dollars) for the service. Unfortunately for me, I was unaware of this practice and never thought that when he opened his desk drawer he wanted me to drop the money into it. Over a month went by and I became curious as to why I was not called down to the division office for an interview concerning the arrest. I mentioned it to an old-timer one day and he told me that as long as I hadn't thrown the clerical man the five dollars, my request was probably never submitted. I made it a point from then on to submit five dollars with each of my scratch copy requests for departmental recognition. It was easier than learning how to type.

As time rolled on in the 90, I developed a feeling for the precinct and the people in it. Most of the Puerto Ricans that I had met were sincere, hard-working people, struggling to make ends meet. A lot of the women without children found work in factories all over Brooklyn, Queens, and lower Manhattan, and many of the men held two jobs, working sixteen hours a day. But on the weekends they loved their "cerveza fría" and, more times than not, overindulged. It was tough enough trying to straighten out a family dispute when all parties were sober, but when all parties were drunk, it was nearly impossible and often proved dangerous. The Black section of the precinct was always the dirtiest: the streets, the buildings, the people, the language. The sympathy I had held for the "victims of society" before I became a police officer was gradually diminishing as I continually came in contact with able-bodied men on welfare who had no more right to a relief check than I did. What was worse (as I saw it) was that most of them pissed the money away on wine, women, or gambling, instead of proper upkeep of their homes and families. Roaches and rats ran rampant in their homes, through nobody's fault but their own. Unfortunately, the hard-working Blacks, the clean, respectable people who cared about life and who knew the value of the hard-earned dollar, were victimized the most by the attitudes and crimes of the lower element of their own race and oftentimes they expressed their own contempt for the "niggers," as they, too, called them. By mid-October I had decided that the best section of the precinct was the Jewish section, but by no means was that a bargain, either. I found the Hasidic Jews to be a religious people, set in their own ways, but far too nosy, unclean, and prejudiced against the Blacks to suit me.

I sensed deep-rooted feelings of prejudice in almost all the patrolmen in the precinct, White and Black, and felt myself slipping, also. Like the others, I had let independent incidents and my feelings toward individuals affect my attitudes in general.

On October 17, I was transferred to Safety Unit "A."

CHAPTER 4

Manhattan is divided into two safety units, "A" and "B," and without a doubt, "B" is the better assignment of the two.

When I was there, Safety Unit "A" consisted of the lower half of Manhattan and ran from Battery Park at the southernmost tip, north to Twenty-first Street, river to river. Some of the areas it encompassed were the Bowery, the Financial District, the Fulton Street Fish Market, the Meat Packing Center, Chinatown, Little Italy, City Hall, Greenwich Village, and its crosstown counterpart, the East Village.

A day on the Bowery was depressing, with decrepit bums and bottles of the cheapest wines strewn all over the sidewalks and gutters. The tramps hampered traffic and were constantly struck as they weaved their way from car to car, wiping windshields at red lights to earn enough money for more booze. In the Financial District, most notably Wall Street, the day was spent directing pedestrian traffic more than vehicle traffic, because wall-to-wall people, especially at lunchtime, and narrow streets kept most of the motorists on the periphery of the area. After a day at the Fulton Street Fish Market it was necessary to fumigate the uniform; at the Meat Packing Center a barrage of angle-parked trucks snarled traffic from morning until night; and main truck routes to and from various bridges and tunnels kept traffic moving at a snail's pace in Chinatown and Little Italy. Inundated with requests for directions at City Hall, I found days there uneventful and dull. The only places I enjoyed working in Safety "A" were Greenwich Village and the East Village, where I was hardly ever assigned.

Safety Unit "B," on the other hand, stretched from Twenty-first Street to Fifty-ninth Street, river to river, and included within its boundaries were the Theater District, Times Square, Shopper's Row, Madison Avenue, the fashionable East Side, and the countless restaurants, nightclubs, hotels, and strolling movie stars that New York is so famous for.

The pace is quicker in midtown than it is in lower Manhattan and the traffic is as thick in the daytime as it is at night. With parking forbidden on almost every street, strict enforcement of the Tow Away Program, and the convenience of the subway, office workers, executives, and shoppers leave their cars home. As a result taxicabs far outnumber private vehicles. Because the streets are wider and unobstructed by parked cars, the tie-ups always seem to break more quickly. The Theater District adjoins Times Square and, understandably, traffic flows smoother in the daytime than at curtain time. Taxicabs taking on and discharging passengers in the Shopper's Row, Madison Avenue, and East Side areas slow up traffic considerably, but people usually manage to get where they are going without any undue delays.

The few times later on in the job that I was fortunate enough to be assigned to Safety "B," I worked 4 P.M. to midnight tours and enjoyed myself immensely. On the whole, I figured traffic was traffic no matter where I was, but the pleasant surroundings of a post and the assurance of being able to get a good meal always made for a better day and there was no other area in the city that could boast of a better setting or more palatable food than found in midtown. At night I had the pleasure of eating my meal at one of the many nightclubs in the vicinity, such as the Latin Quarter, enjoying the show at the same time, and in the daytime I had very satisfying meals at some of the fancier hotels around town. I often spotted famous actors and actresses walking around the city, and whenever I could, I approached them for a chat.

The only bad memory I have of Safety "B" is the night I was assigned to Forty-second Street and Broadway and decided to take some "personal necessity" time in the Port Authority Police lounge, one block away. After relieving myself, I sat down to watch the news on television. A "personal" is only supposed to be twenty minutes at most, but I was off post about thirty-five. Near the end of the broadcast, the announcer was interrupted by a hand from off camera in which there was a message.

"I've just been handed a note," he said, "that a wild shoot-out has just taken place on Forty-second Street and Broadway. The getaway car in a robbery mounted the sidewalk at the location, striking several pedestrians, and at least six people are believed dead."

Holy shit! That was my post and I was supposed to be up there directing traffic. I bet every boss in Safety "B" was looking for me.

I ran out of the terminal and up Forty-second Street toward Broadway. As I neared the corner everything appeared normal, and there were no signs of trouble, but a sergeant was in the middle of the intersection directing traffic. I figured they had me cold and that I'd probably lose a couple of days' pay for being off post. More than likely he was assigned to direct traffic on my post until I showed up, so that I couldn't come up with a story such as "I was around, but I guess nobody saw me." I couldn't figure out how they removed six bodies in such a short time, however, and I was amazed at the absence of excitement in the area. I entered the intersection, walked up behind the sergeant as he was waving on a woman stopped in the middle of the street, and cleared the frog in my throat.

"Hello, sarge! I'm Droge," I said in defeat.

"Glad to know you. Listen, do me a favor, will you? Hold up that eastbound lane." He was playing it coy, I figured. All right, I'll play dumb, too.

"Sure. What's up?"

"This broad is a pisser. I'm riding along, spot her go through the light on Fortieth Street, catch up to her over here, and tell her to pull over." All the while he's talking, we're both directing traffic. "She gets so shook, she stalls the car out in the middle of the intersection, and now I gotta get her out."

I looked at his collar and it said "TPF" and then I

spotted his car off to the side, and sure enough in big wide letters it stated "Tactical Patrol Force." He wasn't from Safety "B" and, best of all, he wasn't looking for me. I wondered about the newscast.

The woman finally managed to pull her car to the side of the road and the sergeant took her license and registration to his radio car. I walked over with him, and through the window I asked him innocently: "Any action tonight?"

"Yeah, we just had a big chase a while ago. It started up here somewhere."

Oh, oh! I wasn't out of the fire yet.

"Some guys pulled a stickup and took off. A precinct car spotted them and pursued. They caught up with them on Thirty-fourth Street after they mounted the sidewalk and crashed into a building down there."

"Anybody hurt?"

"Yeah, five or six people were sprawled out on the sidewalk, including the driver of the getaway car. A couple of them looked dead but I didn't stick around to find out. There were about fifty guys up there."

"OK, take it easy, sarge. I've got to get back out in the street here. Nice talking to you." I breathed a sigh of relief and stayed in the intersection for the rest of the tour.

Aside from the aforementioned disparities, Safety Unit "A" had more than double the bridges and tunnels that Safety Unit "B" had and, because of the chaotic congestion at those locations around rush hours, a consensus from either command definitely would have placed a post by a bridge or a tunnel on the bottom of a hypothetical "Most Desirable Post List."

The post I got most often while assigned to Safety "A" was at the base of the Williamsburg Bridge in the slum area along Delancey Street. Peopled with sleazy prostitutes, winos, and drug addicts, the streets of the Lower East Side were wretched to look at, walk on, and work on. A decent place to eat was so hard to find that in three and one-half months, I never found one. I reluctantly ate most often in a Jewish cafeteria with only dairy food on the menu—until the day a rat decided to join me at my table.

My only refuge in inclement weather or when I had to write up summons affidavits was cramped quarters in the rear of a liquor store near my post. I got along well with the owner, a relationship fostered by the fact that a patrolman on the premises in a lousy neighborhood always made good company for store owners.

My only consolation in Safety "A" was that (following the employment of another scientific method of decision making common to the Police Department—a pick from a hat) I wound up working steady tours of 11 A.M. to 7 P.M. with Sundays and Mondays off. It just so happened that Christmas Eve and New Year's Eve landed on Sundays that year and that was the first and last time I was fortunate enough to be off on those dates.

The primary duty of a patrolman assigned to a safety unit is traffic control, which includes not only expediting traffic but also promoting safety conscious practices and compliance with traffic regulations. In addition, if assigned to Safety "B," towing illegally parked cars becomes one of the chores. One day while clearing a block pasted with "No Parking, Parade Today" signs, I learned from a Police Department tow truck operator how to break and enter a car in less than thirty seconds. That experience will definitely come in handy if I ever decide to become a car thief.

Directing traffic is an art in itself. Nobody teaches you how to do it. You just step into the street and start waving your hands with two thoughts in mind: keep the traffic moving and keep from getting killed. Aside from the frustrations, there is also the danger—standing in the middle of a busy New York City intersection during rush hours is not my idea of the safest place in the world.

The way I saw some people drive, I couldn't help wondering how many box tops they had to send away for their licenses. Not only did the cars whiz by perilously close, but there were also swaying chains on the rear of many trucks and getting smacked with one of them could have proven fatal, from either the blow itself, or the fall into oncoming traffic.

There is a certain knack that, if mastered, will enable the patrolman to expedite traffic at even the busiest thoroughfares, but, unfortunately, I was unable to develop that knack, so most of the time I stuck with the lights. If the light was green, I'd wave the traffic on; if it was red, I'd put up my hand and blow my whistle. Some days I felt as useful as screen doors in a submarine.

Because the lights did most of my work, I was able to concentrate on preventing "spillbacks," the patrolman's nemesis in many a traffic jam and a safety man's nightmare. A spillback is when a motorist enters the intersection, finds out there is no room for him, is unable to back up because of advancing traffic behind him, and thus blocks the cross traffic. The cross traffic, then, pulls into the intersection but is unable to flow and everybody is stuck. Afrer experiencing many difficult tie-ups resulting from spillbacks, I wasn't surprised at all to find out that the summons the commanding officer of Safety "A" liked to see issued most was the summons for spillback.

To effectively cut the rise in traffic accidents each year and the injuries and the deaths that resulted from them, we were instructed to enforce the laws indiscriminately and to warn, summons, or, when necessary, arrest motorists, whether their violations were intentional or unintentional. In my short stint in the academy I was informed that sixteen specific moving violations were the main reasons for the heavy amount of accidents throughout the country and they ranged from driving while intoxicated, for which a person was arrested, speeding, for which a summons was in order, and improper lights, for which a warning would suffice. Unfortunately, there wasn't enough time to be instructed on the proper issuance of a summons, so I had to learn that for myself in the street.

At first, having received two summonses for minor violations myself before joining the force, and knowing the frustration and ill feeling that went with them, I wasn't too keen on issuing summonses, but sometimes I felt it was necessary.

The first summons I issued was on Delancey and Essex streets, where there were three signs that indicated "No Left Turn." I waved on a taxicab driver who had signaled to make a right, turned away to wave on the opposing lane, and turned back again just in time to hop out of the way of the cab that was making a left. Not only flustered that anyone would so flagrantly disobey the signs and a police officer, I was also enraged that he had almost hit me in the process. He was stopped for a red light on the next corner and I trotted over to him, collected his license and registration, and issued him a summons.

He was arrogant and told me: "You have to be a certain kind of person to give a cabdriver a summons. This is my livelihood." This made me a bit angrier and I wound up getting into a heated discussion with him that nearly resulted in his arrest. The aggravation from that experience taught me to listen while writing, but not talk. Most of the time from then on that's exactly what I did.

On another occasion, at the same intersection, the light was not working properly and I was waving cars across, against the red. One man stopped his car on the corner, and when I waved him on he refused to move. I waved him on again and he pointed to the red light and shook his head. I told him to pull his car over to the curb and asked him why he didn't come across when I waved.

"The light was red," he said.

"But don't you know a police officer's directions supersede any traffic device?" I asked.

"You can't tell me to go against a red light if I don't want to. The last time I did that, I got a summons."

"You mean a police officer directed you to pass a red light, then gave you a summons for it?"

"No, my wife was the one who told me to pass the red light. She should have gotten the ticket."

I issued him a summons for "Failure to Obey a Police Officer's Lawful Direction." If there was a violation for being a jerk, I would have given him one for that, too.

I was often offered money by motorists to ignore violations, but I never took a nickle. Some people openly made the offer and others implied it, waiting for me to make the first move. Many times a folded bill would be stuffed inside the person's license, or drop to the ground as he got out of his car. Almost always I was alone and uninfluenced, and still had enough pride to refuse. Not only that, but to me traffic money was very risky. The old-timers, or "hairbags" as they're often called, had a rule of thumb about who was safe to take from and who was not that hinged on appearance. Anyone physically unable to be an undercover police officer was usually considered safe. For instance, if a man was five feet, two inches tall, walked with a limp, wore glasses, and offered money, they would take it. Also, women were usually always safe. The big hole I found in that theory was the fact that the previously described man could well have been the district attorney or a judge and the woman, his wife.

I had never heard of anyone making a bribery arrest, so I just tongue-lashed those who offered and let them go. Besides, even though I had never offered a police officer money when I was stopped for a summons, I came to realize that the image that the New York City Police Department had projected over the last few years was not a healthy one. As one out-of-towner put it after fruitlessly attempting to avoid a red light summons: "Well, at least I tried. New York is the one city in the entire country where you stand a fifty-fifty chance of either bullshitting your way or buying your way out of a summons." I don't know about the part concerning New York's exclusiveness, but, unfortunately, the rest of that accusation is true. It saddened me to find that out.

On the whole, life was too boring, too easy, in Safety "A" and "B," and after experiencing other phases of the job, I feel any patrolman assigned to those commands more than two years risks losing all perspective on what being a policeman is all about.

In December, 1967, while still temporarily assigned to Safety Unit "A," I was detailed to my first demonstration. The theme was draft resistance and the location was the Whitehall Induction Center, an old fortlike building at the foot of Manhattan.

Demonstrations are as much a part of New York City as its skyscrapers or its subway system, but there are two kinds: orderly and disorderly. The former does not necessitate as much police supervision as the latter; but the possibilities of injuries, accidents, lost persons, and other such incidents, inherent with large assemblages, nevertheless require that ample police be present. Police presence at a disorderly demonstration is absolutely necessary to preserve the peace. Shouting and chanting are common with both types, but generally there are acts of misconduct at disorderly demonstrations promoted by threatening and malicious participants. Tempers flare without notice and fights break out sporadically.

My tour was 4 A.M. to noon and the place of muster was the Staten Island Ferry Terminal, two blocks from the center. The early morning air froze any skin exposed to it and the only way to keep warm was to drink coffee. In my entire life before that detail I must have had a total of two gallons of coffee, but in those three days alone, I drank at least triple that amount. After receiving our assignments in the Ferry Terminal and walking over to take up our posts by the Induction Center, there wasn't much to do until 8 A.M. except stand around and shoot the breeze. Barriers were erected on every street surrounding the center and it was our job to make sure that nobody passed them.

At around 8 A.M. every morning a screaming, wild group of from five hundred to a thousand braved the winter weather and converged on the area. Apparently formed up a few blocks away, they were well equipped with flags and signs that ranged from "Fuck the Draft" to "Hell No, We Won't Go" to "Thou Shalt Not Kill," and some marched with a style that hinted at past military training. Made up mostly, but certainly not entirely, of long-haired youths dressed in shabby clothes, they set up picket lines around the building, chanting and singing antiwar slogans and songs all the while, in an effort to thwart any inductee's entering. Unknown to them, however, every future soldier had been contacted days in advance and arrangements were made for him to meet a police escort a few blocks away to guide him into the center.

Aside from tussling with prowar demonstrators who showed up on the scene, the mammoth crowd often stormed the barricades en masse, swinging their signs and flags at patrolmen as they did so, and not a day went by without an arrest. Regardless of the patrolmen's political outlooks, they all, to the man, were against violent demonstrations. Some officers I spoke with sympathized with the cause, but defended the center with as much verve as the rest of us and, in fact, one sympathizing officer made an arrest on the second or third day.

Over one hundred plainclothesmen and detectives were assigned to the detail and each day they were given buttons to wear on their clothes so that we could distinguish them from the demonstrators; one day it was green, one day it was orange, and one day it was yellow. With long hair, beards, and shabby clothes, some of the plainclothesmen made it a point to wear the button in the most conspicuous spot.

On one particular occasion I spotted an aide of the mayor leading a group of people toward my barrier; no one was wearing a button, not even the aide. They charged the barrier, trying to break through to the center, and a battle ensued. After a few moments of nightsticks hitting their marks, the demonstrators gave up and retreated. It was rather disconcerting, to say the least, to see someone who was supposed to be on your side, working against you. Others noticed him, too, and when the word spread, many patrolmen spoke their minds openly, denouncing the aide and the administration. I didn't say anything, but in my mind I seconded most of the disparaging remarks. Incidents such as this constantly contributed to the demoralization of the force throughout my career.

CHAPTER 5

On February 1, 1968, after seven months of learning the job in the street, having had the seeds of bias planted in my head, having formed most of my opinions on the best ways to handle various situations, which weren't necessarily the most legitimate, but certainly the most practical, having depended heavily on the more experienced patrolmen in the street to teach me the ropes, and having been almost constantly exposed to their prejudiced outlooks and venal ideas, I was sent back to the Police Academy for formal training. It was like closing the barn door after the horse had escaped.

In two weeks we were off probation and, under the Civil Service Law, full-fledged patrolmen. Under Police Academy rules, however, we were still considered recruits and treated as such. Needless to say, the instructors had their hands full trying to teach us by the book, because we had learned by now that the job in the street is just not done by the book.

The rules, regulations, and procedures of the job, as taught in the academy and as applied on the street, were vastly different. The first thing many of the more experienced officers had said to me when I worked in the 90 and Safety "A" was to forget what I had learned in the academy. Things are done differently out here, they told me and they were right. Some of the forms that I had been taught were used daily in the precinct, couldn't even be found, and when I questioned some of the officers they hadn't even heard of them. The procedure of checking in with the station house every hour while on patrol was hardly ever followed and, if it was, many times the answer from the switchboard operator was: "Call me when you need me, otherwise, don't break my balls." And on and on and on.

I had become cynical during my nine months on the job as I became aware of the realities of police work and as I saw what it was really like. This state of mind hardened when I contrasted reality with the ideals taught in the classroom.

The instructors constantly emphasized our status as professionals yet neither they nor the people in the street treated us as such. As recruits in the academy, we were not allowed to use the elevators, we were given "gigs," or delinquent points as used in high schools, for various infractions, we were not to be out after midnight, and heaven forbid we wander into a place that served liquor. In the street over the past few months, my being spat upon, verbally assaulted, and the target for objects ranging from cigarette butts to soda bottles indicated how much respect I had received and how professional the people thought I was. They wouldn't have done those things to a doctor, yet I was out there to help them as much, if not more, and they did them to me. The stories my father had often told me of the respect he had given the patrolman on the beat and my own reminiscence of similar respect shown, haunted me in the academy. I constantly wondered why we were not taught in realities instead of ideals, to prepare us better for the shock of the street.

Aside from the cynicism, the instructors also had to contend with the cocky attitudes of a lot of the men. When we were first assigned to the academy, nine months before, everyone was green and unsure of himself, but the second time around that mode was replaced by an overall rebellious atmosphere, which portended trouble right from the start. Having had a taste of the street, the men were anxious to get to their permanent commands, regardless of the fact that they knew little about the law. Many men lacked the discipline necessary for proper control of the classroom and defiant outbursts often disrupted the class for several minutes. In an attempt to rectify this lack of discipline, some of the instructors meted out misweighed punishments for insignificant infractions and the men resented it.

At each command I was assigned, the other probationary men and I had compared notes as we went along about all aspects of the job, legitimate and illegitimate. In the academy recruits talked, and in some instances bragged, of their "scores" in the street, as if there was no chance that another would turn them in. There wasn't—the "code of silence" prevailed.

Wisecracks in the classroom about corruption were laughed at by other rookies and ignored by instructors. There was still no constructive advice on how to handle the *problem* of corruption. No one thought of it as a problem. The inference was that you were old enough to know the difference between right and wrong and that was it. If you did something wrong and you were caught—tough luck; if you did everything right, there was nothing to worry about.

There was no appreciation of the fact that most of the men had never before had the opportunity or occasion to have to choose between honesty or dishonesty on the police level. When did I, in an office in the telephone company, ever have to decide whether I should take money or not, or for that matter what to do in case someone wanted to give me a free meal, knowing that I wasn't supposed to take it? And how did the rest of the men in my class differ—the truck driver, the baker, the plumber's assistant? In their new role they would be put upon to not only decide what to do when offered these things, but also to make that decision in a matter of seconds. Ten or twenty dollars to overlook a traffic summons was one thing, but hundreds or maybe thousands of dollars to overlook a serious crime was another and certainly should have merited some consideration from the instructors.

Men who had worked all over the city, from the northernmost reaches of the Bronx to the southern tip of Brooklyn, spoke of payoffs to themselves or others and the stories were basically consistent. For the most part they centered around gamblers who paid quite regularly, but they also included tow truck operators on accident scenes, city marshals on evictions, and other various "contracts" or "scores." Though I had taken money in the 90, I was still so unfamiliar with the preponderance of corruption existing in the street that I was amazed at not only the nonchalance with which the patrolmen took the money, but also the ease with which they talked about it.

Though late in coming, there was an exhausting amount of rigorous mental and physical training, but at least it wasn't necessary to go over "How to Go Sick" again and everybody was happy for that. I studied long and hard and spent many a night in bed with a book. There was so much to cover and so little time to cover it, for nobody knew how long it would be before the next demonstration or riot forced us out into the street again, probably to stay. We delved deeply into the more important subjects but simply skimmed over the ones the instructors decided we could learn for ourselves, if necessary.

The most enjoyable hours in the academy were spent in the firing range, learning how to shoot, in the swimming pool, learning water rescue, and on the third-floor rear staircase, looking through the window, watching the nude models pose for the art school next door.

The gym classes were brutal and many times a patrolman would collapse from exhaustion or puke up his lunch. It was interesting to note how many men were in such poor physical shape, even though their very lives might one day depend on their condition. Some men couldn't do ten push-ups or run around the gym three times without needing oxygen. On the other hand, there were a few men who had developed their bodies quite well and could have easily outshone the instructors. I was somewhere in the middle.

Every class included lessons in judo, boxing, first aid, and the proper use of a nightstick. I had a gratifying experience one gym class when during a boxing lesson I was matched against a patrolman whom I had come to dislike in the 90. We were supposed to pull our punches when practicing new techniques, but the temptation was just too great and I floored him. For some reason or other, after that he didn't want to be matched with me in the gym anymore.

Instead of just barking the commands and then watching, the instructors exercised along with the men, in a sense justifying their most strenuous "requests." Unlike the academic instructors who were sergeants or above, the gym instructors were all patrolmen with a sergeant in charge, though he never conducted any classes. Some of the instructors were young men and one, in fact, had just graduated out of the last class, March, 1967. Unfortunately, instead of sympathizing with the men and appreciating their anxieties to get out of the academy, he antagonized them and acted in a puerile manner, all too often overstepping his bounds. He made his presence at an otherwise uneventful gym class completely rewarding one day when, not knowing how close to the rear he was, he fell off the instructor's platform in the middle of a jumping jack. The class was hysterical for about ten minutes and shouts of "encore" echoed into the halls. Another instructor, stocky with a short crew cut, not only looked like a Marine Corps drill instructor, but acted like one also.

Being off probation with close to a year on the job and still not knowing where or when we would be permanently assigned, victimized by rumors of graduation dates that came and went, experiencing more and more disruptions in the classrooms and pressure in the gym, the class was just bound to explode; and one day it did.

"All right, let's do fifty jumping jacks," the young instructor bellowed from the front of the class. The men were spread before him in rows of twelve, from one end of the massive building to the other. Because the academy was overcrowded with recruits, an armory about a half mile away with inadequate shower facilities and no lockers was being utilized. We had to change into gym gear in the grandstands and pile our uniforms in a heap on benches, which disturbed some of the men and certainly didn't help relieve the ill feelings that existed. "By the numbers. One, two, three, four, one, two ..." We finished the fifty breathing heavily and his gravelly voice blared again. "That was terrible. Now we're going to do another fifty and this time we're going to do them together. By the num ..."

"Aw, fuck you," said a voice from the rear. It had started. The frustrations and anxieties had peaked and the mutiny had begun.

"What was that?"

"Fuck you," said a different voice from the other side of the floor.

"OK, let's make that one hundred jumping jacks."

Now many men moaned aloud.

"One-fifty," he screamed, determined to break our backs once and for all.

"You do them, champ, we'll watch you," came another anonymous voice, again from the rear. The other two instructors assigned to the class that day were walking within the ranks, but were unable to detect who it was that was calling out. Inspired by the brashness and the frustration of the instructors, one by one first and then in clusters, the men sat down.

"Stand up," shouted one instructor.

"Fuck you," someone shouted back and in a moment all were seated. The instructor on the platform stepped down and went into the office to call the sergeant at the academy. Huddled together in the center of the floor, we remained that way with catcalls and obscenity flying both ways for about a half an hour. At that time the sergeant in charge steamed through the side door with fire in his eyes.

"Stand up," he commanded, ready to explode, and everyone obeyed. His stern face and slanted brows hinted at his vehement anger. "In all my years in the department, never before have I witnessed such flagrant acts of insubordination. Now, I don't know what's gotten into you men, but whatever it is, it had better end right here and now. This is a gym class and you're to follow instructions. Those who don't, no matter who they are or how many they are, will be dealt with accordingly. Now you mark my words, I'll do everything in my power to get them thrown off the job and, by God, I mean it." His voice was cracking and I for one believed him. "Do you understand?"

All stood silent.

"Do you understand?" he shouted louder.

"Yes," was the reply.

"Yes, what?"

"Yes, sir!"

"Now, get down on the floor. By the numbers, twenty-five push-ups. One, two, one, two . . ."

The class continued normally, but the point was made and from then on the sergeant supervised every gym class personally. As a gesture of goodwill he even suspended exercises one day and brought down our Patrolmen's Benevolent Association delegate, so we could voice our grievances openly. Unfortunately, he had represented us poorly over the months and any time a patrolman went to him with a gripe he would tell them, "Don't make waves." Appearing before the men as a whole was probably the worst thing he could have done, for the men took their ire out on him, verbally ripped him to shreds and asked him to resign right on the spot. He didn't oblige, but a few months later he received the same reaction from a class after us and put his papers in.

Near the end of March all the probies called their "hook." A hook is a person who claims he can get you the exact assignment you want and sometimes he can. But most times he just says he can. In the telephone company we called him a "rabbi," and coincidentally, my hook was a friend of mine in the telephone company whose brother was a sergeant in headquarters. He was supposed to be instrumental in new assignments for recruits fresh out of the academy, and I was assured of any precinct I asked for. In return he asked nothing, but I had planned on giving him a couple of bottles of Scotch. I felt I was getting a good deal because some of the men were buzzing with stories of payoffs of hundreds of dollars, depending on the position, location, or detail desired. I told my hook I wanted to go to either the 62nd precinct in Bath Beach or the 66th precinct in Borough Park, both a hop, skip, and jump from my home and both high on the list of "Country Club" precincts. If they were impossible, I listed as my next three choices the 61st precinct in Sheepshead Bay, the 68th precinct in Park Slope and the 63rd precinct in East Flatbush. Anywhere in Brooklyn except Bedford-Stuyvesant, I told him. I wanted to be active and make some good arrests, but Bedford-Stuyvesant was reputedly the roughest and most dangerous Black section in the city—even worse than Harlem. My hook told me he'd take care of it.

Rumor after rumor arose pinpointing the date of graduation and the men grew tense. The instructors had heard the rumors also and were hurrying through the syllabus to make sure they touched everything, disregarding the prescribed order and manner of presentation. They covered all areas, but our heads were spinning. We had taken three of the four required academic examinations, but nobody placed too much stock in them, for there was justifiable doubt that anyone, especially being off probation and under the protection of the Civil Service Law, would or could get fired for not passing tests on material so shoddily covered. Because of the uneasy feelings and the constant flak, the instructors were as anxious as we were to hear an official announcement of our graduation date. It never came.

CHAPTER 6

The killing of Martin Luther King on the afternoon of April 4, 1968, took place in Memphis, Tennessee, but triggered waves of tension throughout the country. New York City was no exception and in order to be fully prepared for any Black uprising, again we were temporarily assigned to the street. This time I was sent to the 9th precinct, in the East Village section of lower Manhattan. It runs from Houston Street to Fourteenth Street, from Broadway to the East River, and is considered the busiest precinct in Manhattan South. Because the city's administrators were so sure of trouble from the Negro quarters, all members of the force were ordered to perform twelve hour tours, the rookies being assigned 8 A.M. to 8 P.M.

In the East Village live rich and poor Whites, Blacks, and Puerto Ricans. But, most notably, the East Village is the home of the original Hippies. Long hair and beards started right there and were popular when the rest of the country was wearing crew cuts and aspirin-sized knots in their ties. It was considered such an unusual community a few years ago that tourist buses made regular passes so the people could ogle the "freaks."

On any given night the couples in love, strolling hand in hand down the street, along the water, or through Thompkins Park, add to the unique atmosphere of this Bohemian neighborhood. They may be girl and boy, girl and girl, boy and boy, girl and dog, boy and dog, girl with boy and dog, or any combination thereof. They may also be White and White, Black and Black, Black and White,

White and Yellow, Black and Yellow, Red and Black (Yes, Virginia, some Indians still live in New York), Red and White, Red, White, and Blue (figure that one out), or, again, any combination thereof.

On the weekends the East Village is inundated with thrill seekers and what the real Hippies call "Plastic Hippies." The former are lured by the fact that in most any doorway they can buy grass, hash, speed, LSD, STP, DMT, XYZ, EFD, or whatever else turns them on. The latter are the people from around the city who dress up in their wildest clothes, the clothes they are embarrassed to wear in their own neighborhoods, and come to the East Village to "hang out" because they know nobody will laugh at them down there. They want to blend with the "in crowd," but they are easily discernible because they are the ones with shoes, or without holes in their bell bottoms. As one real Hippie once told me: "These people envy the freedom and independence of the Hippie and for the weekend they let their hair down in an attempt to be as free, or at least to project that image. But they will never be as free because they are slaves to the dogma of society that kowtows to conformity and when Monday morning rolls around they can be found doing the same old thing, the routine they had escaped for a while." In essence, they consider them synthetic, thus the label "Plastic Hippie."

There are few private homes in the area and most of the people live in apartment houses. The clean ones smell of air freshener or incense and the occupants are usually wealthy, but most of the buildings are dirty and smell of insecticide or urine and the occupants are usually unemployed. The inferior condition notwithstanding, it is expensive to live in even the dingiest East Village apartment and for this reason, in addition to their aversion to work, many of the local residents form "crash pads" that consist entirely of wall-to-wall mattresses. As many as twenty people might share a two-room apartment, paying the rent with pooled money obtained through panhandling or thievery.

There are department stores galore up around Fourteenth Street and, as long as the tramps don't bother you, you can always find a bargain down on the Bowery. There's *kielbasa* and *keeska* in any of the Polish butcher shops along Avenue C or pizza and sausage sandwiches in any of the snack shops along Avenue A. When I was there, you could see a burlesque show with buxom strippers, a play with an all-Black cast, and a rock show with dancing, amoebalike lights, all within six blocks of each other on Second Avenue.

The hub of the village is St. Mark's Place, between Second and Third avenues, and on that one block alone gather more people at one time than any other five blocks put together in the area. Aside from the wildest discotheque in town, there are shops to buy sandals, beads, leather crafts of all kinds, T-shirts adorned with pictures of anything from Mickey Mouse to a vagina, headbands, neckbands, incense, water pipes, hash pipes, regular pipes, cigarette-roll paper, marijuana "roach" holders, and probably any other conventional or unconventional product on the market.

Most of the shop owners were friendly, but none more so than two Polish sisters who owned a small restaurant in the middle of the block. Once seated at a table covered with a red-and-white checkered cloth and a candle, you could order the specialty of the house, *kielbasa* and boiled potatoes, or anything from spaghetti and meatballs to chow mein. They always invited me in when I had that post and it was nearly impossible to pay for my meal. "You're our guest," they would say. I always offered, but never insisted, and made a point of leaving a tip for them, large enough to pay for the dinner. That arrangement made us both happy.

Two doors away at the Electric Circus Discotheque, which cost four dollars to get in, unless you took your shoes off, in which case it was three fifty, a popular rock group, two song and dance acts, and a light show filled the bill twice a night, seven days a week. The immense building was painted bright blue with multicolored trim and housed over three hundred screaming teenyboppers with no problems. The bulk of the crowd ranged from sixteen to twenty and there was no drinking on the premises, but from the blank, glassy-eyed looks on most of the customers' faces, there was no need for alcohol.

When the nine or ten of us from 67-17 arrived, the precinct was practically devoid of patrolmen. The major portion of the men had been sent to Harlem to bolster the forces preparing for riots. In addition to a skeleton crew in the station house and a few old-timers cruising the neighborhood, we made up the entire complement of the 9th precinct.

On my first tour, I was assigned to a radio car with another rookie and we spent the day running from one job to the next, taking longer than the regular men because we were so unfamiliar with the streets. For that matter, we weren't too familiar with the radio car and the radio because neither of us had ever before ridden without being assigned with a more experienced patrolman. Although it seemed we were called over the radio every fifteen minutes, I'm sure we must have missed at least half a dozen calls because our ears were not attuned to listening for Nine Charley, our code name.

One of our assignments was an ambulance case on First Street and it took us a good twenty minutes to find the house. It was on the top floor of a four-story tenement occupied mainly by Puerto Ricans. A middle-aged woman had fallen from a ladder, cut her leg on a glass-top table on the way down, and was lying on the kitchen floor, unconscious. At least that's what we were told, but from the looks of the disheveled room, the bruise on the woman's cheek, and the sweat on the drunken husband's brow, I guessed they had had a fight and he had connected with a roundhouse. But I was just guessing.

I took the necessary information about the woman from the husband while my partner attended her leg. Blood was coming out slowly and the floor was covered with it.

"This doesn't look so good, Ed," my partner said. "Did Central say the ambulance was coming?"

"I don't know. I'll go down and check." I walked down to the radio car, started the motor, and waited for the air to clear before calling Central.

"Nine Charley to Central, K."

"Go ahead, Charley."

"Is there an ambulance responding to that First Street job, K?"

"Wait a second, Charley . . . Bellevue holding, K."

"10-4."

I didn't really know what "Bellevue holding" meant, but

I thought my partner would, so I didn't ask over the air. I knew he was referring to Bellevue Hospital, which was in the area, but I couldn't figure out what he meant by holding. I went back up the eight flights of stairs, entered the apartment, and bent down next to my partner who was apply pressure to the gash in the woman's leg.

"What's the story?" he said.

"Bellevue holding," I answered.

"What the fuck does that mean?"

"I don't know. I thought you would. Well, whether they're coming or not, we're going to have to carry her downstairs, anyhow, so let's take her down now and if the ambulance hasn't arrived by then, we'll take her in the radio car."

"OK."

We picked the woman up and sat her in a kitchen chair. We borrowed the husband's belt and strapped it around her to keep her from falling off. She was a slight woman and only weighed about 120 pounds. We carried her down to the radio car and the ambulance still hadn't arrived, so we placed her in the rear, letting the husband get in next to her for the trip to the hospital.

I picked up the phone on the dash. "Nine Charley to Central, K."

"Nine Charley, go ahead."

"This unit has one female and one male in the car, proceeding to Bellevue Hospital, K."

"10-4, Charley, I'll cancel the ambulance. Advise when they leave the vehicle, K."

"10-4."

It was lucky that the husband had come along because we didn't even know where Bellevue Hospital was. It would have been a switch for a police car to pull up next to a pedestrian and ask for directions. With the turret light flashing, we got to the hospital in a few minutes, carried her into the emergency room, gave the nurse the proper information, and left. We never saw her again. We found out a little later that "Bellevue holding" meant that Bellevue didn't have any available ambulances and the dispatcher was holding the job for the next available one.

We were so busy answering jobs for the first six hours that we didn't have a chance to eat. At about 2 P.M. we rode over to St. Marks Place and Third Avenue to grab a sausage sandwich. Outside the snack shop was a breathtaking blonde dressed in a white mini-skirt, high enough to reveal beautifully proportioned, tanned legs. She wore hardly any make-up but her face was radiant and needed nothing to evince her beauty. She was being embraced and fondled by a swarthy, orangutanlike Black man, shoddily dressed and at least ten years her senior. To me it appeared she was enjoying it, but my partner was a bit suspicious and as we walked by he tipped his hat and said: "Good afternoon. Is everything all right?"

"Fine, just fine," she replied. The Negro responded with an indignant smirk.

"That kills me," he told me inside. "A beautiful piece of ass like that screwin' around with that Black 'skel.' I don't get it. Why is she with him? She looks like an actress or a model. She should be dating rich movie stars, but, instead, she picks him."

I didn't say anything, but I reflected on it, too. Up to this point in my life, I had never given interracial marriages or relationships any serious thought. Anytime I had seen a Black man with a White woman, or vice versa, I didn't think bad of them, rather on the contrary, I admired their courage to be able to stand up to the scorn and abuse they were subject to. But since becoming a policeman I had been brainwashed with constant anti-Black talk and had become increasingly biased. Before joining the department, I would have been unaffected by the couple out front, but now I was revolted. My partner couldn't stop talking about it, and because he was driving, he cruised through that block, or parked on it, every chance he could in the next half hour. They appeared to be window-shopping and had slowly worked their way up and down the street twice. After at least five passes, we rode down the block on the way to a job and the blonde was alone, standing by a bus stop. I don't know where the Negro was. My partner couldn't resist and he pulled the car to the curb, motioning at the girl to approach.

"Hello, again," he said with a serious face. "Please don't think me rude, but I must ask you a question that's been on my mind all day."

"Sure," she said with a big smile.

"You're a beautiful girl and you could probably have any man your little heart desired. Why do you pick him?"

"Well, it's really none of your business but if my telling you will make you feel better ... last year I decided to dedicate the rest of my life to the propagation of the Negro race. ..." I stopped listening; I didn't want to hear any more. She went on to explain further to my partner for about three more minutes, however, until he smiled and politely interrupted her.

"Thank you, but we just got a job over the air and we really must go." He rolled up the window and pulled away quickly. His face was flushed and the veins on his forehead were clearly defined.

"A whacko," he said. "A beautiful piece of ass like that and she's a whacko."

I agreed. She was a beautiful piece of ass.

After a day or two, most of the regular men had been reassigned to the precinct and I saw little of the inside of a radio car after that. The union members of my former employer, the New York Telephone Company, went on strike while I was assigned to the 9th and occasionally my post was in front of the telephone building on Second Avenue and Thirteenth Street. Some of my old friends were assigned by the union to picket in front and the day passed quickly as I stood outside, reminiscing with them. On my meal hour, they took a break from the picket line and we ate lunch together in a fancy restaurant, or grabbed a quick hot dog at an umbrella stand so that we could catch the burlesque show a couple of blocks away. I had such a good time those few days that I was a bit sorry when the strike ended and they went back to work.

I enjoyed walking a foot post most of the time, especially if it was Special 4—St. Marks between Second and Third avenues. When assigned there, the day passed quickly with never a dull moment. There was always something to do or something to see. I stopped into all the shops on the block to let the merchants know I was around if they needed me and each one of them expressed a combination of appreciation and bewilderment. With the advent of the radio car and the trend toward its more extensive use, the day of the footman was passé and a patrolman stopping into a store just to say hello was indeed remote. I was gratified by their favorable reactions and in fleeting moments felt like I was really accomplishing something, just by being in sight.

The Village was filled with runaways, mostly young girls, many of whom were fugitives from wealthy homes in Long Island, suburban Connecticut, Cape Cod, and other eastern seaboard, well-to-do communities, where they could probably have any material thing they wanted. But what they wanted, money couldn't buy and in quest of this unknown quantity, they fled. For some reason they felt that this happiness could be found in the East Village, but not long after their arrival realized they were mistaken, and instead found only misery.

A night on Special 4 did not pass without my being besieged by distraught mothers, fathers, or even distant relatives, of runaways, equipped with photos of the child, on the back of which were physical statistics, descriptions of the clothes they were wearing when last seen, habits, friends, rewards, and the name, address, and telephone number of the parents and guardians. These usually well-dressed, bejeweled seekers scoured the Village in hopes of finding their missing child and invariably wound up on St. Marks Place.

The back wall of the station house was covered with pictures and pleas to the officers to keep an eye out for the runaways and some of the mercenary men did just that, looking forward to the reward with as much avarice as a bounty hunter of the Old West.

I found a young girl one night who confided in me that she had come to New York with little money and, searching for friends, met up with a female member of a "family." She was invited to stay at their crash pad, where she met the rest of the members, seventeen men and six women. The first night went by without a hitch, but the second night she was involuntarily "gang banged" by every male member and forced to participate in homosexual activities with the female members. She estimated about ten hours of continuous sex. She was then considered a member of the family and for two months panhandled and stole to contribute to its support. She was too frightened and embarrassed to do anything but cooperate. When I found her, she had run away from them and was wandering aimlessly along Third Avenue. She cried throughout the story and I feel the only reason she told me was because she had to tell someone. I tried desperately to find out where the "family's" crash pad was, but she would not tell me and said that even if I found them, she would not prosecute. She asked me never to tell anyone, especially her parents, and, until this writing, I have not mentioned it to a soul. When her parents came in from Connecticut to pick her up, they offered me a three hundred dollar reward, but the happiness on the girl's face when they arrived and the thrill that I was a small part of it was rewarding enough and I refused.

CHAPTER 7

When I wasn't in a radio car, on a strike post, or walking a foot post, I was assigned to City Hall on demonstration details.

City Hall is an old graystone that looks just like any other City Hall around the country, with a wide, stone-stepped stairway leading past a row of pillars into the main entrance. Inside there are well-dressed men and women forever hustling through the halls, into and out of the office of the mayor or the maze of smaller offices maintained for his staff and other officials. Directly in front is a parking area, which holds approximately twenty cars, and encircling the building is a small, well-kept park, filled with trees and lined with benches for lunchtime pigeon feeders.

Whenever there was a strike in the city, which seemed to be more days than not each year, the members of the striking union demonstrated at City Hall. Whenever a politician, most notably the mayor, said something against the grain of a club, group, or faction of the city, they demonstrated at City Hall. Whenever a new bill or tax was introduced into the State Legislature that displeased the residents of a particular community in the city, they demonstrated at City Hall. In essence, whenever people were not happy in the city and they wanted to let everyone know, they demonstrated at City Hall and for this reason a detail with as few as twenty men and as many as two hundred men, depending on the size of the demonstration, was assigned there to keep the peace.

THE PATROLMAN: A COP'S STORY 69

I didn't mind the peaceful demonstrations so much because if the crowd broke up before 4 P.M. there was a good chance we would get an "early blow," instead of having to report back to the command. At a disorderly demonstration, where fights flared up and the people got really out of hand, there was no telling when we would get dismissed and on some occasions I wound up working an hour or two overtime. On the norm, however, after two, three, or at the most four hours, even the most irritated demonstrators tired of standing, marching, or shouting and the crowd would break up and go home.

Because I hated traveling on the subway in uniform, I took my car to every demonstration. The parking conditions by City Hall were horrendous and on two different occasions, while assigned to a demonstration, my car was summonsed on an expired meter.

One morning, en route to City Hall, I heard on the radio that a Black faction (I missed what they were to protest about) was to be demonstrating that day and a small turnout was expected. Figuring it would be a short day and not wanting to risk another summons, I decided to pull my car into the parking area in front of the building. The driveway leading there was cordoned off by stanchions because it was supposed to be for the exclusive use of city officials, but every now and again on a detail, I had noticed a policeman or two park their cars there for the day.

When I arrived that morning, I simply pulled into the mouth of the driveway, got out, moved the stanchion, pulled my car into a space at the end, and replaced the stanchion. Until it was time to go home, I wasn't going to let anyone know I had parked there, because if a boss found out he might have made me move it.

On the west side of the building was a stairway that led to the basement and it was there that the men mustered in the morning. My watch had stopped, so before I got inside I didn't know that I was late. I was scheduled for a 9 A.M. to 5 P.M. tour and it was then nine-ten. The men, about twenty in all, were lined up in the hallway facing two sergeants, a lieutenant, and a captain. Had I been quiet, my entrance might have gone unnoticed, but I sneezed and drew the immediate attention of all present.

"What's your name?" one of the sergeants asked. Just from the sound of his voice, I guessed he was a ballbreaker and hoped I would get assigned to the other one.

"Droge, sir."

"What tour are you supposed to be doing?"

"Nine to five, sir."

"And what time is it now?"

"I don't know, sir. My watched stopped."

"Well, you're late and when you're assigned here again see to it that you're on time. Is that clear?" Now I knew he was a ballbreaker.

"Yes, sir."

I stepped back into the ranks and the sergeant walked to the other end of the column.

The guy beside me gave me a poke in the ribs with his elbow and whispered out of the corner of his mouth. "He just got here himself, the hump. He's just trying to make a couple of points with the captain."

"Yeah, he sounds like a real ballbuster," I said.

The other sergeant counted heads and there were twenty-two of us. I knew from previous details that there would be two men assigned inside to handle a phone or run errands for the captain and that the twenty men left would be split into two groups of ten, assigned to each of the sergeants. The captain cleared his throat intentionally loud and glanced up and down the ranks to make sure he had everyone's attention.

"Now listen, men. We don't expect a large turnout today, so there shouldn't be any trouble. I don't want to see any of you men conversing with the demonstrators, or for that matter, with each other. Just stay on this side of the barriers and let them do all the screaming and yelling they want on the other side. I don't exactly know what they're protesting, but I understand it's a Black group, unhappy with something. Now you all know the tension the city's felt in the past couple of weeks and the summer is coming up, so we don't want to provoke anything or give anybody an excuse to riot like they've done in the past. Just keep to yourselves and don't start anything. I don't want to see any arrests out here today unless you have the authority of a superior officer." Pointing to the last two patrolmen on the extreme right-hand side of the column, he said: "OK, you two men come with me." The three of them walked past me, down the hall about fifty feet, and turned right, into a room designated as temporary headquarters for the day.

The lieutenant then directed the sergeants to take ten men apiece and deploy them around the building. The sergeant I had designated as a ballbreaker counted the first ten men from the right and huddled them off to the side. I breathed a sigh of relief. The other sergeant took the remaining ten and huddled us up right where we were. He took our names, shields, and commands and copied them next to posts on a long mimeographed sheet of paper. My post was directly in front of the building by the parking area and I was glad to have it so I could keep an eye on my car. Before the sergeant had copied all the names, the lieutenant interrupted.

"By the way, if any of you have your car parked in front of the building, move it. Any car parked there in a half hour without authorization will be tagged and towed."

Shit! Now I had to go find another spot and I knew that was nearly impossible. About the only spaces available were by parking meters and I would be lucky to find one of those. And even if I did, I wouldn't be able to leave my post to keep throwing dimes in the meter. Meter maids swarmed over the area each day and I was bound to get another summons.

The sergeant finished taking the names and, as was customary, told us to break up into two groups of five to go for coffee, one group at a time. I wound up in the first five and, after parking my car on a meter about a block away, I joined the four other patrolmen in a coffee shop right across the street from the park. Over a regular and a danish I learned that the demonstration was supposed to start about noon. We shot the breeze about the captain's speech and everyone agreed he was wrong to tell us not to take any action without a superior officer's say-so. One of the men asserted, and again we all agreed, that if a patrolman failed to discharge proper authority in maintaining peace at the first sign of misconduct at a demonstration, he fostered such behavior. After a half hour of old war stories, we returned to our posts so the other five men could go for their breakfast.

There were six or seven cars parked out front, all shiny Cadillacs, Lincolns, and other expensive limousines costing at least six thousand dollars apiece, probably more like eight or nine. I found out later that they belonged to city councilmen who were inside at a conference. I laughed to myself at having unknowingly tried to pass my Volkswagen off as belonging to one of them by parking alongside, earlier in the morning. I spent the better part of the next three hours doing nothing more than admiring both the cars and the pretty girls strolling through the park. The sun was shining and the skies were clear for the first time in a while and the park was filled with more than the usual number of office workers from the vicinity on their coffee breaks and students from the neighboring college, whiling away the time between classes.

At about eleven-thirty, dribs and drabs of Blacks with signs and flags arrived and clustered at the southernmost tip of the park. The bigger the crowd got, the noisier it got, and I sensed I was in for a trying day. I had learned from past demonstrations that part of the policeman's lot was to stand silent while the protesters shouted violent and profane epithets aimed at upsetting him. Regardless of what the main theme of the demonstration was, the police always managed to garner their share of disparaging remarks. Having had the utmost respect for the police before joining the department and never having addressed any one of them in a manner unbefitting that respect, it was hard for me to swallow that kind of ridicule without being able to retaliate with as much as a simple question like "Why?" But it was all a part of the job and maybe it was all a part of maturation to stand there and take it, as much as I didn't like it.

By twelve o'clock, a chanting, howling group had formed and started to slowly make its way through the park, heading straight for me. Another patrolman and I closed the barriers up tight and, where we could, overlapped them so no one could pass without either going over or under. The cars in the parking area were only about a foot away from the stanchions and didn't allow us much room to operate. I mentioned to the sergeant that it would be a good idea to have them moved, but he shrugged off the suggestion and said: "Just as long as the demonstrators

The Patrolman: A Cop's Story

stay on the other side of the barriers the cars are all right where they are."

About two hundred strong, comprised mainly of young adults between eighteen and twenty-five years old, and led by a husky, bearded man with a bullhorn, the angry mob of Blacks arrived at the stanchions in front of me shouting things such as: "Equal rights for the Blackman," "Down with the White honky mayor," "Let freedom ring," and of course "Kill the pigs." I still didn't know what the demonstration was all about because those slogans were screamed at every demonstration. Aside from another patrolman, the sergeant, and me, there was no other police officer within fifty yards of the crowd, the sergeant having spread them out to the sides of the park and to the rear of the building. We all knew right away that more men would be needed up front and the sergeant waved the eight other patrolmen assigned to him closer to the demonstrators. He sent one of the men into the basement with a suggestion for the lieutenant or the captain to come out and bring the other sergeant and his ten men from the rear of the building to the front. He left and was back in a minute with the captain, and he and the sergeant conversed right behind me.

"What's the trouble, sergeant?"

"We'll need more men up here, captain. There are a lot more demonstrators than we had expected."

"All right, I'll send up five men from the rear. Do the best you can until I see what the story is with reinforcements. Don't do anything till I get back."

"Yes, sir," he said and the captain walked away. A few moments later five men joined our ranks and the sergeant filled in some of the gaps between the cars.

The protesters continued to scream and shout and a few had worked themselves up to a real frenzy. Up to this point the only contact being made was between themselves as they jockied for positions closer to the barriers. Presently, however, the more worked up of the group began climbing on the stanchions and in an instant many more followed suit.

The patrolman next to me approached the barriers and politely urged the people to get off. He was met with a glob of saliva in the face from one of the more arrogant youths in front of him, a muscle-bound six-footer, about nineteen years old, and, before the patrolman could react, the youth jumped backward into the crowd to freedom. There was no way the officer could have gotten through the crowd to catch him. All the protesters laughed and the patrolman's face grew a deep red. The captain appeared from nowhere and cautioned the patrolman to maintain himself. From a safe distance behind me, he asked the crowd to get down off the barriers. When they laughed at him, he ignored them and instructed the sergeant to let them stay there.

About an hour passed, which seemed more like an eternity, and the ever-increasing crowd of Blacks had not relented one bit; in fact, they were worse. They taunted the patrolmen up and down the ranks, just waiting for one to blow his cork so that they might in some way blame him for any trouble that followed. The majority had forsaken their original cause and concentrated on jeering at the police. I was the subject of hundreds of debased remarks from various people in the crowd, but the ones I noticed the most were shouted from the youth who had spit at the other patrolman. He had worked his way up from the rear and was now seated upon a barrier right in front of me. Every time he yelled something he looked me straight in the face with a contemptuous smirk on his face. I watched him carefully, planning my strategy if he decided to spit at me. I would grab his legs, pull him off the stanchion, and arrest him, regardless of what my orders were. We had all taken enough abuse from these people and it was entirely out of hand.

Mounted on the barriers and swinging their arms at us, the demonstrators reminded me of apes in a zoo, except for the absence of bars. One of the officers wandered too close and a long hairy arm from the middle of the crowd reached out and grabbed his hat. A loud cheer went up as the hat was tossed to the rear of the crowd and promptly stomped on until it was unrecognizable. The officer charged at the man who had grabbed it and took a tight hold of his coat, trying to pull him over the barrier. In seconds the crowd around reacted and grabbed the patrolman by the arms, trying to lift him over the barrier. Two other officers and I pulled the patrolman free, but not before we had all taken some blows on the arms and head. The only one I knew for sure had hit me was the arrogant youth so fond of spitting at police officers. Another loud cheer went up and the people in the rear started pushing. The crowd starting spilling over the barriers and mounting the hoods of the cars.

Again the captain appeared from nowhere, this time with the sergeant and his remaining five men from the rear of the building, again he politely asked the unruly mob to get off the cars, and again they laughed at him. A few of the Blacks jumped to the roofs of the cars and reached out for him, knocking his hat to the ground, but he withdrew quickly, retrieving his hat on the way.

In moments the cars were swarming with demonstrators, jumping up and down shouting now: "We want the mayor. We want the mayor."

For twenty minutes they proceeded to absolutely demolish every car in the parking area, smashing the windshields, flattening the roofs by jumping up and down, ripping the chrome from the sides, and for twenty minutes we just stood there and watched. Not one person made an effort to stop them, including me; it would have been suicide to try.

Presently, two buses roared up the driveway and gray-uniformed recruits, about sixty in all, piled off and lined up on the stairs of City Hall. At the same time, six or seven men, mounted on riot-trained horses, galloped from the street and stationed themselves at the base of the stairs. I was steaming as we stood waiting for the order from the brass to disperse the mob. It never came.

At this time the protesters started throwing everything they could get their hands on at us, from rocks to soda cans to glass they had ripped from the cars. The bombardment lasted only a short time, but I got banged with a soda can that opened a gash on my forehead and the ballbreaker sergeant, catching a brick square in the chest, collapsed like a sack of potatoes, before the sergeant in charge of my group finally had had it up to his eyebrows and decided to wait no longer. "Let's get 'em!" he shouted.

That's all any of the men had to hear and with nightsticks firmly in hand, heads bursting with rage, we rushed the demonstrators. The first ones in were the mounted men and, at the sight of charging horses, the protesters scattered like their tails were on fire. The horses had been trained to raise their legs, kicking their hoofs outward, and nobody wanted to get too close. They were successful in their attempt to get the crowd moving but the barriers prevented them from dispersing them completely.

Eyeing the punk who had hit me before, I ran full force at one of the stanchions, hurdled it with comparatively little trouble, and closed in on him in a couple of strides. I lashed out with my nightstick, swinging laterally with all my might, and caught him square across both shinbones. He screamed in pain and dropped to his knees, burying his head under clasped hands. I turned and trotted away while two other patrolmen converged on him and whacked him some more.

People were running everywhere, screaming, as angry patrolmen unleashed their wrath. "Clear the park," someone shouted. My mind was red with rage and I hit anybody in my way. In the middle of the park I was confronted by a Black man much bigger and stronger than I. I slowed my trot down to a walk as I approached him and told him to leave the park. "Fuck you, pig," was the reply and no sooner had he said it than I lanced forward with my nightstick, my left hand near the front and my right hand on the grip in the rear, jamming it deeply into his gut. He moaned and bent forward in pain. I withdrew my nightstick from his stomach, swung the rear quarter up swiftly, and smashed it on the bridge of his nose. He fell back like a ton of bricks and his head thumped painfully on the concrete walk. I stood ready for him to get up, but he lay there apparently unconscious. Again I turned and trotted away. By the time I reached the end of the park, almost all the protesters had fled. A White man in a suit was sitting on a bench watching what was happening and ignored me when I told him to move.

"Get out of the park," I repeated.

"I'm not a part of this," he claimed. "Why should I have to move?"

"Because I'm telling you."

"Well, I choose not to."

I grabbed him by the knot in his tie, lifted him to his feet, and shoved him out of the park.

"I'll have your job for this," he shouted. "Do you know who I am?"

"Do you know who I am?" I countered. "I'm the police officer who told you to move and you refused. And I'm the police officer who's gonna lock your ass up if you don't get out of here right now. And I'm the police officer that's gonna enjoy breaking your nose while I'm doing it, too." I was glaring at him with my eyes wide open, and if he had said another word, I would have smacked him. But he recognized the wrath in my eyes and straightening his tie, mumbling under his breath, he wisely moved on.

By this time the park was clear and some bosses were blowing their whistles back by what was left of the cars, waving at us to return. I walked back slowly, feeling the strain of the battle and wiping the blood from my head with a handkerchief. More reinforcements had arrived, including plainclothesmen and detectives. The streets being flooded with people running from the park, traffic was jammed up all around City Hall. Car horns were honking, people were still yelling, and the bosses kept blowing their whistles. My head was aching.

As we lined up in columns of twos for a head count, a deafening roar from the block perpendicular with the park filled the air. The protesters had regrouped and were again chanting and taunting, this time in the middle of Broadway, holding up traffic for blocks.

Up to this point, not an arrest had been made, but an inspector quickly barked instructions to all the detectives to spread out and arrest anyone breaking the law. A large group of them set out across the street and the uniformed force followed with the same instructions.

Again screaming people ran in all directions and for the next ten minutes bedlam spread to three square blocks on the west side of City Hall. No sooner had I entered the street nearest the park when I saw a detective, with his shield on his lapel, making an arrest. I ran over, assisted him in cuffing the prisoner, and walked back with them to the patrol wagon waiting in the rear of the park. In all, nine arrests were made that day.

Spotting a coffee wagon by the patrol wagon, I walked over, got a cup of regular, tilted my hat to the back of my head, and sat down on the running board to relax.

Before I had finished the coffee, the word spread that it was all over and I walked to the front of the building to line up for another head count. All men present and accounted for, we were dismissed at the scene. I walked toward my car, thinking of what it would have looked like if I hadn't moved it in the morning. From about fifty feet I was able to discern a parking ticket slipped under my windshield wiper, rattling in the chilly wind that had just started up. I left it where it was, got in the car, and drove home. I didn't remove it for three weeks, letting it be a sorrowful reminder of a very demoralizing day.

CHAPTER 8

Late one afternoon, in the first week of May, 1968, nine other rookies and I sat nervously in the back room of the 9th precinct station house, waiting for the departmental mail to arrive. We had heard that earlier in the day orders had been issued assigning us to our permanent commands and everybody was anxious to find out what precinct they would be working. To pass the time we chewed our fingernails and ribbed each other about bad assignments. Even though my friend from the telephone company had assured me that his brother would be able to arrange my assignment to the 62nd precinct, I wasn't counting on it.

We had been waiting over an hour, when a patrolman entered the station house with the evening mail tucked under his arm and he handed it to the desk officer. The lieutenant, realizing our anxiety, fished through the various papers until he came up with the orders and brought them into the back room personally. "Here you go, fellas," he said as he tossed them on the table. "Good luck!"

For an instant everybody just stayed where they were, then darted toward the table, jockeying for a position to get the best view. The lieutenant just chuckled, probably recalling his rookie days, and walked back out to the desk.

The precincts were arranged numerically, with men's names listed underneath each one. I focused on the 62nd precinct list, but, after scanning it twice, realized I wasn't on it. I jumped to the 66th, but I wasn't there either. By now five or six had found their own names and had cleared the table for those of us remaining. I looked at the 67th and 68th but still no luck. Finally, when I got to the 80th, I found my name.

"Where the fuck is the Eight-O?" I asked nobody in particular.

"Never heard of it," said one guy.

"Me neither," said another. "Sounds like the jungle, though."

I borrowed the desk copy of the Rules and Procedures and quickly turned to the back, where all the precinct boundaries are defined. Sure enough, the Eight-O was in the 13th division—Bedford-Stuyvesant. So much for my hook. The station house itself was located on Grand Avenue and Park Place and its boundaries were Fulton Street and Eastern Parkway to the north and south, New York Avenue and Vanderbilt Avenue to the east and west. I wasn't familiar with that area of Brooklyn at all, so after we all shook hands, promising to keep in touch, I left the 9th to take a ride through my new command.

The closer I got to the Eight-O, the more Blacks and less Whites there were around and the more dilapidated the neighborhood. Once inside the confines of the precinct, I rode haphazardly up and down the streets to get an idea of the environment. Along Nostrand Avenue, the first sign I noticed, painted brightly atop a storefront, read: "Black Panther Party—Brooklyn Headquarters." I cruised by slowly, rubbernecking in the window, and saw about five or six similar-looking Blacks, in their late teens or early twenties, goateed and Afroed, dressed in army fatigues with bullets strung around their necks. *Oh great! I'm just in time for the revolution.*

The area was made up mostly of tenements, from three to six stories high, the bulk of which were in dire need of repair. Clotheslines, laden with wash, were strung not only from the rear of some buildings, but also from the front, across the side streets. Bars and grills far outnumbered any other type of business and not one store in the entire neighborhood was without an iron gate out front.

Three times that night, while riding through the area, I noticed people throwing garbage bags out their windows, and the streets were filthy with refuse. A stench, most likened to human waste, permeated the air so thickly I could almost taste it. More than once I thought I would vomit.

Most of the streets were narrow and burdened with double-parked cars. Apparent addicts and winos were everywhere, nodding in doorways and lying in the gutter. The sleaziest group of prostitutes I had ever seen were lined up along Fulton Street, the length of the precinct, openly propositioning everyone who passed, including me.

It seemed every motorist in the area had a heavy hand on the horn and music blared from record shops, rendering my car radio inaudible.

I drove home, having seen all I cared to, and told my wife where I had been assigned. I wasn't thrilled with Bedford-Stuyvesant, but she was even more disappointed. A rash of recent news about policemen being assaulted and killed in the line of duty in that section had made her afraid.

"Don't worry, honey, I'll be all right," I said, trying to comfort her. "It can't be as bad down there as people make it sound. I'm a police officer, not a prima donna. I can't expect to go where I want to go, I've got to go where they need me and, apparently, that's Bedford-Stuyvesant." I don't think she was listening. At first, just a tear slipped down from the corner of her eye, but she couldn't hold it in any longer and burst out crying. I put my arm around her, laying her head to my chest. "C'mon now, cut that out."

"I can't help it, Ed. I'm so scared for you."

"What would you have me do, throw in the towel without even giving it a chance? You know I can't do that. I'll tell you what. Let's both give it a try for a little while and if it's really that bad, I'll see if I can work something out." That seemed to satisfy her temporarily and we didn't talk about it for the rest of the night. After all, I figured, working in Bedford-Stuyvesant couldn't be that much different than where I'd been assigned so far.

I wasn't overly fond of Blacks in general, but I was certainly far from a bigot. I never took an active part in the advancement of the Negro race, but I wasn't ashamed, like most people I knew, to have Black friends visit my home. Nor was I a hypocrite, like a neighbor of mine who said he wasn't prejudiced, but if a Black family moved next door, he'd sell his home. What bias I had formed in the 90th precinct was completely forgotten over the next seven months and I began working in the 80th with a good frame of mind.

However, I would find out over the next three and one-half years that, though I, as a police officer, would be absolutely necessary in certain instances, I would be called with the greatest reluctance and would rarely feel welcome in anyone's home. In the ghetto I would be treated like a slovenly servant, taunted and debased with derogatory remarks and subjected to bias and prejudice from the Blacks that would quickly reverse my heretofore sympathetic attitude. I would see able-bodied people, entirely capable of work, receive welfare payments and laugh at the stupidity of my government, saying: "Why should I go to work, when I can get paid to stay home." Every day I would see their friends and relatives come up from the South to jump on the bandwagon and get in on the easy money. I would be told, "I pays your salary, motherfucker," by these recipients of tax-free relief checks, when, in fact, it was just the opposite, because my tax dollars paid for their narcotics and booze. I would be faced with the hate and resentment against police and authority inherent in the Negro quarter. I would be filled with anger and frustration at their militant attitudes. I would enter their roach-infested, rat-ridden apartments to deliver their children, to take their sick to the hospital, to help bury their dead, yet I would be spat upon and assaulted, shot at and injured by these very people whom I had aided, and I would grow to hate them for it. Losing all perspective, I would grow to hate not only the people of Bedford-Stuyvesant, but all Blacks in general because of them, and I would be cynical of any good they appeared to project. I would become no different from any other White patrolman in the Black ghetto.

I had been assigned to the 14th squad and my first tour of duty was 8 A.M. to 4 P.M. As I approached the red-brick, fortlike building in the daylight for the first time, with its flag flickering in a brisk wind, it reminded me both literally and symbolically of the Alamo. The radio cars outside were dented and scraped, and in need of a washing. A little police scooter, with its motor running, was left unattended on the sidewalk. I somehow managed to carry all my gear from the car in one trip and, with my hat knocked askew, from behind a pile of rain gear, winter uniforms, and other paraphernalia, I entered the station house and approached the front desk.

"Patrolman Droge, sir," I said to the desk officer, barely able to make him out.

"Oh yes ... Droge. I saw the orders. You're assigned here now, huh?"

"Yes, sir."

"OK, take that shit upstairs to the third floor and see if you can find a locker. When you're finished doing that, report to the clerical office to fill out your personnel cards. And when you're finished doing that, report back here to me."

"Yes, sir." I climbed the stairs to the third floor and threw my gear on a bench. I was a bit taken aback at the sight of the locker room—the floors filthy an inch thick with dirt and the paint peeling from the walls and ceiling. A bare bulb hung in the center of the room and a click of the wall switch failed to light it. The only locker I found unused was as dirty as the floor, so I went looking for something to clean it up. I found the bathroom on the same floor and it was in worse shape than both the locker room and the inside of my locker put together.

Two of three sinks were caked with grime and the third was clogged with stagnant water. Pipes jutted from the wall where the fourth was supposed to be. A foul smell made me want to leave right away, but I stayed to look for some utensils. There was no soap in sight and a thin roll of tissue by the toilet was the only paper. It appeared someone had forgotten to flush until a pull of the chain proved the tank inoperable. Cobwebs in a stall shower hinted at its infrequent use. Finally, overcome by the stench and the unhealthy appearance, I abandoned my search for a cleanser and went down to the second floor to seek help in the clerical office.

I was met there by a middle-aged fellow, impeccably dressed in a blue suit, who identified himself as the clerical officer, Patrolman Vito Polacella. With the small butt of an unlit stogie wedged neatly into the corner of his mouth, sharply defined cheekbones, brown squinted eyes, and a shock of carefully combed black hair atop white sideburns, he reminded me of a highly refined gangland boss, except he spoke with a Brooklyn accent. While shaking his hand, I introduced myself.

"Hi! Ed Droge. I wonder if you could help me out. I found a locker upstairs, but it's a little dusty. Do you have anything I could use to wipe it out?" I tried my best not to show my dismay at the overall poor condition of the station house, but he seemed to sense it, anyway.

"Some shithouse, huh? This fuckin' place is gettin' worse every day. It shoulda been condemned years ago." He disappeared behind the door of a closet for a few seconds and emerged with some rags, soap, paper towels, and bleach. "Here, kid, this oughta take care of it. When you're finished up there, c'mon down. I got some cards here I want you to fill out."

"OK. Thanks!"

Only after thoroughly cleaning out my locker and fixing the broken hasp on its door, did I look at my watch and it was twelve-thirty. I held my breath while washing up, then went down to the clerical office to Patrolman Polacella. He gave me some cards to fill out and by the time I got back to the lieutenant on the desk, it was five and a half hours after I had seen him before. He was writing something, and when he finished, he glanced his eyes up at me without moving his head and said: "What happened to you?"

"Nothing, sir. I just finished getting my locker squared away and filling out cards for Patrolman Polacella." Sensing he didn't think I would be so long, I felt a little bad. The last thing I wanted to do on my first day was get on the wrong side of any bosses.

"I thought maybe the stink on the third floor knocked you unconscious." With that, he started laughing uproariously, taking his glasses from the tip of his nose and laying them on the blotter in front of him. He was almost completely bald, had small ears close to his head, and his laugh revealed a mouth full of rotten teeth. I didn't find his statement the least bit funny, but for his sake, and mine, I faked a laugh along with him.

"Go ahead, take an hour for meal," he said, catching his breath for an instant. "About the best place around is the Greek's up the block. At least it don't have no roaches." I wondered how he passed the grammar questions on the lieutenant's test.

"Thanks!" I walked over to the Greek's and had a soda. I wasn't so sure he was right about the roaches and shuddered to think what the other places in the precinct looked like, if this was the best. I was back by two o'clock and sat in the back room reading the paper for a while before the lieutenant called me out to the desk.

"You're in a radio car with O'Shaughnessy for the rest of the tour. He's right out front."

I went out to a beat-up old Chevy, with a big dent in the door and a broken turret light, and climbed in. Sitting to my left was Gargantua, his belly touching the bottom of the steering wheel. If he weighed an ounce, he weighed 250 pounds. A ruddy complexion and a dark red nose contrasted pleasantly with bushy eyebrows and thinning hair. The front of his uniform was stained terribly and his collar was frayed beyond repair. I was beginning to think that everything in the ghetto eventually deteriorated and only the future would prove how close I was to the truth.

"Bill O'Shaughnessy," he said, sticking out his hand.

"Ed Droge."

"First day here, Ed?"

"Yeah, I'm in the 14th squad."

"Oh! You'll be working with a nice bunch of guys. What are you, right out of the academy?" He spoke with a constant smile, and when he faced me I detected a faint smell of alcohol.

"No. I've been bouncing around for about a year now. I've worked in the Nine-O . . ." And for the rest of the tour I told him briefly what I had done in the past year and he told me as much as he could about the Eight-O.

He told me that the precinct was one of the smallest in the city, with a total complement of only around 160 men. He told me a couple of places where I could eat roach free when I was hungry on a day tour or a four to twelve, and a couple of places where I could "coop," or lay up, when I was tired on a late tour. He told me that the men referred to the precinct as the "anus of the world" and said I'd find out why soon enough. He told me that

Mother's Days, the first and fifteenth of each month when the welfare checks came in the mail, were the busiest because everybody was high on booze or dope. He told me the addresses of a few buildings where junk was trafficked heavily, one of which would become my primary source of narcotics arrests, a rat's nest on Pacific Street. He told me that Fulton Street and Nostrand Avenue was probably the most crowded corner in the precinct, if not the earth, and warned me not to stray there alone. He told me I'd probably wind up getting the shitty assignments in the beginning, but not to despair, they couldn't last forever. Finally, before we parted at the end of the day, he told me to be careful in the Eight-O, it was a dangerous place to work.

CHAPTER 9

For the first few months, being the newest member in the Eight-O, therefore still a "rookie," I bore the brunt of unwanted assignments. A typical week consisted of two tours "flying" and three tours on "fixers," or vice versa. Occasionally, I would ride in a radio car, but it seemed no more than once a month. A "fixer" is a specific location within a precinct that the commanding officer deems worthy of special attention, for example, a Jewish synagogue or Yeshiva. When assigned there, you are required to remain in front of the premises for the entire eight hours, not to wander, and to go to a meal at the nearest location only when relieved by another officer. Needless to say, those posts were quite boring. To "fly," in police parlance, is to perform a tour of duty outside of the command.

I flew mainly to two commands: the 88th precinct and the 73rd precinct. Heaven knows the 88th had more patrolmen than the Eight-O, but for some reason or other (it probably looked good on paper), they recruited us to patrol the periphery of Pratt University, because of a rash of muggings and assaults. Though we were assigned there specifically for their protection, the college students never even smiled hello and were always one index finger short when giving us the peace sign. The 73rd precinct, in the East New York–Brownsville section of Brooklyn, always needed reinforcements when one of their weekly riots broke out, especially the one over the control of the school board, in which several people were arrested and injured every day for two weeks. I could never figure out where all the people came from that made up the huge crowds, for riding through the Seven-Three was like riding through Nagasaki in 1945. Almost the entire precinct was a shambles, with block after block of half-torn-down houses, uninhabitable. But the crowds kept showing up.

There were three fixers in the Eight-O to which I was assigned more than any others and they were: 19 Grant Square; Fulton Street and Nostrand Avenue; and Brooklyn Jewish Hospital.

Grant Square was a lousy post, because on it was a Yeshiva to which busloads of Hasidic boys came every day, many from the Nine-O area. If I stayed directly in front of the building, like I was supposed to, I was swarmed under by nosy kids and inundated with questions, so I usually stayed across the street, facing it, and none of the sergeants seemed to mind when they came by to sign my book. The existence of that fixer was fostered by the fact that the commanding officer of the 80th precinct was Jewish. The only consolation in receiving that post was a "guarantee" of a square meal from a restaurant nearby, one of three I came to trust during my stay in the Eight-O. Unfortunately, they all closed around six o'clock, leaving me very hungry on four to twelves and late tours unless I brought a sandwich, which I often did.

Bill O'Shaughnessy wasn't kidding when he said Fulton and Nostrand might very well garner the "Most Crowded Corner in the World" award. With a subway stop downstairs, a bus stop on every corner upstairs, and two square blocks of stores surrounding it, the intersection was constantly swarming with people and vehicles. During rush hours, people were elbow to elbow; and cars, bumper to bumper. The corner resembled an all-Black Times Square; every weirdo in the neighborhood passed through during the day or hung around at night. On one corner was a bank and on the remaining three were fried chicken and rib joints.

Because of the crush of the people, fights sprang up sporadically and the patrolman with the post was hard tested to keep the incident from mushrooming. Originally, right after the '66 riots, four patrolmen, one each from the 80th, 79th, 77th, and 88th precincts, were assigned to the intersection, each one taking a corner, but sometime in 1969 the Eight-Eight and Seven-Seven got out of it, leaving two men, two corners apiece. At first Eight-O instructions were to stand on the southwest corner and not to stray, but after a while the post was broadened the length of the block, west to Bedford Avenue.

Some of the Black patrolmen in the precinct so loved the post, with plenty of girls to look at, people to talk to, and music to listen to from a pair of record shops, that to get it they would often trade their seat in a radio car with a White patrolman, who was only too happy to oblige. I dreaded Fulton and Nostrand not only because of the confinement, but also because of the wall-to-wall people.

A tour, especially a late tour, in Brooklyn Jewish Hospital, guarding an injured prisoner, was without a doubt the best fixer of them all; at least that's what I thought in the beginning. All you had to do was handcuff him to the bed railing to make sure he couldn't go anywhere and the rest of the tour you could sit and read, or take a nap. Aside from being aggressive and yearning to ride in a radio car more often—so I could be where the action was—I didn't mind pulling the hospital assignment. One late tour I was rudely awakened to the fact that not all the action was out in the street.

Assigned to the Intensive Care Unit to guard a prisoner on the critical list, I had been convinced by the needles in his arms, tubes in his nose, bandages on his head, and the night nurse's report that he would not be stirring, so I left him uncuffed. He was charged with possession of a weapon, a .25 caliber automatic, which was plucked from the bloodied floor beside his body moments after he had stuck it in his ear and pulled the trigger. There was no doubt in my mind that this man was a psycho. As I dozed in an uncomfortable chair at the foot of his bed, I couldn't help thinking that had I done that, I would have surely succeeded in killing myself.

I was in more of a trance than a sleep, listening to the steady beeps from a panel of screens with jumping lights, which kept a constant vigil on the condition of the unit's patients, when the night nurse tapped me and motioned toward the prisoner's bed. He was sitting up, staring out the window and I regretted not having cuffed him, but thought to do so then.

As I slowly approached, he turned away from the window and, not even noticing me, recklessly ripped the tubes from his nose and arms and the bandages from his head. I turned quickly to the nurse, instructing her to phone for more police assistance. Completely naked, he jumped out of bed facing me, staring into my eyes as if I were the only thing between him and freedom. I was.

The ward was dark, with only the nurse's desk lamp shining, and, but for the steady beep-beep from the electrocardiogram machines, was unearthly silent. From the corner of my eye I could see that the patients in the surrounding beds were all awake and, critical or not, propped up, taking keen interest in what was happening.

I placed my right hand tightly on the handle of my holstered gun, extended my left hand in his direction, and, taking a step toward him, said in my most authoritative voice: "Get back in bed. What do you think you're doing? Get back in bed." He was a light-skinned Black man, about six feet two inches tall, 210 pounds, in his late thirties, and built like a weight lifter.

Without warning, he slashed out with his left hand, like a giant grizzly swatting, and caught me flush on the right side of my face. I fell to the floor and my head throbbed in pain as the blood rushed to my temple. He started at me and I was so nervous, my hand instinctively whipped my gun from its holster and pointed it at him like a divining rod to water. He stopped in his tracks and shifted his stare from my eyes, to the gun, then back to my eyes. I jumped up from the floor and straight-armed him in the chest, trying to push him back toward the bed, but he didn't budge.

He started walking toward me again and my mind darted back to an academy gym class: "Whenever you're confronted with a psycho, never put yourself between him and the only way out. When the adrenaline flows strongly, even a little man can build up a temporary immunity to being hurt. You'll find that maybe your bullets won't even stop him."

I was scared shitless. The only way out of the ward was a swaying door behind me, so with each step he took

The Patrolman: A Cop's Story

toward it, disregarding the gun like Superman does in the comics, I took a pace backward. I kept telling him to get back to bed, all the while thinking of how to explain my shooting an unarmed patient, heretofore docile, on the critical list, in the Intensive Care Unit.

As we entered the hallway and started toward the elevator, I realized if that naked muscleman got on, I'd have to get on with him and that would be too confining and too dangerous. I decided I would have to stop him anyway I could before the elevator came to the floor; I'd probably have to shoot him.

He pushed the button and I glanced quickly to the floor indicator. It showed 3; two more floors to go. "Get back to bed," I yelled in a last-ditch effort to end this nightmare, but he ignored me. My legs were shaking and my brow soaked with perspiration as I drew the hammer back and pointed the gun at his heart. He just stared at me. The elevator stopped, and as the door opened, I started squeezing the trigger.

Suddenly, like an answer to a prayer, two uniformed officers sprang from the elevator, and, realizing the situation, quickly grabbed one arm apiece of the now enraged and violent prisoner. I joined in the struggle to get him back to bed, but the three of us couldn't even get him back through the swaying doors. In a few moments, two more patrolmen responded to the call and the five of us carried him to bed. Apparently resigning himself to defeat, he relaxed completely and I was easily able to cuff his right wrist to the iron railing, riveted to the bed. He lay still, eyes closed, and panted heavily.

The four other patrolmen and I huddled by the doorway, warily watching the resting giant.

"What happened?" one asked.

"The guy's a psycho," I said. "He shot himself in the head and the bullet must've nicked his brain."

"Whew! He's strong as a bull."

"You ain't kidding. I thought I was going to have to shoot him."

"I wouldn't blame you a bit. The meat hooks on a guy like that should be considered lethal weapons." By now we had taken the conversation into the hallway.

"Well, he doesn't look like he'll give you any more trouble tonight, but if he does, don't hesitate to call."

"Thanks, fell . . ." A loud crash interrupted.

We ran back into the ward just in time to see the prisoner pick up a chair by his bed and heave it through the already broken window with his left hand; his right was still cuffed to the railing. His arm was bleeding profusely; nevertheless he grabbed everything in sight and threw it out the window. Before we could reach him, a bedpan, two pillows, and a vase of flowers all dropped five stories. I jumped on his back and he reacted with a swift jerk of his elbow into my stomach that knocked the breath from my lungs. I recovered quickly and was able to throw my left arm around his throat, squeezing with all my might as I withdrew my jack. I hit him three times in the right ear, striking the very spot where he had shot himself. Thick, deep blood gushed from the wound and poured down his body and onto my uniform. I sprang away from him, awed by the fact that he was apparently unaffected. He was growling like an animal and swinging his outstretched arm toward me in vain. Though my shirt was now hued a deep red and his chest was completely covered with blood, I don't think he was even aware he was bleeding. The five of us rushed him at once and threw him down in bed, another patrolman cuffing his left wrist to the left side railing. To restrain him from kicking his feet, we tied blood-stained bedsheets tightly around his legs. Again, apparently capitulating, he lay still.

The room was a mess, with broken glass scattered everywhere and blood on the walls, beds, and floors.

"This guy's unbelievable," one of the patrolmen said. "He's not human."

"Do me a favor, will you?" I asked him. "Bring me up a walkie-talkie, so I can get you guys in a hurry if I need you."

"Sure, Ed. But even if he starts up again, he ain't gonna be able to get out of that tie-up."

"Just the same, I'd like to have it."

They agreed it was a good idea and about fifteen minutes after they left, two returned with a walkie-talkie.

I moved my chair closer to the base of the prisoner's bed and spent the next few hours reading a magazine with

THE PATROLMAN: A COP'S STORY   93

one eye and watching him with the other. Around 6 A.M. I was enjoying a fresh-brewed cup of coffee when he awoke and he stared at me with icy eyes that raised the hackles on my neck. He grunted and growled, while occasionally tugging on his shackled wrists, until, with a spine-tingling screech at the top of his lungs and a sudden surge of inhuman strength, he ripped the right railing from the bedside. Like Frankenstein's monster breaking loose, he pulled and jerked at the left-hand railing, but it wouldn't come free. I yelled into the walkie-talkie and in seconds I could hear sirens fast approaching. With the entire weight of my body, I was able to pin his right arm to the bed, as the railing hung limply from his wrist.

In moments, the ward was flooded with policemen, and after ten minutes of thought, we strung three sets of handcuffs together and pulled each of his arms as far down toward the floor as they would go, cuffing them underneath the bed. The previously adamant doctor-in-charge reluctantly agreed to a 50 cc. shot of a knockout drug and at around 7:15 A.M. all was peaceful again.

This was the first of three incidents, all within my first few months in the 80th precinct, which made me wary of people in general, especially Blacks, and unable to trust any post as an easy assignment. In addition, it kindled close relationships with many young officers, who fought beside me.

The next was my first arrest in the Eight-O, in which I charged a female, who refused to identify herself and was booked as "Jane Doe," with various violations of the Administrative Code for running a cabaret-type operation in her home. I was riding in a radio car that night and my partner and I responded to a call for "man with a gun." When we rang the bell of the address given, the female answered the door and admitted us to a swinging party, with a jukebox blaring and drinks for sale. I didn't find anyone with a gun, but she was violating the law, so I arrested her. As I was leading her out to the radio car, her apparent boyfriend, a big, dark man, about six feet, one-ninety, stood in the doorway. Asked to move very politely by my partner, he responded by punching him square in the jaw, knocking him to the floor. I immediately retaliated with a commanding blow of my nightstick across the side of his head and he went down like a ton of bricks, unconscious. I had opened his head with the blow and he had to be treated at the hospital, then released. Because of this incident, I was made to appear at the Civilian Complaint Review Board, better known as CCRB, charged with police brutality. The charge was proven false.

The Civilian Complaint Review Board, a panel of police officials and civilians, was created by the city administration to closely watch the department and answer, investigate, and prosecute all allegations of police misconduct. To me it was a glaring symbol of an antipolice faction. The men in the department didn't want it. The citizens of New York didn't want it, as evidenced by its defeat in a referendum vote, even though the administration tried to confuse the public by making a no vote mean you supported it. But, still, through legal loopholes, the administrators shuffled some papers and instituted it, anyhow.

To be found guilty of an accusation investigated by the board meant a change of command, a loss of pay (or both), or dismissal from the force.

I was made to appear before the board several times, with charges ranging from "improper language for a police officer" to "throwing a prisoner through the station house window." I admit the circumstances surrounding the latter incident certainly warranted an investigation, but it was handled so shoddily that I seriously contemplated leaving the department in disgust.

Another officer and I had arrested a one-eyed man for possession of a large quantity of narcotics and were leading him into the station house when he broke away, ran about five feet and either tripped, or, with full intention, smashed his head through the glass of the front door. He began bleeding profusely and everyone inside, including the lieutenant behind the desk, ran to his aid. He violently refused to be helped, however, and would have preferred to bleed to death. Blood was everywhere. My uniform was soaked and the lieutenant's previously spotless white shirt was now a deep red. A patrolman ripped the shirt from his own body to apply to the wounds, but the prisoner kicked out and struggled, refusing to be treated. It was absolutely necessary to restrain him to apply first aid and it saved his life. (Later he was to refuse treatment at two hospitals.)

At this time he had made no accusations that I, or anyone else, had thrown him through the window, because, in fact, nobody had. But a woman, who was passing by outside and looked in, saw him bleeding so badly with all the police around him and misinterpreted our efforts to aid him for a brutal, unprovoked attack. "They beat him unmercifully," she was to say later. The first thing she did, of course, was to call CCRB and lodge a complaint. In minutes two members of that outfit were dispatched to the Eight-O, one of whom was equipped with a camera. They arrived in a short time and, though they, too, had difficulty dealing with the prisoner at first, finally succeeded in gaining his confidence. They shuttled him into the captain's office, where pictures were taken and a statement was evoked that I had pushed him through the window. I was told to report in two days for an "initial interview." Interrogation would have been a better description.

I reported to their office on Park Avenue South and Seventeenth Street in Manhattan and was seated in a room with two investigators (their side), a PBA delegate (my side), and a tape recorder (neutral). The delegate, a thin man, about fifty, with a ruddy complexion and bloodshot eyes, told me to tell the story exactly the way it happened and to stop if he put his hand up, a signal that I might be saying something I shouldn't. The tape recorder was started and I related the details exactly the way I had seen them. I pointed out that it was possible the prisoner had tripped, but it looked more to me as if he had put his head through the window on purpose. When I had finished I was a bit taken aback that the PBA delegate was—head down, arms crossed—sound asleep. (He had shifted the sides to three to one against me.) I was told later by the investigator that he thought my story ludicrous and he was definitely recommending further investigation and a hearing.

Weeks of anguish passed and I gathered all the information I could to support my claim and negate his. I found that the prisoner had been arrested one year before in the Eight-O—for burglary. I found that on that occasion he had to be psychoed because he wouldn't stop banging the front of his head against the wall in the detectives' office. I found that he had an extensive history of mental disorders and had been a patient at an insane asylum. I found that in the past he had been shot in the head—the reason he had only one eye. I found that he had made several complaints against police officers before, all of which had been unsubstantiated.

The investigators at CCRB found nothing. When I showed them all the information that I had uncovered, they were astonished. With his pictures in front of them, they didn't even know he had one eye.

But the hearing was held just the same. The accuser, the hearing officer, a PBA attorney (I told the PBA I didn't want the same delegate), the other police officer present at the arrest, and I sat around a huge table in an otherwise empty room. There, the prisoner changed his story from my pushing him through the window to six or seven officers picking him up bodily and throwing him through. The hearing officer was so embarrassed he apologized to me, but it didn't help much. I had lost much faith in the city administration for instituting a kangaroo court of this nature and in the Police Department for allowing it to continue. Had I depended on either the PBA or the CCRB investigators to properly research the facts, I might have been found guilty and dismissed from the job.

For any readers with lingering doubts, may I report that a few months later the same one-eyed man, arrested by another Eight-O patrolman, put his head through the same station house window. I rest my case.

The final incident involved the Black Panthers. A large crowd was gathered outside Panther Headquarters, listening to a man with a bullhorn, who was shouting obscenities about the police and advocating the overthrow of the government. Three other officers and I were directing pedestrian and vehicle traffic, trying not to listen, and everything ran smoothly until the crowd got too big, blocking the sidewalk. One of the other officers maneuvered his way through the group to ask the man with the bullhorn if he could move the assembly inside, so that people could walk by unobstructed, but apparently the Panther misinterpreted the officer's intentions and swung the bullhorn at him. The officer defended himself and we ran to his aid. Engulfed by the crowd, a wild melee ensued in which a 10-13 radio call—assist patrolman—was necessary to free us. Two Black Panthers were arrested and two officers were injured. By the time the free-for-all ended, no fewer than sixty patrolmen and six hundred ranting and raving Blacks were on the scene. I accompanied the arresting officers to court later and witnessed the most outrageous, indignant flaunting of authority that I have ever seen. Black Panther members filled the courtroom, smoking, howling, spitting at the officers as they walked by, refusing to take their seats or take their hats off when told to do so, and generally disrupting all official proceedings. One member even urinated in the rear of the courtroom. The judge, a bit senile and shaking in his robes, ignored the pleas of the officers to at least hold the prisoners until they were properly identified, and legally released them on the spot. If there was a moral victory won that day, law and order didn't win it.

The last two incidents made me critical of the policies of the administration, both in the courtroom and on the job, and whenever other officers and I would get together over a beer in a bar or at one another's homes, the subject would inevitably come up. There were many opinions asserted about the overall plight of a policeman in today's society, about the thanklessness of the job and the low morale of the men, about the difficulty of effectively arresting and prosecuting criminals even with the aid of the upper echelon in the department and the judiciary, and the impossibility without it.

"You know, those humps in City Hall don't make this job any easier," one of about six patrolmen said as we huddled around two pitchers of beer at a rear table of a precinct bar. As was the custom, we had stopped "for a few" at the end of the four to twelve, to shoot the breeze. The conversation had started out about girls and, as it always did, evolved into a forum of distaste for the way things were being run.

"What do you mean?" someone asked.

"Fuckin' CCRB. That's what I mean. I was down there again yesterday. Some mother-fucker accuses you of something and right away you're put on the defensive. No matter what the guy says, they investigate it."

"If you want to call it that," I chimed in.

"Right. Like the way they investigated the guy who claimed Ed put his head through the window. Now that was an outright lie. The way I hear it, the investigator who came down that night probably put the words right in that guy's mouth. But what can Ed do about it? He can't sue for defamation of character, even though the charge was unsubstantiated. You're guilty till you prove yourself innocent on this job. It's a God damn shame."

"It's like being a second class citizen," somebody said.

"And the laws they make. Christ, the way these civil rights decisions are going lately in the Supreme Court, pretty soon they'll be taking our guns away and making sneakers part of the uniform, so we can run after the humps." He paused for a moment to guzzle a half glass of beer, then, gathering his thoughts, continued. "And the fuckin' Knapp Commission. We got enough to worry about in this shithole without having to worry about getting nabbed by the Knapp Commission."

"Our own bosses don't help matters much either, you know. They're so busy trying to score brownie points for promotion that all they do is hurt us."

"Yeah, like telling you not to take any action without them giving the OK. I was up in the Seven-Three during them school board riots and that's all they told us: 'Don't do nothing until a superior officer approves.' What the fuck do they expect us to do, wait until somebody gets killed before we can make an arrest, just 'cause they're worried they'll get jammed up if the situation gets out of hand? By the time a boss approves, the situation could be well out of hand."

I wanted to relate my experiences at City Hall, but I couldn't get a word in.

"While we're on the subject," one of the guys said, "there's another thing that bugs me. When a patrolman makes a good arrest, some boss always manages to sneak in and steal the credit. But if something goes wrong, the patrolman takes the blame."

The most militant in the group, a former GI, banged his fist on the table, knocking two glasses to the floor. "The real reason this job sucks is the ignorance of the people," he said. "What the hell do the people in Staten Island or

Queens care about you being down here fighting a war; and that's exactly what this is—a fuckin' war. Not just law and order against disorder, but Black against White. We're down here keepin these mother-fucking monkeys in line like ... like a doctor checkin' the spread of some disease—if he gets too close he might catch it and die, but if he don't try to contain it, it'll spread uncontrollably and everyone will die. The White people in all-White neighborhoods don't give a good fuck about the Blacks. Unless, of course, if they move next door, or rape their daughter. Then you see how pro-Black they are. But they say they care, because that's the vogue; you gotta sympathize to be in the 'in crowd.' What do they know about what's happenin' in the ghetto? My wife doesn't even know what I go through down here. Sure, I tell her it's rough and that working down here is like being back in Vietnam, but she doesn't really *know*. You've got to experience it to know."

"You're right. Nobody knows. All them asshole liberals know is what they read in the newspaper or what some schmuck tells them on the six o'clock news. But unfortunately they run the country. They oughta make riding in the back of an Eight-O car for a week of four to twelves and a week of late tours one of the requirements for getting a degree."

"Do I detect a bit of cynicism?" somebody said facetiously. "Do you have any prejudices against liberals?"

"Does a hobbyhorse have a wooden dick?" he answered. Everybody laughed.

But much of what was said was not funny and conversations like this were quite common among the men. I listened to many an angry old policeman, and many an angry young one for that matter, voicing their opinions; and most of the time I agreed.

CHAPTER 10

Not long after my arrival in the Eight-O, I became aware of many opportunities to take money. After 4 P.M. to midnight tours I stopped off for a couple of beers with the majority of men at one time or another and the conversations at the bar inevitably pertained to daily police work, often leading to various corrupt practices in which they were involved. I was felt out and my reactions to these practices were recorded, so that in the future when we worked together, they knew that I was safe.

After my seasoning in the Nine-O and conversations with more experienced men throughout the department, I had come to believe that taking money was a part of the everyday life of a patrolman. To other police officers your participation was another strong link in a chain of fraternity and had no reflection whatsoever on your honesty. Conversely, your refusal meant certain ostracism and a cross-eyed look as someone not in full possession of all his mental faculties. It cannot be emphasized enough that taking money was such a tradition, such a habit, and was so common all around, that the police officers I talked with did not think of it with any more regard than the habit of smoking—you know it's bad for you and you shouldn't do it, but you do it anyway. And in the beginning I held those exact beliefs.

Every rookie is eager to be accepted in a new command and is anxious to show that he is worthy of being "one of the boys." A policeman's best friends are almost exclusively other policemen. This is true not only because the odd hours and crazy shifts make socializing with anyone else on a regular basis nearly impossible, but also because the ever-present danger in the street infuses a bond between men. Any intention of not taking gratuities was gradually whittled away by the growing realization that to do so would mean being without friends on a job in which friends are a must.

Once the basic trust existed between officers, the attitude became even more freewheeling, and when a patrolman was sure himself, or was told by another patrolman that you were OK, there was no attempt to hide daily money pickups. There was little worry that you would run to anybody with your newly acquired information, for the thought of one patrolman turning another one in was practically nonexistent. There was no fear of sergeants because it was rumored that most of them picked up too, and when you were assigned to chauffeur them, you shared the loot.

During this initial period, because I was isolated on "fixers" or "flying" to other precincts most of the time, it was more a matter of hearing about corrupt activities than participating in them, but it wasn't long before I was admitted to an arcane world that affected my entire life. Thinking back now, I am amazed at how much of the hearsay was actually true, and the nonchalance with which it was thrown around barstools all over town in my early stages in the Eight-O. The contact with the people in the street and the various payoffs for different reasons came mainly when riding in a radio car, and I did not get those assignments regularly until the end of 1968.

Because I did not have a steady "seat," that is, ride the same sector all the time, I filled in intermittently in every sector of the precinct, thus becoming familiar with most of the "contracts" and in a matter of months I was fully versed on all common areas of payoffs in the Eight-O, whom to see, when to see him, and how much to expect.

Most police officers I was acquainted with did not feel as strongly against gambling violations as they did against other violations, such as narcotics, so it was understandable that that was the primary area in which money crossed hands. I was introduced to a variety of gambling operations and operators, who would pay varying amounts to avoid arrest.

"They're making a right," my partner, Pete McGreggor, reported to me.

"OK."

"Pull up next to them at the next light."

The car we were following was quite unlike what you would expect three wealthy gamblers to drive around, old and battered, the paint worn thin, but, being their working car, the appearance was calculated. The fewer people who knew who they were, the better for them. Pete knew very well who they were and after that day, so would I.

As he rolled the window down, we pulled alongside at a red light.

"How are you today, Mario? How's business?" he asked of the aging driver whose eyes just about cleared the steering wheel and whose gray hair hung unintentionally long in need of a cutting. He knew who it was without having to turn.

"Not bad, Pete, not bad," he responded as he straightened his back and raised himself by pushing off the top of the seat, digging into his pocket. He lowered his trunk and looked down pensively at his lap for a few seconds, counting, before resting his elbow on the crest of the door, arm upright. His two brothers sat silently, hazy in the background. In a quick lunge, a cobra striking, his arm darted forward, toward the radio car and his hand opened up, releasing the missile. The course was true and it landed on the seat between Pete and me.

"Take it easy, Mario," my partner said as I accelerated quickly.

"So long, Pete," I could hear fadingly.

It was as easy as that.

Undoubtedly the kingpins in the Eight-O, the Cavallero brothers, Mike, Mario, and Al—in alleged order of importance—known gamblers, that is, arrested and convicted in the past for gambling violations, controlled most of the policy and bookmaking activities. There wasn't a man in the precinct or the division who did not either know them, or at least know of them, yet for my entire three years assigned to the Eight-O, to my knowledge they were never arrested. They would ride through the neighborhood in their car and pick up the "action"—gambling records—from the various runners. If you spotted them, you would follow them around for a few blocks to let them know that you knew who they were and what they were up to, and then pull up next to their car, whereupon they would throw eight dollars into the window. That amount was established before I got to the 80th and they were fair game for every sector car in the precinct, every day you spotted them. There was always a laugh when someone brought up the time they threw the folded money so hard one summer day, it went in one window of the radio car and out the other, onto the street.

One of the numbers runners working for the Cavallero brothers was a guy named Vito who owned a small candy store in the heart of the precinct. The money received from the Cavalleros also covered Vito. Every day around 4 P.M. he left his place and made the rounds, picking up action from the various stores in the neighborhood. Because he kept his store, a shabby, sparsely filled establishment, open until 4 A.M. some mornings, I often wondered if gambling was his only illegal source of income. Although I had never received any information confirming my suspicions, I thought he might be selling drugs and one day I sent an informer into his place to snoop around. He returned convinced that Vito was not dealing narcotics. Vito, however, must have caught wind of my suspicion, for one night when I stopped in my favorite precinct bar, I bumped into him and, after buying me a drink, he swore he was only a runner, not a pusher, without my uttering a single word about it.

Shortly after this, I was riding with an officer, John Simmons, who thought that our sector was entitled to a separate "contract" with the Cavalleros, because the major part of their operation in the precinct was in it. He suggested that we follow Vito on his route that day, seize him when we were sure he was "dirty"—had gambling records on him—and threaten to lock him up every day unless we received more money. I wasn't too hot on the idea, but I went along with it.

"We'll wait until he comes out of the cleaners and walks down toward the building," he said as I nudged the bumper of the truck parked in front of us with the rubber bumperettes hanging from the head of the radio car. "He'll probably see us here, so we'll just pretend we're reading or something, OK?" He stared across the street at the dry cleaning store.

"OK," I said mechanically as I looked at my watch. It was four-thirty.

Only a few seconds passed before the door to the cleaners opened and the small, marionettelike Vito stepped to the street. He glanced over, but ignored us, strode briskly to the corner, turned left, and disappeared from view.

"There he goes!" my partner yelled as I jerked the car back, then screeched the tires forward with a sudden shift to "drive," simultaneously flooring the gas pedal.

"OK, hold on," I said, as if I had to, and we screamed around the corner, listing, just in time to see Vito entering an apartment house on Prospect Place.

With the car still rolling, Simmons lashed open the door, skipped free, and ran full speed into the building with me on his heels. I could hear someone scampering up the stairs, probably Vito, and, taking the steps three at a time, we raced up after him. We overtook him on the fourth floor, and my partner grabbed him by the neck, spun him around, and slammed him against the wall, causing the back of his head to strike painfully loud as the dull thump echoed throughout the building.

"What are you running for, creep?" he blasted.

"What are you breaking my balls for?" Vito quivered. "I'm clean, I'm clean."

The sweat poured from his brow, partly from the run and partly from fear. His knees trembled and his voice cracked with apprehension. His curly black hair was unkempt, his clothes disheveled, and his face unshaven. The hallway stunk of stale urine and crusted vomit and added to the displeasure of the confrontation in this tenement typical of the neighborhood. I knew too well that foul, nauseous stench of the ghetto that lingered on your clothes.

My partner rifled through his pockets and came up with fifty dollars, but no action.

"What did you do with it, you hump?" he demanded. "We've been watching you pick it up."

"I'm clean, man, I'm clean."

"We're taking twenty," Simmons said, handing him thirty, "and we want you to give the boys a message. If we don't get more for our sector, you're going to go everyday we're working, whether you're dirty or not."

"OK, OK, I'll tell them," he said, pocketing his money with a spasmodic hand. "Just don't hit me. . . . What do you want?"

"Twenty a week for us."

Just then I realized Vito must have thrown the papers out the open window. I leaned out and looked down to a courtyard every inch covered with soaked debris and garbage, dropped from the windows above. I wasn't about to sift through that junk for a few lousy slips.

"Let's get out of here, this place is making me sick." I coughed, as a diarrheic smell made me wince with disgust. It could have been coming from Vito.

"You tell them, Vito, for your own good," my partner said.

"I'll tell them, I'll tell them."

A few days passed and, seeing Vito on his route, we called him over to the car. He informed us nervously that they had turned us down, and after thinking it over carefully, deciding it might not have been such a good idea in the first place, we didn't pursue it.

Another associate of the Cavalleros, Jimmy "the Screw" Tucaarno, constantly stood in front of his social club, studying passersby with a rugged face as the day's action was processed inside. Bulging at the belly, tall, and square-shouldered, he had the reputation of an accused murderer, but nevertheless, a gentleman. Periodically, if you gave him the eye, cruising on an 8 A.M. to 4 P.M. tour, he would give you ten dollars.

One evening, shortly after the incident with Vito, another officer and I were riding past "the Screw's" social club when I spotted a man with a bulge under his shirt and I told my partner to stop.

"Hey you, come here," I called to the wavy-haired stranger in his mid-twenties, thinking the bulge might be a gun. But before he even reached the radio car, he knowingly picked up his shirt and uncovered a bundle of papers.

"Let me see that," I demanded. "That looks like work [gambling records] to me."

"No ... no, that's not work," he said, passing me the bundle. "That's just store receipts." It did look like store receipts, but I had heard that some sophisticated gambling combines coded their weekly tallies, called ribbons, to look like receipts of this kind.

"Get in the back," I said, removing the rubber band, "until I see what I have here. What's your name?"

"Martin."

"Martin what?"

"Just Martin."

I whirled in the seat, grabbed him by the throat, and gritted my teeth. "Don't be a wise guy and there won't be any trouble. What's your name?" The element of surprise and sudden show of force worked every time.

"Cavallero, Martin Cavallero," he wheezed, before I released his Adam's apple. He didn't look like a Cavallero—not rowdy enough. But his driver's license backed him up and now there were no doubts in my mind that I truly had an enormous amount of gambling records in my hand.

"Let's get away from the club," I suggested to my partner and we circled around the neighborhood a few times, finally parking about a block away from where we picked him up. I was trying to decide if I should lock him up or not.

During this time a lot of things were happening. Martin kept swearing, over and over, that it was not work and that he had nothing to do with his brothers' operation. Known gamblers from all over the precinct kept popping their heads in the window trying to bargain for his release. Vito even came by and offered to take the pinch to spare "the kid." At first, the thought of locking up a Cavallero appealed to me, but a few things entered my mind that made that notion fade. Even though he was a brother of the known gamblers and he was coming out of "the Screw's" club, he said he had never been arrested before and his insistence that what he was carrying was not work made me wonder. I had come to presume that gamblers, unlike most other criminals, were not apt to deny their guilt, especially when caught in the act. But the main thing that threw me was Martin's telling us to keep the bundle, he did not need it. If, in fact, it had been work, he would have had a strong desire to retain it, for if the word ever got out to the bettors in the neighborhood that the record of their bets had been seized by the police, every Tom, Dick, and Harry would storm their policy man, claiming they had a bet on the winning number. You can see the problems that might ensue. He finally offered to pay for his release and we figured a score of this nature was surely worth a healthy amount.

"C'mon, fellas," he ventured, let's work something out."

"What did you have in mind, Martin? This is a lot of work."

"Look, it's not work. I keep telling you, it's store receipts. C'mon, here's ten bucks. Let me get the hell out of here."

I almost fell out of the radio car. This cheap bastard had to be kidding.

"All right, let's take him in," I said to my partner. "This guy must think we're fooling."

"Wait a minute, wait a minute," Martin gulped. "How much do you want? How about fifty?"

"Let's take him in," I repeated and it went like that for about fifteen minutes before he offered six hundred dollars and we found that irresistible. We kept the bundle and let him go, figuring if it was work, in a short time we would be approached with an offer to buy it back.

About a half hour later, the team riding in an adjacent sector informed us that Mike Cavallero, the head of the operation, wanted to see us. We figured this was the pitch and wondered how much he would offer. Instead, when we reached the meeting place, I saw anger in Mike's eyes and knew right away something was wrong.

His massive bulk lumbered clumsily, yet with certainty, toward the radio car. His meat hook hands hung limply at the sides, swaying little. Face stern, bushy black eyebrows slanted downward, he spoke deeply, with authority.

"I want the six hundred back. The kid was clean. That's not work."

"We think it is," my partner retorted, "and you're not getting anything back."

"If I don't get it by tonight, nobody gets anything anymore ... not division, not borough—nobody." He was referring to the division and borough plainclothes units. He walked back to his car, fell in, and drove away.

Naturally, the topic of conversation in our car for the next hour concerned only what we should do. We did not want to be responsible for the end of one of the oldest and probably best contracts in the division, and if the Cavalleros stopped dishing out money, there would be a lot of men pissed off at us. Maybe it really wasn't work, we thought. Finally we decided to give back the money, but not the bundle, just to be sure.

We found "the Screw" by his club. He knew.

"Here, Jim," I mumbled, regretfully handing him the six, crisp, one hundred dollar bills, knowing they would find their way into the right hands.

"You're doing the right thing, kid. . . . Here . . . for your trouble," he said, handing me back one of the hundreds. Like I said, Jimmy was always a gentleman.

Yet another associate of the Cavalleros was Tony Passera, a middle-aged, ever smiling bookmaker, who paid the police daily, operating out of the phoniest front I have ever seen. It was supposed to be a plumbing store, I think, but there was nothing, absolutely nothing inside except little old Tony, taking his bets and staking the sector five dollars a day. The walls were dingy gray, the floors slatted, and a partition that cut the store in two was inches thick with dust. A twenty-five watter dimly lit one quarter of the "store."

You would stop the radio car around the corner, get out, walk inside behind the partition, followed by Tony, get the five dollars, return to the car, and write a visit to a known gambling location in your memo book, indicating there were no violations observed.

Although their operation was the biggest combined effort in the precinct, the Cavalleros did not have their hand in everything and many independents paid for protection. One was Tommy "Bones" Zekia who paid ten dollars per sector car, two sector cars a night, four nights a week, to keep his Ziganette, a card game in which large sums of money can change hands in a relatively short amount of time, flourishing in the Eight-O.

It was well understood that the division and possibly the borough plainclothes units were receiving monthly payoffs for similar protection. During my stay at the Eight-O, Tom, a poor dresser, with uncombed hair and consistently looking as if he had just awakened, had his game reported frequently to the plainclothesmen, yet to my knowledge he was busted only once. Subsequent conversations with him revealed that the pinch was, in fact, a phony arrest, made just to keep the pressure low.

When thriving, the game was run on Wednesday, Friday, Saturday, and Sunday nights, although there was never a foolproof schedule. The tip-off to whether it was on or not was the abundance of parked cars on the usually empty block and the light in the hall. On 4 P.M. to midnight and midnight to 8 A.M. tours, you could pick up the ten dollars as long as the game was in progress. You would park the radio car across the street and eventually "Bones" would come to the hall window. He would send someone else out with the money and usually they made little or no effort at all to hide the payoff. One of the payoff men was a short, Puerto Rican guy and the other a tall, red-headed galoot, straight from a Damon Runyon tale. It got so ridiculous after a while that if you got tired of waiting, you would blow the horn to speed things up. Sometimes we were told by Zekia there was no game going on when we actually believed there was—a suspicion that produced that high number of reports. By reporting it, you would also be able to enter that fact in your memo book, a plus factor for your defense if ever accused in the future.

A dice game and a poker game rounded out the gambling payoffs. On 4 P.M. to midnight and midnight to 8 A.M. tours on the weekend, a payoff of ten dollars to the sector was supplied by the operator of the dice game conducted in the rear of a luncheonette. As with the Ziganette game arrangement, you parked the radio car outside of the illegal activity and, sooner or later, the operator, a spidery black man with a patch over his eye, would come out and give you the "dime." "Patch Eye" invariably appeared unexpectedly from the dark, leaned into the car with a few pleasantries, dropped the money to the floor, and returned to the night—a very mysterious man. The poker game was on Sunday afternoons in a social club on the periphery of the precinct and, again, was picked up in the same manner.

Aside from gambling, money was picked up in a variety of other ways. ...

An average of two or three traffic accidents per week was handled by each sector in the 80th and invariably, soon after the patrol car arrived, a tow truck would arrive, if it was not there already. The reason for this was that each garage had a radio tuned to the police band, which was completely legitimate, and in some cases the tow trucks themselves carried police-band radios, which was entirely illegitimate. A mad race of tow trucks to the scene of an accident was not a rare sight, due mainly to the unwritten law that the first one on the scene gets the job. Most trucks towed only fairly new cars when it was reasonable to assume the owners would have them repaired, although that was not always the case. When there was a tow job at the scene of an accident, the sector car received ten dollars initially, with a possibility of from ten dollars to sixty dollars more if the garage got the repair work. This first payment was in return for a lackadaisical attitude by the officer toward the tow truck driver in respect to the law forbidding solicitation of repair work at the scene. If the collision was spotted by a sector car team before it was transmitted over the air, a private call to the garage could have netted them an additional twenty to thirty dollars.

Sometimes the driver would pay us at the scene but usually we would go to the garage the next day or even the next week, where we could see for ourselves if he, in fact, got the repair work. Some drivers didn't pay and one garage had a reputation of stalling so long you would get tired of going back. If these men showed up at an accident, we made it a point to strictly enforce the law and check their license, registration, medallion, ID card, and the like, and warn them not to solicit repairs at the scene. Conversely, your attitude toward drivers who cooperated was more lenient than normal if you caught them violating the traffic regulations.

When a report of a factory or warehouse break was received, especially on the midnight to 8 A.M. tour, visions of dollar signs or goods danced in some officers' heads. If the premises were secure, a call to Central radio would determine if the owner or alarm company was responding. The chance that the owner would "throw" you something for being present when he arrived, was good, but I never received any payment from an alarm company. If you were able to enter the location, anything and everything was vulnerable to be taken out to the radio car and later transferred to your private vehicle. That became such a habit that I found myself sometimes with things I couldn't use, which I eventually discarded or gave away. The imagination need not be stretched too far to determine what transpired when the circumstances were right at the scene of a break at a liquor store or an appliance store. When the owner reported what was missing, it was assumed that it was taken by the burglar. A shirt factory in the Eight-O was the most constant victim of police pilferage.

Alcoholic Beverage Control and State Liquor Authority violations were found mainly in two places: "After hours" clubs—usually extravagantly finished basements, where one could get a drink after the bars closed; and "juice joints"—usually apartments, where one could buy a bottle of booze on Sunday or whenever the liquor stores were closed. Out of seven sectors in the Eight-O, there was only one that was void of these illegal activities. Although the enforcement of laws in this area was left primarily to plainclothesmen, these spots could also supply a radio car team with twenty or thirty additional dollars a weekend, and possibly more, and a sergeant with an additional fifty or sixty dollars a weekend, but probably more. Understandably, most sergeants were sure to "hit" these places on a weekend and the chauffeur's share varied according to the sergeant. Some split fifty-fifty, whereas others kept more for themselves and gave less to their driver. In fact there was one sergeant, Lou Dalton, who, rumor had it, collected over one hundred dollars from various pickups throughout the entire precinct on a single Saturday night and gave his chauffeur only ten dollars. On other occasions he picked up money and gave his chauffeurs nothing. His reputation was that of the greediest man in the precinct. In fact, undoubtedly, he was the greediest man I knew. Many patrolmen felt that way too, and if it were not for his stripes, I'm sure he would have had a perennial black eye.

After turning out of the precinct on an 8 A.M. to 4 P.M. tour, radio car crews would usually pick up some coffee and newspapers within their sector and sit somewhere to digest them both. If you happened to be working in a sector that contained a check casher—a store designed to profit solely from charges incurred for cashing checks— that is where you would sit. The owners and managers were only too glad to have you around when they opened in the morning because they were prime targets for stick-ups. To show their appreciation, they paid two dollars every morning to the radio car outside. For a stinking dollar apiece, you risked everything. But you never thought about it. If you got called away on an assignment and by the time you returned the place was open, you went in and informed him that you had a job elsewhere, whereupon you received the money anyhow. Transporting money from one store to another with the radio cars was worth five dollars each trip. The number of trips each week was unpredictable.

Also unpredictable were sudden windfalls of money from unexpected sources. The most notable occurred one wintry evening as another officer and I were passing a bar with the radio car. We were hailed by a Black man with a hairless, shiny dome, spread nose, and a walrus moustache over full, crimson lips nestled atop a redwood frame. Each step closer to the car magnified the bulk of this giant. He stuck his head in the window and leaned on thick-wristed branches. His overpowering presence enfeebled me and I could not imagine what he wanted.

"Sorry I missed you last week," he said, dropping fifteen dollars on the seat. We didn't say anything. We had never seen this man before and he obviously mistook us for someone else, but we kept the money anyhow. Until this day I don't know what he was up to.

When the manager of a supermarket wanted to deposit the day's take in the bank, the presence of a patrol car was often appreciated. He would either call the station house and ask the switchboard operator, usually either a patrolman or trainee, to send a car or he would dial

911, the emergency number, and report a phony dispute, advising the men of the true nature of the call when they arrived. Normally he would jump in the rear of the radio car and get a ride back and forth. The reward for this service varied from a couple of packs of cigarettes to four dollars.

When landlords' troubles with tenants resulted in the procurement of a court eviction order, it was given to a city marshal who was compensated by the landlord for its successful execution. You can imagine that taking someone from his home and putting him out on the street was not an easy task and that more times than not, he resisted. For this reason, city marshals liked to have a sector car on the scene of an eviction to preserve the peace, for which the marshals paid to the tune of five dollars per eviction, whether the people were home or not.

On Sunday mornings a regular practice was to enter all open grocery stores and order a pack of cigarettes. The merchants, knowing that they were not supposed to be open—a violation of an anachronistic law, punishable by a fine of up to five dollars—gladly handed over the cigarettes free of charge, in addition to a book of matches containing anywhere from two to five dollars to save themselves the trouble of going to court where they'd have to pay it anyway. For some reason, not many patrolmen took Sundays off.

"Scores" from lawyers were not talked about as freely as the above categories, but often enough to know they existed. The only incident I had in this area occurred when I was approached by a lawyer, Sam Bronstein, in the complaint room of the Brooklyn Criminal Court while I was waiting to draw up a complaint. The charge on the man I had arrested was driving while intoxicated.

"Are you Droge?" I heard him ask a patrolman three seats away down the front row. His voice was melodious, bordering on a female's. He was not as well dressed as some of the attorneys mingling in the courthouse, but his conservative suit and plain, matching brown tie were neat and clean. His spotless teeth showed through a constant smile and his thin, bony body craved nourishment.

"Over here," I volunteered, wondering how he got my name.

"Droge?" he questioned. I nodded. "I'm Sam Bronstein, can I talk with you a moment?"

"Sure, what's on your mind?" I asked as I strode with him out to the hallway.

"You have Lopez, right?"

"Right."

"How does his sheet look? Was he in bad shape? How abou . . ."

"Hey, wait a minute. Who the hell are you, anyhow? Just because you tell me your name is Dan Bronstein doesn't mean you can ask me a hundred questions and expect answers."

"Sam, Sam Bronstein. I'm an attorney. I've been down here for years. You're from the Eight-O, aren't you?" He pinched the bridge of his nose, lowering his head in cursory thought. "Peterson," he exclaimed. "And Villa, Joe Villa. Do you know them?"

"Yes, what about them?"

"I've had cases with them . . . and a couple of other guys, too, from the Eight-O, but I just can't think of their names."

"Jack Peterson is a good friend of mine," I said.

"I'm surprised he never mentioned me, then. I've been working with Peterson for years."

"Working?"

"Well, let me just ask you this. Does this fellow Lopez look like he has money? I don't mean wealthy. I mean— does he have a job? Did he have any money on him when you locked him up? Does he look like he can afford his own attorney?" He spoke very rapidly.

"I'm listening."

"Well, if he does, and if he happens to retain me, I take care of you."

I had never played this game before, but it wasn't too hard to figure out what he meant. "How much?"

"Fifty."

"I'll see what I can do," I said brusquely, walking back inside. I was more concerned with losing my place in the line than convincing my prisoner to hire Sam Bronstein.

Later on, though, leaning against the wall outside of the courtroom, having a smoke, I had forgotten all about

Bronstein when I was approached by a chunky little brunette.

"Patrolman Broga? Are you Patrolman Broga?"

"I'm Patrolman Droge. What can I do for you?"

"I'm Mrs. Lopez," she said. "You arrested my husband last night."

"Oh, hello! What can I do for you?" I repeated, reevaluating chunky to be well endowed, but badly proportioned.

"I wanted to know if you thought I should get my husband a lawyer." I immediately remembered Bronstein.

"I know if it were my wife in there, I would definitely get her a private attorney," I said truthfully. "But that's entirely up to you."

"But I don't know who to go to. I've never needed one before."

"Well, there are plenty of attorneys around. There's one over there," I said, pointing to the conveniently positioned Mr. Bronstein. "Why don't you just go up to him and ask him for his advice?"

"I will ... thanks," she said as she turned and padded her way toward Sammy boy.

At that moment, I felt a bit cheap, but rationalized to myself that, in a way, I had done her a favor by steering her away from using the free Legal Aid attorneys, a group that, because of their overburdening workload, would understandably not be as efficient as a private attorney.

But I was only making excuses for myself. From an inexperienced rookie, it hadn't taken long to evolve into a hardened thief and, ever so slowly, I began to realize it.

CHAPTER 11

The mechanism of corruption was not all I learned in my intermediary stage in the Eight-O. I learned that police officers put their lives on the line every day and that whether they are honest or not has no correlation with their bravery or lack of it. I learned some of the heartaches and some of the joys of being a patrolman. I learned that some people call the police for any reason—because they know they will come. I learned that to millions a police officer is not only an enforcer of the law, but also a doctor, a lawyer, a plumber, an electrician, a baby-sitter, a judge, a jury, a mediator, a coroner, and on and on and on. I learned that however ridiculous the call may seem, the patrolman must answer it, because there will always be that one time he is really needed. I learned that a psycho call or a family dispute could present as much trouble as a bank robbery. I learned that when a police officer knocks on a door he never really knows what's on the other side and because of this he must be ever wary and always on guard. And I never stopped learning how profound Bill O'Shaughnessy's statement was that first day when he warned me of the danger in the Black ghetto.

Visualizing an end to my flying and fixer details, I jumped at an offer to join the scooter patrol in the precinct. The small machines could not compare with the motorcycle that I owned and could not be expected to catch speeding motorists, but they were sufficient for the purpose for which the department had acquired them—mobile patrol.

Zipping through the precinct on a balmy day was certainly better than standing on Fulton and Nostrand or shuffling off to the Eight-Eight for the Pratt detail. However, it wasn't too long before I realized why nobody else volunteered for the assignment. Aside from the natural hazards, such as gigantic potholes and roaming packs of ferocious dogs, which were able to travel faster than the scooters, there were the hates, resentments, and ignorance of the people.

There wasn't a day over seventy degrees that went by without at least three-quarters of the fire hydrants in the area being turned on by the residents. Instead of going to pools or beaches, ghetto children frolicked in the spray from the "johnny-pumps." Although the station house switchboard was inundated with calls from people complaining of no running water in their homes on those days, when the police turned off the hydrants they were called "heartless bastards" who deprived the poor Black children of a little fun.

Some of what the children thought was fun, was often injurious to the scooter patrolmen. Gushing with such great force and often throwing the water the width of the street, the hydrants were always visible from at least a block away. But a favorite thrill for the youngsters was to sit on the mouth of the pump, causing the spray to shoot sharply downward, thus making an approaching scooter patrolman or radio car unaware of its being open. At precisely the right moment the youngster would leap from in front of the hydrant, allowing the potent flow to follow its normal course. In the case of a radio car the result would be two drenched patrolmen and a barrel of belly laughs by the onlookers, but in the case of a scooter man the impact was often so powerful that it knocked the officer to the ground and, despite the risk of serious physical injury, the people laughed, just the same.

I considered myself fortunate for a few weeks, having escaped any dousings, but my luck was short-lived. Traveling down a side street on the way to the station house one evening, I struck something in the road and the rear end of the scooter rose sharply, catapulting me through the air. I landed painfully hard in the gutter, but miraculously I wasn't hurt more than a few bumps and bruises. Looking back to the scooter, motor running, on its side in the roadway, I saw three or four boys running down the sidewalk away from me, howling with laughter at my spill. I didn't think too much of it until I approached the scooter and saw what had made me fall. Almost invisible in the night, a length of thick black cable had been strung across the street, tied to a lamppost on one side and a fence on the other. By the time I realized the boys were responsible, they had vanished. A day or so later I unvolunteered myself for scooter patrol.

A new crop of rookies took up the slack in the flying and fixer details and I saw the radio car assignments that I received as a result a welcome relief. Radio cars, however, were not impervious to violent attacks. One, brand-new, with a little over sixteen miles on the odometer, was reduced to cinders. The two patrolmen assigned to it had been lured into a building on a dispute call, and when they realized it was unfounded, they returned to the street to find a flaming mass. Subsequent investigation revealed it had been fire bombed. Another attempt failed when an incendiary device, which had been attached to the gas tank of a radio car parked in front of the station house, was discovered by an alert patrolman. On other occasions, while on routine motor patrol, rocks, sticks, cans, or bottles, thrown by unknown assailants, constantly struck the car or smashed on the ground perilously close. These conditions didn't instill any amicable feelings in the hearts of the White policemen toward the Blacks of Bedford-Stuyvesant.

On radio motor patrol the job broadened. With from ten to twenty assignments received from Central radio each tour, three to five pickup jobs in the street, an hour for meal and the rest of the time on patrol, there were few boring moments. The assignments ranged from the emergency to the ridiculous, but to the last one, regardless of their apparent insignificance, they had to be answered. A large part were unfounded and proved to be nothing more than a waste of time.

Some people called the police emergency number for anything. I responded to jobs with other police officers where a man wanted us to watch his two-year-old granddaughter for an hour while he went to the library to pick up a book, where a housewife became irate and indignant when we told her we were not equipped to fix a leaky pipe under her sink, where a group of homosexuals asked us to judge their "Fairy Queen Contest," where a man with a toothache wanted us to give him a lift to the dentist, where a woman asked our advice on what vitamins to feed her pet monkey, where a man who wanted to save the cost of an electrician asked us the proper method of rewiring his kitchen, and where, on countless other occasions, we were asked to knock down an apartment door because the occupants had locked themselves out.

Many people, of course, called the police for legitimate noncrime incidents where a patrolman's presence was required, for instance, calls for a disorderly person or group, noise, a family dispute, an alarm of fire, a traffic accident, or an ambulance case. These incidents were handled with less speed and enthusiasm than the crime-related jobs, but usually with the same quality of efficiency.

A disorderly person many times meant a drunk or a prostitute, and if they were bothering anyone, they were sent on their way. Noise complaints were often just a loud party or stereo next door, remedied by a simple request to quiet things down. However, many a burglar trying to break into an apartment was arrested as a result of a disorderly person or noise complaint call and being prepared for such an occasion was always a good habit.

Without a doubt, one of the most monumental plights of the patrolman is having to stand in the middle of a family dispute. The majority of squabbles I handled in the Eight-O were between unmarried couples who were living together, where one of the two had decided to end the relationship. Technically the one with the rent receipts should have been allowed to stay and the other made to leave, but I did not find that to be the best solution. I referred both to court, taking aside the man, trying to persuade him to take a walk or spend the night with a friend until things cooled off. I would never force a man from his own home, common law marriage or not, unless the woman had a court order directing me to do so. Patrolmen who did attempt to throw out the man often regretted it. If they had to use necessary force, the woman would turn against them, and if they locked him up, nine out of ten times, the next morning she would refuse to press charges. Like an umpire on a baseball field, I figured the only friend I had in certain situations—especially family dispute scenes—was dressed in a blue uniform and I sided with no one.

Out of the hundreds of disputes I answered, one is most memorable. My partner and I responded to a job in a multiple dwelling and, climbing the stairs as quickly as possible, we heard a man screaming for mercy. The door to the top floor apartment was open and we came upon an unusual sight as far as conjugal fisticuffs go: the wife was beating hell out of the husband. But that wasn't the only irregular thing and, as we were soon to find out, this was no ordinary pair. They were both about six feet four inches tall and because my partner and I were only five-nine, the first thing we did was tell them to sit down, hoping to gain a psychological advantage. In a few moments we were able to discern two facts from the half-English, half-French ranting and raving: they were newlyweds from Haiti and the wife suspected the husband of being unfaithful. When I took the husband off to the side, I suggested he leave for a while and he told me that was exactly what he was trying to do when we arrived, but the wife had grabbed him before he could make his getaway good. She interrupted us and suggested he leave for good. For several reasons, one of which was his health, he agreed. As he was walking down the stairs, she leaned over the railing and threw her hands out at him, saying: "May the curse of Mobutu be upon you," or something to that effect. Ostensibly they were both superstitious people and believers in some ancient rites of voodoo, for he covered up his face, screamed inhumanly, and fell down the rest of the flight. Apparently unhurt, he picked himself up and ran out the door yelling something that sounded like: "Aaaayeee." Unfamiliar with any New York State law against voodoo, we left.

As in a dispute, the patrolman is hard tested at the scene of a fire. The primary function of a police officer at the scene of a fire is to protect lives and property. Because he is usually on the scene before the Fire Department, he must ascertain the exact location of the fire and be certain there is a responsible person to direct the fire apparatus to it. When necessary, he must warn the occupants of the building and assist them to safety. Once the fire apparatus arrives, it is the patrolman's duty to establish and maintain fire lines around the building.

On only one occasion was it necessary for me to enter a burning building in the Eight-O. I arrived at the scene of a fire and was told there were people still inside. I rushed into the building, not yet too badly ablaze, but congested with clouds of smoke, and on the second floor, I heard the screams of an infant coming from behind a locked apartment door. I kicked the door down and inside found a baby girl, lying on the living room floor, with her mother unconscious beside her. Grabbing the woman's collar with my left hand and the baby around the waist with my right, I was barely able to find my way through the heavy smoke, back to the door, and down the stairs to safety. The Fire Department had just arrived and two firemen were able to revive the woman on the scene; the baby was apparently unaffected. After a short period of crowd control, I resumed patrol, thoroughly satisfied with a job well done.

Though some officers relished an assignment to a traffic accident—mainly for the money they could make—I dreaded the calls because of the mountains of paperwork. Aside from an extensive memo-book entry, anywhere from three to five comprehensive, multi-paged forms had to be filled out, which often required over an hour's time. Almost every phase of my duties was so burdened with paperwork that anytime I could, I avoided it.

An ambulance case meant a maternity, a psycho, a sick or injured person, or a death. On three different maternity calls I was present and able to assist when the baby was born, and on two of those occasions it was a pleasure; on the other the baby was stillborn.

After the experience with the prisoner in Brooklyn Jewish Hospital, a psycho call always kept me on my toes. Whether the patient was violent or not, the assignment lasted anywhere from four to eight hours, depending on how long it took to see the psychiatrist in the hospital.

Routine sick or injured cases were simply handled by waiting for the ambulance or, if necessary, taking the person to the hospital via the radio car. Some were not so routine and required quick first aid action.

In the beginning I found it a bit sickening dealing with severed limbs, pools of blood, screaming people in excruciating pain and all the other gruesome sights and sounds a patrolman witnesses daily on an ambulance case, but after a while I was unaffected by them. The one thing I never got used to was death, however, and the first DOA (literally: dead on arrival; figuratively: any dead body) assignment I received will always stick in my mind.

". . . Proceed to that location and meet a complainant on the third floor, K."

"10-4, Central." I put down the radiophone and turned to my partner that day, Steve Vandalia, a twelve-year-veteran on the force, small, well built, and always composed. "You know, that gets me," I said. "They tell you 'meet the complainant,' but they don't tell you what the complaint is. This guy might want to tell us that the roof looks like it's gonna fall in, three seconds before it happens."

The day was sweltering and my uniform was soaked through with perspiration. Just the week before it had been pleasantly cool with torrents of rain hitting the city, but the summer sun had broken through the last couple of days and made living a little sticky.

"Yeah, I know. Those dispatchers in Central have probably been on the teat so long, they've forgotten what it's like out here in the street," my partner said.

"If they've ever *been* out here. Well, we'll find out in a few minutes what 'meet the complainant' means this time." We pulled up in front of the address given.

As we walked up the stairs, I wiped the sweat from my brow and commented that this was the first job all week that wasn't on the top floor. It always seemed that the majority of jobs I'd get in a four- or five-story building, without an elevator, were on the top floor. Steve laughed, knowing that he had spent more time responding to top floor assignments than I had time on the job. When we reached the third floor hallway we were met by a stout Caucasian male wearing an out-of-date, wrinkled suit, holding a matching fedora in front of him with both hands. He was nearly bald, wore dark brown, thick-framed glasses firmly set on the bridge of his nose, and spoke in a Milquetoast whisper.

"Good afternoon, officers. I'm William Northrupt. I suppose you're looking for me?"

"Did you call?" Steve asked.

"Yes, sir, I did."

"Then we're looking for you. Central radio doesn't give us the caller's name all the time. Just the address."

"Oh, I see. Well, the reason I called was my father. He used to be a policeman, you know. He was stationed over in Manhattan."

"What about your father, sir?" I said.

"Well, he lives in apartment 3-B over here and I haven't heard from him in about two weeks. That's not like my father. He usually calls me at least once a week. I tried calling him, but I got no answer."

"Did he mention a vacation or anything like that?"

"No. He wouldn't go away anymore. He's too old."

"How old is your father, sir?"

"Seventy-two."

At that moment we were joined in the hallway by a short Negro wearing overalls filthy with grease.

Northrupt looked to us, then to the Negro and said: "This is Mr. Washington, the superintendent of the building. I asked him to get my father's spare key. He leaves it with him because he's forever forgetting to take his with him and locks himself out of the house."

"I see. Has your father been sick recently?"

"No. Surprisingly he's a strappy guy. Six-two, I believe. Hasn't been sick in years. Except . . ."

"Except what?"

"He did complain a couple of weeks ago about his heart. He was supposed to go to the doctor . . ."

"Very well, Mr. Northrupt. Why don't we check out the apartment and take it from there."

"Fine."

The superintendent walked over to 3-B with the key in his hand and opened the lock. Seeming to sense what was inside, he stepped to the side to let me go in first.

Again wiping the perspiration from my brow with a handkerchief, I pushed the door in. Instantly I was struck in the face with a gush of steaming, putrid air, causing me to cry out in disgust. The heat was intense, nevertheless Steve pushed past me into the small apartment and ran straight for the living room window to the left. Opening that and the one in the kitchen beyond it, he ran back to me at the door and said: "C'mon, Ed, give me a hand."

"But the sme——"

At that moment he opened the bedroom door to my immediate right and I laid my eyes on the most repulsive, repugnant sight I had ever seen—that of a human body decomposing. Stretched across the bed, half-clad in pajamas, was the pathetic bulk of a man with his eyes popping out of the sockets, his lips a pale green, and the flesh of his face crusted and eaten away by the scores of maggots crawling about it. The body was swollen with liquid, hued a deep black, and certain to burst at first touch. The stench was unbearable, and as Steve moved past it to open the window, I staggered into the hall, gagging nauseously.

Mr. Northrupt had seen the body also and was leaning against the wall, staring into space, repeating, "Oh my God!" over and over again.

In a few seconds, Steve came out of the apartment and suggested I go down to the radio car to call the sergeant to the scene. I gladly obliged.

I took my time down and by the time I reentered the building, the smell had spread to the ground floor. On the third floor Mr. Northrupt was still against the wall and Steve was rolling up newspapers piled by the open door.

"Here, take one," he said, handing me a cone-shaped *Daily News*.

"What do I do with this?" I asked.

He took a book of matches from his change pocket and lighting my cone, then his, he said: "An old trick I learned from a guy in emergency service. The smell of burning newspaper is supposed to neutralize the air. C'mon." With that he walked into the apartment and, taking a deep breath first, I followed. We walked around the living room for a few seconds, then Steve motioned for me to follow him into the bedroom. I had a vivid mental picture of what lay in there and could not bear to see it again in person, so I declined. When my lungs were about to burst, I started walking quickly to the door and, feeling I would have to suck in air any second, I ran. I hadn't yet cleared the doorway when I was forced to inhale a chestful of rancid air. Again I choked uncontrollably and running to the window at the end of the hall, I stuck my head out into the sunshine.

Ten minutes later the sergeant arrived and, upon viewing the body, immediately called a unit of the emergency service division to the scene for removal. When two men from that outfit arrived, they nonchalantly donned their gas masks and entered the foul-smelling apartment, one with a large plastic-type bag tucked neatly under his arm. The other wrote the name and address of the deceased on a tag and tied it on the big toe of the right foot. When he moved the leg accidentally, a thick purple liquid oozed from an opening by the ankle. I turned away and saw no more until they carried the bag from the apartment on a stretcher.

About a half hour later, in the station house bathroom, I learned that the badge on a police officer's shirt prevents him from vomiting only in public.

In addition to noncrime incident calls, the airwaves were flooded with calls of possible crimes, crimes in the past, or crimes in progress. In Bedford-Stuyvesant each year there were more reported robberies, burglaries, larcenies, assaults, and shots fired than any other section of Brooklyn. For that matter the total was probably higher than that of the entire boroughs of Queens and Staten Island together.

A good portion of each tour was consumed by every sector car in taking reports of past crimes. Many pertinent facts were necessary for the report and on the average each call would take from twenty minutes to a half hour, including travel time. On a burglary, for instance, in addition to the person's name, address, and telephone number at home and work, it was necessary to know what time the house was vacated and what time the burglary was discovered, how the entry was made, what articles were taken, how much of each, how much they were worth, what brands they were, and their serial numbers. Finding out that information in a ransacked house took time. Similar information was also needed for other crime reports.

I never put it in writing, but I often suggested to bosses

in the precinct the assignment of one car each day tour and another each 4 P.M. to midnight tour with the patrolmen's sole function being to take reports of past crimes. There would have been no trouble getting volunteers with no midnights on the schedule and it would have served to free the sector cars bogged down with paperwork. But apparently nobody but me thought it was a good idea.

With the vast number of crimes came a closeness among the men who investigated them. Often men were transferred from Bedford-Stuyvesant to other precincts around the city where crimes were comparatively few and far between, and they told me of another world, where being a police officer really meant something to the people of the neighborhood and where a semblance of respect was discernible. Their stories were consistent in reporting the lack of camaraderie in those precincts, however, no close-knit crews, no backups on certain assignments—conditions common in the Black ghetto. As one transferee put it: "There's no policeman like a ghetto policeman."

In Queens, midtown Manhattan, the North Bronx, and Staten Island, nobody even talked to newcomer patrolmen, let alone "bounced" with them after work. Those attitudes turned me off. It was no bargain working in Bedford-Stuyvesant, with five gun runs some nights and continual 10-13s, but at least there was a strong bond uniting all men, and if you cut one, we all bled.

If there were enough cars working on some nights, you could expect a backup unit on every job. Too many times at roll call were we informed that a police officer in the area had been shot, stabbed, or had lye thrown in his face, for us not to be tight. Too many times did we respond to a past burglary run and come upon a burglary in progress. Too many times did we knock on a door, and when it opened, we were face to face with an assailant. Too many times did a "simple" dispute flare up or a peaceful psycho turn violent. No, too many times were we placed in the face of danger not to work and play together; and if nothing else, that's what was satisfying about working in Bedford-Stuyvesant.

With the high number of crimes in the Eight-O came a high number of arrests.

CHAPTER 12

In the New York City Police Department uniformed patrolmen are judged by their activity, that is, the number of summonses they issue and arrests they effect. A man who walks the same post for five consecutive years, and who applies himself, making his presence known, might prevent hundreds of crimes during that time just by being in sight, but, unless he makes arrests and issues summonses, he won't have the reputation of a worker.

This was especially true in an area such as Bedford-Stuyvesant where it was difficult to walk your post five consecutive days without an opportunity for an arrest. But, maybe due to the paperwork or simply to lethargy, some men avoided arrests like the plague and if a patrolman like this ran into one he didn't want, he'd try to give it away to another patrolman rather than let the prisoner go.

It was not uncommon in the Eight-O to hear over the radio some nights: "Anybody looking for a drug arrest?" or "Anyone want a gun collar?" Invariably there was always somebody working who wanted an arrest, especially a quality one, like a man with a gun, a murder, a bank robbery, or a dealer with a large amount of narcotics, and who would take the prisoner off the other patrolman's hands. Some men, in fact, would let everybody know before turning out that they would take any and all unwanted arrests that tour. This practice was known as "catching." A probationary patrolman temporarily assigned to the Eight-O in 1969 was "catching" almost every tour he worked and wound up making over thirty arrests during the summer—quite a good accomplishment for any patrolman, let alone a "probie."

The arrest procedure seems quite complicated at first, but, like everything else, the more you do it the easier it gets. Once the arrest has been effected in the street, the prisoner is handcuffed, frisked, and brought before the desk officer in the station house, who is informed of the details and charges by the arresting officer. The latter then takes the prisoner into the back room or the detective's office and thoroughly searches him—although this is supposed to be done before the desk—confiscating any articles found to be dangerous to life, items unlawfully carried, any evidence, anything useful in escape, or that might be used to damage or deface property. If the prisoner is intoxicated, all personal property should be taken.

If the charge is a misdemeanor (a crime punishable by a sentence not to exceed one year) or less, such as an infraction or violation (offenses punishable by a fine or sentence of no more than fifteen days), the prisoner may be issued a summons to appear in court on an appointed day in the future. This convenience is available only upon consent of the desk officer, upon the sobriety of the prisoner, upon the passing of a rather extensive character background test, which is verified, and is not available to felons or persons charged with certain specified misdemeanors, such as gambling or prostitution.

If the charge is a felony (a crime punishable by a sentence of more than one year) or one of certain specified misdemeanors, the prisoner is fingerprinted. Then begins the onslaught of forms.

The primary form, and usually the first one filled out, is the arrest report. The information required on this form includes: the prisoner's full name and address, any alias or nickname, date of birth, age, sex, color, place of birth, social security number, marital status, occupation, place of employment, resident precinct, and mother's maiden name; the arrest precinct, number, date, and time; the complaint number; the occurrence date, time, and place; the post; the sector; the complainant's name, address, and telephone number; the charges and specific offenses;

whether it was a pickup or warrant arrest; whether the prisoner is a drug addict and if so the amount and type used, for how long, how much it cost, and cause of addiction; if previously arrested for narcotics violation, how many times and what treatment received; whether the prisoner is a citizen or an alien, has been advised of his constitutional rights, has been fingerprinted; the prisoner's physical condition and if he has funds; what telephone calls he makes (allowed three free calls within New York City), the number, the name of the person called, the purpose, and the time; the exact location of the arrest; any aided (injury report) numbers, other arrest numbers, or precinct voucher numbers; the details or story of the arrest; the name, rank, shield, command, and tax number of the arresting officer, and whether he was on or off duty, in uniform or plainclothes; and, finally, the signature of the desk officer.

The other forms that then have to be filled out when applicable include: the arrest disposition report, the precinct voucher (if there is any property or evidence), the request for laboratory analysis of any property or evidence, the gambling arrest report, the supplement to the arrest report, the fingerprint cards, the modus operandi report, and any one or more of numerous specialized forms that pertain to various kinds of arrests.

Depending on the time of day, the prisoner is then lodged in a detention cell or taken directly to court, where another stack of forms must be completed. It is no wonder that some officers are discouraged by this paperwork.

In my immediate quest to earn a steady seat (same partner, same sector, every tour) and my ultimate goal to become a detective, I defied the paperwork and apathy barriers, advancing to number one in a precinct survey under the heading "Summonses Served" (I averaged about thirty-five summonses a month—twenty-five moving violations and ten parking violations) and to the top ten in the arrest department.

I made arrests for robbery, burglary, grand larceny auto, driving while intoxicated, obstructing governmental administration, menacing, felonious assault, possession of a gun or knife, resisting arrest, leaving the scene of an accident, disorderly conduct, and harassment to name a few.

Out of all the arrests I made, however, four deserve special mention—one because of excellent detective work that led to the capture of a woman charged with attempted murder and the other three because of the extreme danger that my various partners and I risked in effecting them.

As my partner and I were cruising slowly through the sector one hot summer day, a report of shots fired in the Eight-O bristled over the radio. The location given was Lincoln Place and Franklin Avenue and when we arrived there, another radio car team was already on the scene, attending to a woman who had received a wound narrowly missing her heart. She provided a description of her attacker, stating it was a Negro female in her mid-forties with a black-and-white checkered dress, heavyset, with dark hair. That description could have fit five thousand women in Bedford-Stuyvesant, so we had our work cut out for us. We searched the vicinity for the weapon and clues and came up empty-handed. We asked neighbors and passersby what they had seen and were told various stories, many of which were obviously fabricated by people who had not witnessed the shooting, but said what they did only to seem important. Two stories that cropped up repeatedly, however, were that a woman indeed had done the shooting and that she had fled the scene in a white car, probably a late model Cadillac.

We scoured the neighborhood in search of the vehicle and found several that fit the description, but none of which, to judge by the coolness of the engines, had been driven recently. One, however, on Park Place around Franklin Avenue had just been parked in a hurry, judging from the angular position at the curb, the rubber skid marks behind the tires, and the heat of the engine. We asked all the people in the vicinity if they knew who owned the car, but nobody was able to tell us. On a hunch I asked a small girl playing skip rope near the car and sure enough she pointed to a house across the street where she said the owner lived—a woman.

We entered the location, guns drawn by our sides, and after knocking on a few apartments, receiving no answers, came to one at which a heavyset woman, in her mid-for-

The Patrolman: A Cop's Story

ties, wearing a black-and-white checkered dress, opened the door. I asked her if she owned the white Cadillac across the street and she said that she did. As I was speaking with her, I happened to look to the floor and by the doorway noticed half of a revolver sticking out of a heavy filing envelope. I retrieved the gun and placed her under arrest. She was positively identified by the victim of the shooting as the woman who pulled the trigger.

What I didn't know then, but eventually learned through further conversations with both parties, was that the woman who did the shooting had suspected the victim of "fooling around" with her husband. To the former's great chagrin, New York State does not believe in the slogan "all's fair in love and war" and she was indicted by a grand jury.

The next arrest in my order of worth occurred early one spring morning while I was assigned to a radio car in the northeast section of the precinct. My partner and I were on routine patrol and stopped for a red light when a man, waving his arm out the window frantically and yelling incoherently, pulled his car alongside. My partner opened his window and asked the man, a Negro in his mid-twenties with an unusually large pompadour, to calm down so we could understand what the trouble was.

"Some guy just tried to stick me up," the man said.

"Where?"

"Back on Fulton Street."

"OK, pull your car over and hop in."

The man followed instructions and in a moment the three of us started out to find the assailant. The Negro informed us that he was coming from a party and on the way to his car was stopped by another Negro, also in his mid-twenties, wearing a dark jacket and pants, who asked him for a cigarette. He gave him one and then continued on to his car. No sooner had he started the engine when the man reappeared by the car door and with his hand stuck in his pocket as if he had a gun told him to hand over all his money or he'd blow his head off. Instinctively the intended victim stomped on the gas and sped away, leaving the would-be holdup man standing in the street.

After cruising the area for a short while we came up behind a man who fit the description.

"I think that's him," the complainant said.

"You think?" I asked.

"Well, I really can't be sure from behind and, besides, I was so scared. You know."

"Yeah, I know. All right, I'll pass him by. Take a good look."

"OK."

I passed the man who was walking rather slowly with both hands in his jacket pockets and his shoulders hunched in the morning chill, then turned to the complainant in the back seat.

"Well?"

"I can't be sure."

"We better check him out, anyhow," my partner said and I pulled the car to the curb. The man kept walking slowly toward us and I was certain from the apparent confusion in his face that he was not the one we were looking for. I walked right into his path to ask him to identify himself.

"Excuse me, sir. May we talk to you for a moment?"

"Sure," he said removing his hands from his pockets. In his right one was a pistol and he pointed it at my chest. My knees buckled from the shock. He was no more than two feet away and I instinctively lunged at him, grabbing his right wrist with both my hands, pushing the gun skyward. My partner, who was right behind me, grabbed his left arm and together we spun him toward the radio car, smashing his back against the rear door handle.

"Drop the gun," I yelled into his ear. He said nothing and continued to struggle. Just as I had seen in the movies, I repeatedly slammed his gun hand against the car until, with the fourth or fifth jolt, he relaxed his grip on the pistol. My partner grabbed it and quickly slid it into his pocket, while I removed my handcuffs from my belt.

The complainant, who had watched the whole scene from the rear of the radio car, now emerged from the street side and came around to the curb. "That's the guy," he said. "I'm sure of it now."

"Me, too," I said as I placed the cuffs on the first, but certainly not the last, man to ever point a pistol at me. "Me, too."

The third arrest was rather unique. A flat tire and no

spare on the way to a midnight to 8 A.M. tour resulted in my being late and instead of being assigned to a radio car I was given the Fulton and Nostrand fixer. In shooting the breeze with the other officer assigned to the corner, I mentioned that I had a strange premonition that something would happen that night, but I wasn't quite sure what. He laughed. At about 4 A.M. he retired to the back seat of his car a block away for a couple of hours of sleep and he told me I was welcome to stretch out in the front seat, but I declined, preferring to stay on post to see if there was anything to my premonition.

The time moved slowly and the passing motorists grew sparse until about 6 A.M. there wasn't a soul in sight. At that time I decided to take a walk the one block length of my post to break the monotony. I tried all the store doors on the way, not moving on until I had assured myself that each place was secure.

As I moved closer to the corner I was overcome with a weird sense of déjà vu: I felt I had been through this all before; I had walked this same block at this exact time on another day. I knew that I had to be mistaken, but when I approached the restaurant on the corner, I became ever so cautious. I could not yet see the front window, but somehow I knew it was broken. I could not yet see inside, but somehow I knew there was a man in there. I was scared.

When I reached it, the first thing I noticed was the broken front window. When I looked inside, and I knew exactly where to look, I was not too surprised to see a man, with his back to me, trying to break into a vending machine.

I put my hand on my gun and almost involuntarily yelled: "Hey, you!"

The man turned and with solid white eyes prominent, his dark black skin covered with perspiration, he stared at me with a fearful look. I had never seen the man before, and yet I felt I knew him.

"Come out of there," I said and with that he ran straight to the pitch black rear of the restaurant. I stood by the broken window, with my hand on my holstered gun, and strained my eyes to see him move, but I saw nothing. In my rush to get out of the station house earlier,

I had forgotten to take my flashlight, but I knew from visiting the place in the daytime there was no exit in the rear. Without a light I would not enter and with me outside he could not leave; it was a stalemate.

Because everything I had done thus far was exactly the way I seemed to remember doing it on another occasion, I tried to think what would happen next, but could not. Suddenly my mind flashed a picture of the Black man lying motionless on the sidewalk by an iron gate, his face bleeding, with me standing over him, gun drawn. The vision lasted only an instant and was gone. I dismissed it as an overworked imagination.

I stood outside for about ten minutes and only one person passed by. I asked him, a male Negro, late teens or early twenties, with a black guerrilla hat covering his Afro, to call the precinct for me. Without batting an eye or losing his stride he said: "Fuck you, Whitey!" and kept walking. I should have expected no more.

Another ten minutes passed and I saw a car coming. Because I heard no sounds from the back of the restaurant and saw no movement, I began to doubt whether I was correct on the rear exit and relaxed a bit, figuring maybe he had escaped. I stepped into the street to hail the car, taking my eyes from the front of the store for only a few seconds, when the sound of glass breaking turned my head back quickly.

With his left arm across his eyes and his right hand wielding a meat cleaver raised high, he burst through the glass window and ran directly at me. Again the vision flashed in my mind, then was gone. The fear was gone from his eyes. I saw only intent. "I'll kill you," he yelled as he swung the cleaver forward at my head.

I had no time for anything but to move my head a few inches and I felt the weapon brush past my ear. On the downswing it caught my trousers and slashed a gaping hole in them. The Negro's momentum carried him past me a bit, but he immediately whirled and swung at me again, this time laterally, aiming for my neck. I ducked, narrowly escaping the blow. Again his momentum carried him past me and this time he ran.

I withdrew my revolver and immediately fired a warning shot into the air, but he did not stop. I ran a few steps after him, then slowed to take aim.

"Hold it or you're dead," I yelled.

He turned, but showed no signs of halting. At the exact second I squeezed off my shot, he fell. As I trotted toward him, the vision flashed for the third time. But he was too near the curb and on his side instead of his back.

When I reached him the first thing I did was bend down to remove the cleaver that he still clutched tightly in his hand. As I did so, he suddenly sprang to life and swung at my revolver, the blunt side of the axlike instrument striking my wrist, knocking the gun to the ground. I kicked out and luckily jolted the weapon from his hand. He slammed his fist to my chest and the impact sent me flying backward the width of the sidewalk until I crashed to a stop on an iron gate. It was obvious he was much stronger than I. He rushed me and cocked his arm for another blow, but I raised my leg with all my might, burying my knee in his groin. He fell to his knees and again I kicked out, catching him square in the chest with the heel of my shoe. He slumped to the ground in pain.

I ran to the gutter and retrieved my gun. As I reapproached the Negro he was pulling himself up by the iron gate. I walked straight up to him and smashed the butt of my revolver into his face, splattering blood in all directions. He fell to the ground and lay exactly the way I had pictured, as I stood over him, gun drawn.

Obviously somebody had thought to make a phone call, for in moments three radio cars, lights whirling, sirens screaming, simultaneously converged on the scene. The first officer out ran to my side.

"What happened, Ed?" he asked.

I couldn't stop thinking of the uncanny experience: the premonition, the déjà vu, the eerie feeling, the vision. "The strangest thing," I said, ready to tell him. But I couldn't bring myself to relate the real story.

The fourth arrest was a closer call to death than this.

CHAPTER 13

The radio car creaked when it struck a pothole, and potholes were everywhere. The left rear fender rattled as it hung precariously from two weak bolts and, with the lock broken, the trunk was tied closed with a piece of twine. The horn ring was missing, as were the front armrests, and the steering wheel squeaked when turned to the left. The dashboard and the front seat were stained with coffee and the rear seat with stale blood, a malodorous reminder of a multitude of beaten prisoners and their victims. The floor, caked with dirt, was strewn with cigarette butts and other litter. The grimy upholstery above was ripped in several places, exposing the bare metal of the roof. The operator of the vehicle sat on the *Sunday News* to avoid impalement by a protruding spring. In all, the car was deteriorated, but it went quite unnoticed for so too was the neighborhood; they went together well.

"What do they look like, Billy? What are they wearing?" I asked of my most reliable informant. In the past Billy Cutter had supplied me with information leading to numerous narcotics arrests in return for a laissez-faire policy toward him and his habit. A small, slithering character, his deep black figure was barely discernible as he lay across the back seat to avoid being seen. Should he ever be suspect of aiding the police, he would suffer the violent consequences. It was in my best interest, too, that every precaution be taken, for I would have a tougher time making good "collars" without Billy. I had already lost one informant that year through carelessness and I wasn't about to let what happened to him happen to Billy. I guess my earlier source was right when he said he thought a pusher had seen him in the rear of the radio car and that it might get back to the wrong people. Later, rumor had it they drove a three-foot pipe up his ass until brown liquid spewed from his lips, then dunked him into a cement-filled oil drum and threw him in a river, a la Mafiosa. No wonder he had been so scared.

My partner that night was Pete Karthas. He had been working toward a degree in sociology and his life-style was that of a liberal. But that was before joining the force. Now, after four years as a patrolman in the ghetto, learning about life in the school of hard knocks, he was a suppressed racist like most of the men in the command. He was about six feet, one-ninety, proficient in various Oriental martial arts, and able to take good care of himself in a brawl. He was twenty-seven, but his pride and joy, a thinned-out version of a Pancho Villa moustache, made him look about five years older.

As Pete guided the radio car slowly through the Black jungle, carefully avoiding the more crowded streets, I surreptitiously talked with Billy. The temperature was below freezing, but the cold never drove the people of Bedford-Stuyvesant indoors. It always amazed me how much more active the neighborhood seemed at night than in the day. I was supposed to have taken over the wheel at eight o'clock but I didn't feel like driving then and, as he had done many times before, Pete remained the operator of the vehicle. As recorder, it was my job to make notes on our assignments and handle the radio.

"One has a blue or black leather jacket on and the other one is wearing a brown, three-quarter-length coat. They're both about six feet, dark as me, and the guy with the leather jacket has an Afro. They're right in the front hallway," Billy said.

The address on Pacific Street was a notorious, six-story building with thirty-six apartments, riddled with dope. It was as easy to buy a deck (grain) of heroin or cocaine there as bread in a supermarket. In the past few months dozens of narcotics collars had been made throughout the building, but addicts still came from far and wide to "score their horse" there. If the dealer in one apartment was all sold out, the junkie needed only to get the word on which of the half-dozen or so other apartments selling junk was well stocked.

The huge doors at the main entrance opened into a front hallway, followed by a long corridor with a staircase at both ends. A repulsive stench hung in the air and struck you immediately upon entrance. Roaches crawled everywhere and crusted bile clung to the walls. The halls and staircases were suprisingly well lighted except for the rear flight to the roof, which was pitch black. A probe with a flashlight there invariably showed the stairs covered with used matches and empty glassine envelopes—telltale signs that addicts frequently used this spot to "get off." The doors to the apartments were made of a light metal and most were reinforced from within by bolts and bars that even the most proficient burglar could not penetrate, though the dents and scrapings around the handles showed how many had tried. Some apartments were vacant and the locks were broken, allowing some junkies to use them as "shooting galleries." The doors to the apartments where drugs were sold were often impervious to anything but a sledgehammer, with which every good narcotics division police team was equipped.

Occasionally an entrepreneur from a different neighborhood, familiar with the building's reputation, would station himself in the front hallway, stealing business by catching some of the flow of users as they entered, convincing them that he had better "smack" than sold anywhere and saving them the trip inside. The drug traffic was heavy and usually he would be able to siphon a large share, but he would never get all the business, for some junkies, as long as they had a choice, would always go back to where they had bought last and where they knew they would get good stuff, rather than take a chance with someone new.

Because it was risky—in that the hallway dealer didn't want to get caught by the established dealers inside and, because he was a stranger, he was always taking a chance that the buyer was an undercover man, while the apartment pushers had regular customers and would not sell to someone they did not know—the peddler was rarely in the hall two nights in a row or, for that matter, longer than three or four hours on any one night. For this reason, when you learned that there was a pusher in that hallway, you had to move fast.

"Any guns, Billy?" I asked.

"I don't think so, but you can never tell with them dudes. You know."

"How much stuff?"

"The guy with the leather coat has at least two bundles (about twenty-five decks to a bundle). . . . I don't know about the other cat."

"OK, listen! I'm doing days next week, so I won't see you until I go on midnight to eight's the following week. You be around?"

"I'm always around," he said, smiling. I couldn't help noticing how white and even his teeth were. "It's just you don't see me all the time. But I see you. By the way, I meant to ask you, what was the story with the woman you was carrying out of that building that time I passed by? She didn't look so good ... matter of fact, neither did you."

"All right, get the fuck out of here," my partner said brusquely, pulling the car over to the sidewalk on a quiet street.

"Take it easy, Pete," I said, turning to face him, "he's here to help us." After all, Billy was risking his life to give us two collars. The least Pete could do was talk nice, but he just shrugged and slapped the steering wheel in disgust. "I'll see you in a couple of weeks, Billy," I said, "and I'll let you know how we made out."

"I'll know," he said, looking all around to make sure the street was clear. He opened the door quickly, jumped out mumbling what sounded like "good luck," and walked briskly away from the radio car with his hands in his pockets, his shoulders raised in the cold, and his coat collar up around his ears.

"Don't tell me to take it easy in front of that weasel anymore, Ed," Pete said, pulling away from the curb. His tone was firm, yet polite. "I can't stand that fuckin' guy."

"I'm sorry, Pete, I didn't mean to come off bad. It's just that he's given us more collars than anybody else—and good ones. Besides, he's your stoolie ... you cultivated him in the beginning."

"Yeah, I know, but I just can't stand the fuckin' guy

now. And when he starts talking about things that don't concern him, like that woman, I get pissed off."

"Yeah, I know what you mean."

"All right, forget it. Let's go get those guys in the hallway. You drive," he said, revealing a little dissatisfaction with me in his voice. It was ten o'clock. "That's another two hours you owe me," he added before he got out and walked around the front of the car while I slid over behind the wheel. The chill in the night air materialized as smoke in his breath. Up until then I wasn't really sure if the incident had affected Pete as it had me, but now I knew. As much as we had grown to hate the Blacks in general, because we were policemen, because we mostly saw them at their worst, and because we were White, there were certain times when we wept with them. One, not too long ago . . .

On a misty evening Pete and I were cruising slowly through the precinct when a young Black girl, about nine or ten, came running out of a tenement, waving at us frantically, shouting, "Hey, police! Hey, police!" I pulled the radio car to the curb and she told us that her mother was upstairs, having a baby. She said that her neighbor had gone off to call for an ambulance and had not returned yet. We jumped out of the car and rushed inside to help. She lived on the top floor of a four-story building that looked like it should have been condemned ten years ago; maybe it was. The wooden stairs were wide enough to support only the front half of the foot and sagged dangerously and uncomfortably downward. There were far too many slats missing from the railing rendering it weak and useless. A pale green paint was peeling from the walls and ceiling; there were no lights and a smell of chicken and grits clashed with urine.

The door to the woman's apartment was open and the closer I got, the more discernible were the sighs of pain. There, on a grease-stained couch, with a tattered, chartreuse dress hitched high around her hips, her legs spread apart and the head of a baby protruding from her vagina, lay a frail woman in severe pain.

There was no time to remove my jacket and, while Pete comforted her and took the information for the report, I quite nervously, yet acting nonchalant, washed my hands in the dish-filled sink, squatted by the couch between the woman's outstretched legs, cursorily wiped the blood from her thighs with a napkin and placed my fingertips on the cheeks of her ass, allowing the baby's head to rest gently in my palms.

The head was completely covered with a filmy, slimy substance and with each contraction, as a bit more of the infant came out, a thick, rich blood oozed from between it and the walls of the mother's vagina, and dripped onto my hands, the couch, and the floor. To keep my hands dry, I alternately wiped them off on my pants.

The extent of my childbirth training in the Police Academy was a one-hour film of an actual birth that I saw twice. In essence, it stressed three main points. 1. Don't pull or tug on the baby, just accept it as it emerges; 2. Save the placenta, or afterbirth, and bring it to the hospital with you; and 3. As long as the woman will be seen by a doctor within a reasonable amount of time after the birth, don't cut the umbilical cord.

Well, at least I saw the film—Pete was out sick the day they showed it. Nevertheless, both of us had helped deliver babies before. But no matter how many times you do it, you still get nervous bringing a life into the world.

The woman was perspiring profusely and was crying out in excruciating pain. I kept telling her to take it easy and thought a conversation between contractions might steady her.

"What do you want, a boy or girl?"

"A boy," she said. "It's just got to be a boy."

"What's the matter with girls?" I asked.

"I got eight girls, I want me a boy ... bad, real bad."

"Do you have a name picked?"

"Michael."

"That's a nice name. After your husband?"

"I ain't got no husband," she said contemptuously.

The daughter answered a knock at the door, and when she opened it, an ambulance attendant, all in white, strode mechanically to the couch as if he had been there before. Just then the woman screamed at the top of her lungs, arched her back, and dug her nails into the cushions of the couch. The baby came more than halfway out and crimson slime squirted in all directions. I felt light-headed and gasped for air but was only able to gulp a nauseating stench. The waist of the child was at my hands as my forearms cradled its head.

"Do you want to take over, doc?" I asked the attendant, hoping he would accept.

"Not now. Don't worry, you're doing fine," he said with an accent I couldn't quite place. In a split second another demonic screech filled the air, the mother went rigid, and the infant was out. The umbilical cord ran limply from the newborn's belly into the mother's womb.

"It's a boy!" I shouted.

"Oh, God! Thank God!" she sighed, relaxing her back. Her pelvic area was still heaving.

The baby wasn't breathing.

"Here, doc, you better take over," I said as I handed him the infant. I felt a little faint and sat down on a nearby camp chair. The attendant, with his back to me, was working feverishly, trying to start the baby's heart. In all, he tried for fifteen minutes, but to no avail. The baby was dead. He would never get a chance to see the world.

The mother was beside herself with grief when she realized and cried incessantly. She was in the state of shock when we carried her and the stillborn to the ambulance. I didn't feel so well for the rest of that day.

Pacific Street, treeless and comprised mainly of multiple dwellings, was only three short blocks away from where we had let Billy off. Dimly lit with two drained, flickering streetlights and two completely nonfunctional, it invited the crime that festered there. Loiterers, prostitutes, and other assorted drug addicts or winos, all potential muggers, lingered everywhere and frequently unaware wanderers and unprotected residents would fall victim to a robbery, burglary, larceny, or assault. Double-parked cars, some of which were cabs waiting for a junkie to return with his score, tested a driver's skill. The wheel squeaked as I turned into the block. I pulled up just shy of our target and my partner and I exited the car, approaching the building from the side to be able to surprise our prey within. We quickened our pace the last few feet and burst into the hallway expecting to startle two pushers. Instead, there was no one. Not a soul around. We advanced into the corridor quietly, listening for someone, but, nothing. I was stumped. It wasn't like Billy to give us a bum tip and he had said he was here just fifteen minutes ago. It was too early for them to have left for the night unless they were chased by someone inside.

"They must have left," I said.

"If they were here at all," Pete murmured, confident that we had been duped by our informer.

"Let's go see if we can find Billy."

We left the hallway and were getting back into the radio car when I looked up the block, behind us, and saw two men standing about seventy-five feet away, with their hands in their pockets, eying us peculiarly. One had on a brown coat, the other a black leather jacket. Pete hadn't noticed them, so when I started the engine, I warned him: "They're behind us. . . . I'm going to back up." I dropped the lever into reverse and stomped heavily on the gas, simultaneously turning my head to see where I was going and laying my right arm across the top of the seat, steering with my left. The car jerked backward, whipping Pete forward, forcing him to brace himself on the dash. The rear end rose sharply and the tires squealed as we accelerated tailfirst. Expecting us to drive off, the two suspects were dumbfounded. As we drew nearer them, the one with the black leather jacket and Afro seemed vaguely familiar. My mind raced to remember where I had seen him before. The brakes screeched the car to a halt and I swung open the door perfunctorily, as Pete exited his side.

Usually, from this point on, it was routine. Once confronted by the police, the majority of narcotics suspects stayed put. If they were "dirty," they would either toss the dope away or keep it hidden on their person, praying that the "pigs" didn't find it. Often the search was illegal, but it had to be done. There were always the few, however, who would run away. This was especially true if they were confronted in an open area, like the street. Usually, heroin addicts offered little resistance—the opium content of the "juice" they shot into their veins sapping their strength. On the other hand, dope peddlers were not reckoned with that easily. Because most dealers knew the effects of heroin and realized that the enormous profits derived from its sale would only go toward satiating their increasing desire, if hooked, the smart pushers were not addicted. Knowing also that the charge for selling drugs was a felony, they were induced to run and resist.

If only these two men would stay put, I thought; it would make things a lot easier. As I had done many times before when approaching suspects, I placed my right hand on my holstered revolver. But I wasn't really ready for anything because I was trying to remember where I had seen this man before.

Unexpectedly, the man with the brown coat bolted, running back toward the corner. Instinctively I took a couple of steps until, out of the corner of my eye, I saw Pete racing after him. I turned toward the other man, and my eyes widened in terror. About six or seven feet away, he held a gun in his outstretched hand, pointing it at my head. It suddenly came to me that I had never actually seen him before; rather, he resembled exactly the picture I had in my mind of the man who had shot at Patrolman Jimmy Kruger a couple of weeks earlier. . . .

"What happened, Jim?" I asked him on the tour change, as he sipped nervously at a cup of coffee in the back room of the station house. He was obviously shaken. "I heard you were shot at tonight."

"Yeah, Ed, some mother-fucker up on Pacific and Bedford. I never saw him before, but I'll never forget him."

"What did he look like? . . . Black, of course."

"Black as the ace of spades, with an Afro and a dark leather jacket. About five-eleven, one seventy-five. Another guy with him, too, but I didn't get a good look at him. I just know he was a nigger."

"Did you let any go at him?"

"No, I didn't have a chance."

I knew so well what he meant. Sure, it was easy to Monday morning quarterback and wonder how anyone could get shot at without shooting back and to boast about what you would have done if you were there—but if you weren't right on the scene, you could not say for sure what your reaction would have been. I had spent weeks explaining to people why I hadn't shot the burglar with the meat cleaver. It seemed nobody could understand.

But, of course, nobody else was there except me and the burglar. So I knew exactly what Jim meant when he told me he didn't have a chance—I didn't have to know the circumstances.

A cracking thunder, the loudest I have ever heard, brought me hurtling back to this world. It was a familiar sound, but never before was it so God damn loud. A searing, blinding flash rushed toward me. My God, I had been shot. I felt limp and paralyzed. My knees weakened and a cold sweat formed on my brow. Why me? Why did I have to get shot? These fuckin' niggers. I don't belong down here anyhow. They don't want White police. We push them around, they say. Well, fuck them. Why don't we just leave them alone and let them kill each other off. Then there won't be any problem.

Wait a minute . . . I remember now. That whistling and that sting. Maybe . . . maybe that was the bullet. Maybe I'm not shot. Oh, God, maybe I'm not shot.

I opened my eyes and patted my face and chest with both hands, ecstatic that I found no hole, no blood. My right ear was ringing in high pitch. He missed. Holy shit, he was that close and he missed. Thank God! Thank God . . . if there is one.

My mind began to clear, then clouded with a lust for revenge. It so obsessed me that fear was shoved aside. My vision focused on the Black who had just, by the narrowest of margins, failed to end my life prematurely. Running hard for his life, he was still only about thirty yards away. I took a few steps, then stopped abruptly, drew my service revolver and, raising it with outstretched arm, elbow locked tightly in place, pulled the hammer back. With a tight grip and a firm, independent movement of my index finger, I aligned the front sight with the rear, aiming my weapon at the base of the Negro's spine. I was rather a good shot and felt confident of hitting my mark. The short fall of the firing pin to the bullet's primer was all that separated him from death.

"Nigger," I thought as I squeezed the trigger. The racism inherent in all White police officers working in a Black ghetto, which was constantly nurtured, yet suppressed, had finally peaked. But did it make a difference if he were Black or White? Either way, I would not be wrong to shoot and kill this man. Had he not just attempted to take my life? There is something sacrilegious about shooting at a policeman. He is the last line of defense and anyone capable of shooting at him is capable of anything. Was I not then justified in an attempt on his life? He was a menace to society—a drug pusher. Who knows how many other people he has shot in the past or will shoot in the future? No, I would not be wrong to kill him, only for singling him out as Black.

He pivoted off his left foot and darted to the right between parked cars, knocking to the ground an old woman getting out of a double-parked car. Two men had already gotten out and were standing nearby. The bystanders saved his life. I would not jeopardize innocent lives, no matter how heinous his crimes. I lowered my revolver and galloped after him to get a better shot, but I had not gone far when I heard my partner call out.

I glanced over my shoulder, still running, to see him in a fierce struggle on the corner. Fists and feet were flying everywhere. What had happened to all his experience in the martial arts? Had he finally met his match? Or his master? If I go back, this other guy is sure to get away. I'll probably never get another crack at him, and revenge is so sweet. But then, which is more important: to exterminate a potential murderer, for the good of society, for revenge, and possibly to satisfy my suppressed racism, or to aid my partner, perhaps save his life? I was not so enraged as to lose all perspective, and decided that a good life saved was better than a bad life ended. I discontinued the chase and ran back toward my partner as fast and as hard as I could.

They were really fighting it out when a roundhouse caught Pete on the side of the head and his foot slipped on an oily manhole cover beneath him. The man wheeled and darted quickly away just as I reached the scene. Damn—if I had known he was going to run away I would never have come back. But then, maybe he wouldn't have run away unless I did come back.

Pete was recovering from the blow and managed to say: "I'm OK—get him!" Without stopping, I took off after the assailant. I was breathing heavily now, having sprinted full tilt for about two hundred yards and my breathing created little puffs of steam. My throat rasped with each gulp of the frigid night air. My chest pained with each expansion. A buzz-saw-type hum reverberated in my right ear and my head felt swelled inside a hat two sizes too small. The muscles in my thighs and calves begged me to stop running, but I continued on mechanically. I forced myself to the rapid pace of my prey, vowing not to let up until I had him. I had already let one get away, after he had taken a shot at me no less, and I wasn't about to come up completely empty-handed. It would be bad enough having to explain how the man that pegged the shot escaped without having to explain the other.

I wasn't gaining any ground on him, but I could see he was panting heavily. He wouldn't be able to keep this pace up for too long either. He had to stop sooner or later and I hoped that when he did he wouldn't have too much fight left in him because I was exhausted. *Where the hell is Pete, anyway? What is he doing—waiting for me to come back?*

The figure in front of me kept turning around, probably hoping that I would give up the chase. Every time he glanced back I shouted in what was left of my most authoritative voice: "Hold it!" or "Stop or I'll shoot!" or something else equally fruitless. He seemed about ready to collapse. I was gaining. I withdrew my jack and wound the long leather thong from my thumb across the back of my wrist, bringing it comfortably into place in the palm of my right hand. With my left hand I unbuttoned the handcuff case on my belt. I was only about twenty feet away now and all ready for combat when he turned again. But this time he stuck his arm straight back and in his hand was a gun.

Oh, no! Not again. It had never entered my mind that *he* might have a gun. The other guy had the gun, not this guy. How stupid of me. But at least now I had an instant to react. I freed my right hand of the jack, letting it drop to the ground, and withdrew my revolver. With his arm bouncing as he ran, the Negro fired, and again the night filled with the report of a gun, but this time it sounded rather dull—just a short, quick "pop." The flash from the nozzle showed the path of the bullet to be high and to the left, but I stooped low just the same. Without even aiming,

I instinctively returned the fire and mine, too, was high, though to the right.

He immediately threw his gun down, but continued running. I could probably get away with shooting him anyway, even though the law says you are not supposed to shoot an unarmed fleeing felon, but then I would be faced with having to live with myself, knowing I had murdered someone, no matter what his crime.

With a tremendous burst of speed and my mind blurred with thoughts of vengeance, I closed the gap in seconds. I holstered my revolver and, from about two feet, I dove forward with open arms, aiming my right shoulder for his spine. I hit waist high and my momentum carried us both forward for a few feet before we crashed to the sidewalk. I fell on top of him—following the advice of a gym instructor in the academy, who had told us repeatedly, "The body of the person you're fighting with is a lot softer than the ground. So if you're going to fall, fall on him if you can." He wheezed in pain as the air gushed from his lungs. The coarse rock of the sidewalk scraped him from his face to his shoes while only the skin of my knuckles was peeled a bit.

I jumped to my feet before he had a chance to recover and I grabbed him by his collar with my left hand and by his belt with my right. He was on his hands and knees as I ran forward a little bit and jerked him past me, headfirst into an iron fence one of the residents had so thoughtfully erected in front of his house. He saw it coming so he put his head down just before it smashed square against one of the bars. It made a "ping" sound and the railing rattled noisily for a few seconds. Barely conscious, he fell sideways, away from me. He was propped against the fence with his legs sprawled toward the gutter and his head steaming in the chilled air, as thick blood trickled into his eyes and down his cheek.

"No more," he sighed in defeat. "No more." Convinced he had had enough, I let him be. Sirens wailed in the distance. Help was on the way. Pete was probably searching for me. I could only hear with my left ear. My right was filled with an unearthly hum and my head felt as if it had been pierced with a knife. It would be five weeks before I could hear right again.

As I glanced up the block behind me, a hard blow bounced off the back of my neck and threw me involuntarily to the ground, my left leg twisting beneath me. The huge Black figure looked about seven feet tall as I peered up at him from the street. He had played possum and still had plenty of fight left in him. He took a quick step toward me and kicked me in the chest, and again in the side of my head. I rolled away, whoozy, but sprang to my feet as he rushed me again. I grabbed frantically for my jack before remembering it was lying on the sidewalk somewhere, a couple of blocks away. He connected a left to my lip. My head was pounding. His eyes were furious as he telegraphed a roundhouse right. I ducked it easily and, from underneath, straightened my knees abruptly, forcing the rigid trunk of my body upwards, cracking the hard part of my head into his jaw. It hurt like hell, but it hurt him more. It sent him reeling backward the width of the sidewalk and slammed him against the iron fence. I withdrew my revolver and ran straight at him. I was tempted to shoot him, but instead, with all my might, I slashed sharply down with the barrel of the gun, catching him square across the left cheek, ripping the skin from his face. He shouted and grabbed at his cheek with both hands, but I wasn't letting up this time. With all the strength I could muster, I kicked him in the groin and he crumpled over in pain. In a smooth, fast, underarm arch, I swung my gun and caught him across the bridge of the nose with the barrel and trigger guard. I heard something crack. He fell to his knees, his hands clasped tightly against his face.

I remembered being taught in the academy: "Never let up on him until you are sure he is through. Don't give him a chance. You're not out there to fight clean fights. If he had you on the ground, he wouldn't stop. If you have cause enough to fight someone, you use whatever methods you can to win; to stay alive. That's the main objective—winning. It's not the means that count, it's the result. There is no such thing as a draw. There is only one winner and it had better be you or one of these days we'll find you laying dead somewhere." I knew from experience that he was right. My head was throbbing and my hands were shaking.

Again he screamed: "No more. No more."

I kicked him in the face, knocking him flat on his back. As he writhed on the ground, I kicked him in his ribs again and again. I was oblivious of the surroundings, of the cries for help, of the pain in my ear and my leg. I was aware of only one thing: this man had tried to kill me and now I was making sure he would never be able to do it again.

"That's enough, Ed," Pete said, pulling me away from the limp bundle on the ground. "He's had enough."

The seven-foot giant of a few minutes ago didn't look so big now. I stood silent, staring at the blood oozing slowly from his head. The sidewalk was covered with it. Some of it was mine, my lip and forehead being cut badly and my left leg slightly, but most was his. Now my ear hurt more than ever and my left knee felt swollen.

I stepped toward the crumpled body, withdrew my cuffs and, pulling his arms behind his back, squeezed them tightly over each wrist. I took a deep breath. It was all over . . . almost.

I had to go back and retrieve his gun—if it was still there. By now, somebody could have easily picked it up and without it I had a very weak case. Regardless of the facts, if I did not recover the gun, I would be unable to produce the most essential piece of evidence in the shooting when I brought the prisoner before the bench. In all likelihood, the case would be thrown out.

"Help me get him in the car," I asked Pete as he opened the back door. "We have to go back for the gun."

The prisoner was conscious but unwilling or unable to get up and get in the car, so Pete and I picked him up and threw him there headfirst. I limped as quickly as I could around the radio car and hopped in.

"Better call off the 10-13, Ed. It came over just as I was pulling up . . . Herkimer and Bedford."

"Where the hell were you, anyhow? Waiting for me to give up the chase and come back?"

"By the time I got back to the radio car, I had lost you. Sorry, Ed."

As we pulled away I grabbed the phone and transmitted: "Eight-O Charley to Central, K."

"Go ahead, Eight-O Charley. What is your location? Do you need assistance, K?"

"Negative, Central. This unit has one prisoner from Herkimer and Bedford and is en route to Atlantic and Bedford for a weapon search. Call off the 13 but have an available Eight-O unit meet us forthwith at that location to assist in the search, K."

"10-4, Charley. Attention all units in the thirteenth division. Nothing further at Herkimer and Bedford. Resume patrol. Eight-O Charley is on the scene and advises that no further assistance is necessary ... all units resume patrol. An available Eight-O unit for a 10-85 with Eight-O Charley at Atlantic and Bedford, to assist with a search, K."

"Eight-O Edward on the way, K."

"10-4, Edward, Atlantic and Bedford, 10-85 Eight-O Charley."

"10-4."

We arrived at the scene just as Eight-O Edward did. Eight-O Frank was already there.

"I'm looking for a gun, an automatic I think," I shouted to the others as I hopped out of the car. "He threw it somewhere over ... Never mind, I've got it!" I said as I spotted it in the gutter. I was in luck.

When I got back in the car I turned to the bloody figure sprawled across the back seat and said: "Now I've got you." He spit at me, but it fell short. We rode to the station house to start the long process of booking the prisoner.

Four hours later, I was finished.

On my way home I thought of the irony of the job: one day you almost bring a life into the world, another day you almost take two out.

CHAPTER 14

Attached to each arrest is the frustration of the court proceedings. At first, the courthouse was a whole new world for me. We hadn't studied court procedure much at the academy, so once I was exposed to it I found that a patrolman had to thoroughly familiarize himself with so many rules and regulations that much of my free time was spent studying the process. After a while, though, I got it all down pat. Then I found that the knowledge didn't help matters and going to court—a long, drawn-out, exasperating affair—became a thorn in my side.

The first time I ever stepped into any courtroom was as a police officer. The occasion was the arraignment of the one-legged gunman in the Nine-O—my first arrest. I learned very little at that arraignment, however, because I had been taken under wing by two salty detectives from the Nine-O squad, who knew all the ins and outs of the "game" and who went out of their way to get me through the ordeal as quickly as possible. They couldn't do enough for me—they even filled out all my forms. I was grateful when I walked out of the courtroom with them relatively early in the day, but I was also just as ignorant about what I was supposed to do as when I had entered.

At that first arraignment the case was postponed until the next week and sent before a Family Court judge in Manhattan. It seemed a bit silly to me that a gun charge would be handled in a Family Court, but who was I to argue? My reservation proved correct, however, for the judge read the court papers quickly and in less than five minutes postponed the case until the next week, sending it back to Brooklyn Criminal Court. It remained there until the defendant pleaded guilty a few weeks later.

With Safety Unit "A," the Police Academy, and the 9th precinct in between, almost one year elapsed before I made my next arrest—the first one in the Eight-O—and by that time I had forgotten what little I had learned, anyway.

As my activity increased in the Eight-O, so too did my court appearances and, with nobody's coattail to hang on to, I was on my own. I sometimes found myself going to court not only on half of my working days each month, but also on a few of my regularly scheduled days off. On the first few arrests, I floundered a little bit, which was to be expected, but after a while I became familiar with all the proper procedures for an officer at court.

The first thing I learned about was the arraignment. Both the United States Constitution and New York State law dictate that a prisoner is to be brought before a magistrate as soon after arrest as possible for the purposes of determining bail. The time a police officer first takes his prisoner to court, however, naturally depends on when the arrest is made—judges do not sit twenty-four hours a day in New York State.

In Brooklyn, for a printable offense (one for which fingerprints are taken) the prisoner must be booked at the station house and brought to court before 9 P.M. or be lodged in a precinct cell overnight, until court opens in the morning. This is due mainly to the fact that it takes an average of two and one-half hours for the processing of the prisoner's fingerprints. They are sent to Manhattan, checked for accuracy, and fed into a computer that returns form DD 24, "the yellow sheet," which contains the prisoner's entire known criminal history—the date of arrest, name and address given, borough or city arrested, charge, arresting officer and disposition, date, judge, and court.

For a nonprintable offense the prisoner must be brought to court before 10 P.M.

Statistics show that the highest crime period in New York City is between 6 P.M. and 2 A.M. and the majority of my arrests fell within those hours. That resulted in my being unable to make night court most of the time. Therefore I had to lodge the prisoner and go to day court the next morning. Because the Eight-O was not equipped with cells, all prisoners had to be lodged overnight in other precincts. If there was room in a bordering precinct, such as the 88th or 71st, it wasn't too bad, but on some occasions Brooklyn was hopping so much that there wasn't an available cell in the entire borough. In that case the prisoner had to be lodged in a Manhattan precinct, which tacked at least an hour's traveling time on to the next day's schedule.

The first thing to do on the morning of an arraignment is to make arrangements for a patrol wagon to take you and the prisoner to the rear entrance of the courthouse. Kings County Criminal Court, a huge, eleven-story building with high ceilings and no air-conditioning, is located in the downtown area of Brooklyn and is broken up into various parts: Part IA is for all arraignments; Part IB1 is for misdemeanor dispositions; Part ID1 is for felony dispositions; Part III is for adolescents; and so on. When I was a regular customer, they were constantly changing the part numbers and their designations, so there was no surefire way of telling what part you were supposed to report to, but I got along all right.

After you sign yourself and your prisoner into a logbook, you lodge the prisoner in a detention cell and fight your way into a jam-packed elevator to begin a day filled with mounds of paperwork, crowds of people, long lines, and God-awful, monotonous waiting.

Your first stop is the complaint room, where you draw up an affidavit of complaint, relating the details of the crime and arrest. If the people of the State of New York are the complainants, you sign the affidavit. If there is a citizen complainant—as there would be with a robbery, burglary, or grand larceny auto, for example—he signs the affidavit.

The complaint room is a rectangular-shaped room with considerably less space than necessary to accommodate the enormous number of police officers, civilian complainants, and witnesses who visit it each day. Rows of plastic chairs and wooden benches extend out into the corridor to seat as many people as possible. Poor ventilation renders the room stuffy most of the year and unbearably ovenlike in the summertime. Clerks sit in little cubicles where they type up your report of the incident.

Upon entering, it is necessary to sign in and receive a number, as you might receive in a busy bakery. I do not recall ever receiving a number lower than 100. In fact, on one occasion I was given number 164 while the officer with number 28 was working with the clerk—there were 136 people in front of me!

The line moves slowly with usually only two clerk-typists to take care of the entire complement of officers and civilian complainants. If you are not present when your number is called, you lose your turn, making lunch out of the question unless they're nowhere near you. The clerks go to lunch, however, and often there are no replacements for them, thus slowing the line even more. When one is late in returning or a scheduling error overlaps their hours, which happens occasionally, the line is at a complete standstill.

On a crowded day it is senseless to think you will be finished in anything less than three hours. There is over an hour's worth of forms that must be completed, so for a while you are busy. But for the other two hours or so, it is rather boring unless you're equipped with a good book or a crossword puzzle.

When it's finally your turn to see the clerk, you relate the details of the arrest, whereupon he translates them into "deponents," "defendants," "wherefores," and other legal jargon for the affidavit.

You leave the conglomeration of papers there, where they are collated, while you report to the detention cell, sign out the prisoner, and take him for an interview with a probation officer. He asks the prisoner personal questions about his job or family—if he has either—to determine his eligibility for parole. There is no real way to verify anything he says, so many of them lie their heads off, hoping the judge will believe them and parole them. Because there are usually only three probation officers handling the entire influx of prisoners, conditions are the same as in the complaint room—a long wait.

After the prisoner is interviewed, if his yellow sheets

have arrived from Manhattan, he is photographed; if they haven't, another wait.

With the yellow sheets in hand, the prisoner interviewed, photographed, and relodged, you're off to the complaint room again to pick up the collated mass of papers thus far accumulated. The next stop is the adjoining docket room where every case is given a number. Unless every form is present and properly completed—the officials of the court are punctilious—the case will not be docketed and you are again in for a long wait. If luck is on your side, the stack of papers, in book form, is forwarded to the courtroom, Part IA.

The courtroom is a large room with rows of churchlike pews capable of accommodating no more than 250 people comfortably. The first few rows on the left are reserved for police officers and on the right for attorneys. The judge's bench—just as it is depicted on television and in the movies—is raised on a platform and set behind a wooden railing. Again, the ventilation is practically nonexistent and in the summertime the heat is murder. All courtrooms throughout the courthouse are similar.

You sit there until your case is called, which may sometimes mean hours. When your case gets close to the top of the pile, the court officer who stands in front of the judge calling the cases, known as the bridgeman, directs you to sign out the prisoner from the detention cell and into the "bullpen," or waiting pen, where he can be interviewed by either his private attorney or the Legal Aid attorney that the state provides at no charge. If the prisoner uses the free Legal Aid attorney, which the majority of Blacks ordinarily do, the procedure is sure to add at least another half hour onto the wait because the staff is so undermanned and because half of the men who work for them are fresh out of law school and fancy themselves Clarence Darrows.

If you are not at this point in the proceedings by approximately 4:45 P.M., you might as well go get something to eat, because day court closes at five and night court doesn't open until eight.

When you are finally called before the bench, you stand to the extreme right. To your immediate left is the assistant district attorney, next to him is the defense attorney, and on the extreme left stands the prisoner. Behind you is at least one court officer. The bridgeman reads aloud the charges and the details of the arrest from the affidavit, which you swear is true, the defendant's attorney enumerates all his client's good points (on some occasions living at the same address for more than three months and being employed more than two weeks are the best they can offer), the judge sets bail or paroles the prisoner and decides the date and part for the next time back in court.

If the prisoner is paroled, he is warned that failure to appear on the assigned date means an additional charge will be added to his case. He then walks out of the courtroom, many times never to be seen again. If he is remanded, he is put back into the bullpen until you have retrieved the court papers defining his bail, then taken back to the detention cell. There you must fill out another handful of forms before he can be sent to the county jail. Those are the last forms you fill out at court, but your day is not over yet.

If there is any evidence in the case, it must be taken to the property clerk's office, located in the 78th precinct in Brooklyn. Narcotics must first be taken to the police laboratory for analysis and a gun to the ballistics unit for testing—both places located in the Police Academy in Manhattan. In nearly five years on the job, I never once visited the lab, ballistics, or the property clerk without having to stand in a line and wait. Once the evidence has been submitted to the property clerk and you have returned to the precinct to sign out, the day is over.

It should be understood that this description is based on an arrest with one prisoner. Any additional prisoners increases the paperwork and the waits considerably. That is why if there are six or seven people arrested at once, in a crap game, for example, two officers very often split them.

On each succeeding court appearance, it is necessary to have all evidence with you, which means reporting to the property clerk in the morning, where you wait in a long line to withdraw it, and in the afternoon, where you wait in a long line to return it. This is bad enough for the men in the 78th precinct and surrounding precincts, but for someone stationed in Canarsie it's a real pain in the ass.

Because none of the judges start working before 10:30 A.M., the next stop in the morning is the coffee shop, where—no fault of the department—you unfortunately have to wait for lousy service and even lousier food at a high price, no less.

After breakfast you walk to the courthouse, sign in, look for your case on the calendar of the part to which it is assigned, and squeeze into the sardine-can elevator for the ride to that part; there are no parts lower than the sixth floor—a fact that discourages walking up the stairs.

Unless the defendant is under nineteen years of age, your case is assigned to a disposition part. About 250 other cases are also assigned there each day, and on your first trip back after arraignment most of them are ahead of you on the calendar. What it amounts to is that you will pop yourself out of an elevator filled to capacity and have a little time to regain your composure while walking across the corridor before sucking in your stomach again in order to fit into a courtroom bulging with people.

The quarters are so close that in the summertime it is impossible to wipe the sweat from your brow without wiping the person's next to you, and when you return the handkerchief to the pocket from whence it came, you're liable to find out it's his, anyhow. Because many people waiting to be called have been charged with pickpocketing or jostling, it is not a good idea to carry too much money around. If you're a single guy, it's a lovely place to meet a girl (what the hell, even if you're married) and get to know her real well before you leave.

If you are lucky enough to get a seat, you sit squashed in a pew, and are not allowed to talk, read, or smoke (thank God). With an hour out for lunch (at 1 P.M. the place empties and at 2 P.M. all the people flood back in), you remain all day long, until finally around 3:30 P.M. you are called—only to be told there's not enough time for your case. It is then adjourned to another date in the same part, where you do the same thing. Each time your case is adjourned, however, it moves up the calendar, until about the fourth time back you have an outside chance of being reached before 3 P.M. and sent to another part for a preliminary hearing.

When that happens, there is little cause for excitement, because invariably the hearing part is too jammed to reach you that day and the case is adjourned from there, anyhow. To top things off, it is sent back to the same disposition part where, by now, you know everybody by their first name. You have gained nothing but a higher position on the calendar. In order to get anything accomplished, it is necessary to get called in the disposition part before lunch, whereupon you stand a good chance of getting called in the hearing part before 4 P.M.

Many men, especially rookies, unaccustomed to speaking in front of people, find a preliminary hearing rather difficult to handle; but everyone makes it through without dying of embarrassment. When you are called, you take the stand next to the judge and, after being sworn in and stating your name, shield, and command, you are asked by the assistant district attorney to describe the circumstances surrounding the arrest. After you have done so, the defense attorney has the right to cross-examine and, regardless of your testimony, when he is finished he perfunctorily moves to dismiss on the grounds that the people have failed to establish a prima facie case, that there is reasonable doubt that a crime has been committed, or that, if there was a crime committed, his client committed it. Nine out of ten times, the officer's testimony is sufficient for the judge to deny the motion.

After the preliminary hearing, the case is adjourned again and sent back to the good old disposition part, where the same rigmarole has to be hurdled before it gets to another part for a motion to suppress the evidence. A motion to suppress the evidence is a motion in which the defense attempts to prove that the evidence is inadmissible for some reason or other; that it was seized improperly, for example. The procedure is just about the same as a preliminary hearing in that you take the stand and tell the story, but the percentages that the judge will grant the motion are higher. This is especially true in narcotics cases where, because of a recent Supreme Court ruling that hinders the police officer severely, a great deal of the evidence is seized improperly.

If the charge is a misdemeanor, after the motion to suppress, the case is sent back to the disposition part for the final time before trial. If the charge is a felony, it is then waived to a grand jury where, after listening to the officer's and any other witnesses' testimony, the jurors decide whether to indict or not. A grand jury is made up of citizens of the county, selected at random, who are sworn to investigate any crimes tryable in their jurisdiction. There are from sixteen to twenty-three members and there must be at least sixteen present to constitute a quorum. Twelve or more of those members must agree on an indictment. If they indict, the case is then forwarded to the State Supreme Court.

Up until this point the defendant is continually given a chance to plead guilty to a lesser charge and receive a lighter sentence, in order to save the state the time and expense of trying him—a sort of legal deal. But many men choose to go all the way, and once the trial starts, no deals are possible. The facts that they are eligible for parole relatively soon and that one-sixth of the sentence is deducted for good behavior are taken into consideration when making their decision, I'm sure.

One of the few cases I ever lost was at a trial with a three-judge bench. The charge was grand larceny auto. I got an uneasy feeling as the defense attorney and the three judges exchanged first name greetings before the trial. I had caught the defendant driving a late model Chevrolet that had been reported stolen. At the time of arrest he offered no excuses. At the trial his attorney stated that the defendant had borrowed the car from a friend and had received from him a registration that he neglected to look at. The attorney then produced a registration that had no similarity to what the real one looked like except it was for a Chevrolet—for a Chevrolet of a different year, with different license plates, with a different serial number, of a different color, and so on. The defendant had no registration of any kind on his person when I arrested him. When the attorney finished presenting his case, he laughed with a wry smile at the judges and they, to the man, laughed with him. Their decision was 2 to 1 in favor of acquittal. I was surprised it wasn't

3 to 0. I was too embarrassed to tell the complainant who owned the stolen car about what I thought had transpired.

Because it is such a long time from the start of a case to the finish, other cases overlap and on occasion it is not uncommon for an officer to go to court with three, four, or five cases on the calendar. That's bad enough if they are all in the same part, but if you have to hop around the courthouse all day, it adds to your misery. During one period of my time in the Eight-O, fifteen of twenty-nine of my cases were pending a final disposition—over 50 percent.

The number of adjournments from the arraignment to the final disposition is unpredictable, but in some cases it goes to around twenty. That means twenty trips to court for the officer and, if there are any, for the civilian complainants and witnesses. It also means twenty days of waiting, and forty trips to the property clerk. It is no wonder, therefore, that, after they are credited with the arrest, many men couldn't care less what happens to the case and consider going to court one big frustration and headache.

Moreover, Criminal Court was not the only court I had to attend. Averaging thirty-five summonses a month, I spent a great deal of time in Traffic Court, an old brownstone building in the East New York section of Brooklyn. There were a lot less forms to be filled out, but just as much waiting at Traffic Court as there was at Criminal Court. You waited in a police room, however, where only policemen were allowed and where there was room enough to stretch out on a bench if you wanted. When you were notified that your case was up in the courtroom, you proceeded there and had a seat until it was called. The layout was the same as the Criminal courtroom, except there were no freebie Legal Aid attorneys or members of the district attorney's office.

Because of all the red tape involved in a "not guilty" plea on a traffic summons, most of the cases were backlogged a year or more. It was indeed difficult trying to remember the events surrounding a particular summons you had issued one year earlier. If you could not recall, you simply told the judge and there was nothing else to do except dismiss the case.

On one occasion I did not have the vaguest remembrance of a summons I had issued and was about to tell the judge when the defendant pulled a piece of cardboard from his attaché case with a diagram of the area involved and arrows pointing in the direction of the flow of traffic. Before I had a chance to say I didn't remember, he proceeded to describe the incident exactly and, unfortunately for him, before long I totally recalled the summons. If he had kept his trap shut long enough for me to say something, he would have beaten the case; instead he was found guilty and fined fifteen dollars.

Such are the hassles of an active patrolman and I often wondered if it was worth it. Because whether you worked your ass off or hid out every tour, whether you worked in the Black ghetto of Bedford-Stuyvesant or the rich White neighborhoods of Queens, whether you got stabbed in the back by an assailant or patted on the back by a bartender, whether you went to court on your days off or went fishing, you still got paid the same amount of money.

The day I got my steady seat I almost convinced myself it was all worth it.

CHAPTER 15

"Congratulations, Ed," said my friend, Charlie Cole, as I walked through the front door of the station house. It was my first day back from vacation and in my anxiety to get back to work I had arrived a bit earlier than usual for a 4 P.M. to midnight tour. I liked Charlie. He was always abreast of everything happening in the precinct and with an ever-present smile he liked to be the first to tell somebody good news.

"For what?" I asked.

"The captain gave you a seat. You're gonna be riding sector David with Ray Manetta."

"No shit?" I was ecstatic. My activity had paid off.

"As soon as they get it squared away upstairs in roll call, you'll be working in the 17th squad." He paused and looked at me a bit admiringly. "Not bad, Ed. You know I gotta hand it to you; you did your thing—you locked up every hump you came across, you didn't give no collars away, and you banged out twenty or so movers a month—and now you got your seat." What he lacked in grammar and diction was more than made up in his pleasant appearance and delivery. About six feet one, early thirties, he was a bit on the skinny side but gave the impression of being very wiry. He wore the uniform impeccably, with his hat brim and shoes always shined brightly. Dark, bushy eyebrows accented soft brown eyes, but the first things you noticed when you glanced at his face were two bony cheeks. "What're you here—a little over a year? Some guys are here ten, even fifteen years and still don't have a seat. And some of the guys that do, don't deserve it. Fuckin' Montrose and Harris ain't filled out an arrest form since I been here. They got their seats with the last captain. He was from the old school and put guys in on seniority, not performance."

"Thanks, Charlie, I'm glad you feel that way. I know a lot of guys felt I was putting the pressure on them by working hard. You know, like the sergeant might expect the same results from them. One of those 'if he can do it, you can do it' type things."

"What're you talking about? Nobody ever said nothin' like that to me. As far as I know, there ain't no pressure, neither. Hey, give credit where credit is due, I always say. If you want to bust your ass knockin' the jock off these niggers, go right ahead. I know how bad you wanted that seat."

"Thanks, Charlie."

"No thanks necessary, Ed." With that he walked past me toward the door. "Good luck and be careful."

"10-4," I said. I couldn't get the smile off my face.

Because your very life depends on your partner and you probably see more of him than anyone else, except just possibly your wife, you and he must have a unique rapport. Your compatibility must extend beyond friendship and social life to the attitudes and mechanics of good police work. Sometimes the instinctive or preplanned knowledge of where your partner is and what he is doing when you become separated at the scene of a crime can make the difference in catching a criminal or saving a life, be it your own or another's.

Ray Manetta was a strapping guy, about six feet tall and 175 pounds of solid muscle. As a kid he had trained rigorously, lifting weights and exercising, to develop himself into a veritable brick wall. He had taken a serious interest in boxing and had compiled an impressive record as an amateur before joining the department. Not without paying the price, however, for a broken nose slightly distorted an otherwise handsomely rugged face.

We hadn't worked together much, but he had the reputation of being active and, of course, capable of handling himself well in a scrap. He was a little older than I and had a few months more on the job and in the precinct. He had made as many arrests as I, if not more; and quality arrests, no cheapies like disorderly conduct or harassment. He seemed to be a shy, withdrawn guy, yet he and his wife always showed up at the precinct functions. Without really knowing him, I thought of Ray as an all-around good police officer and I was happy to be his steady partner.

Over the next year I would get to know Ray Manetta like I've known no one else in my entire life and feel closer to him than my own brother. We would share our innermost thoughts and secrets. I would penetrate his shield of quiet reserve and see him as a happy-go-lucky, come-as-they-may guy. I would uncover a dry, but clever humor and laugh more knowingly at some of his wit than at any other man's. I would discern a sharp intelligence behind his pugnacious appearance and envy his aggressive attitudes. And a bond would develop between us such as few men ever achieve.

I would learn that I had been 100 percent correct in my assumption he was an all-around good police officer. Without a doubt he would be the best partner I ever worked with. We would make many arrests together and fight many a brawl, winning most of them. He would truly justify his reputation as a scrapper. We would both develop not only the synchronized speed and timing of professional athletes, but also a sixth sense that would enable us to split up on an assignment, he going around one corner or up one staircase, and I the other, yet know exactly where the other was and what he was doing. We would spend an enormous amount of combined energy and much of our own time working to reach whatever goals we set. We would gain a reputation through the precinct—with both officers and civilians alike—of, simply enough, a duo of hard-working, tough policemen.

We would be constant companions—on the job and off. Together eight hours a day inside the radio car and sometimes eight hours outside, on occasion we would be with each other more than with our families. We would go "bouncing" many a night and drink until our stomachs burst. And when one of us was too drunk to make it home, we would both sleep in whoever's house was closer. The next day we would exercise together to keep in shape.

We would go big-game hunting and skiing together in the winter and to the ball park and racetrack in the summer. His family would be frequent guests in my living room and mine in his. His wife would befriend my wife, his kids would play with my kids. He would help me carry furniture when I moved and I would help him fix his jalopy whenever it broke down. We would celebrate each other's birthday and treat each other as kin. We would trust each other implicitly.

In effect, we would grow to love each other, Ray Manetta and I, as only two police officers and two "brothers" can. We would develop a mutual respect and friendship that seemingly appeared unshakable. But in the not too distant future, I would be asked to do something that would irreparably break that friendship and utterly destroy that bond of love and respect.

CHAPTER 16

Whether you call it horse, stuff, H, junk, dope, shit, scag, smack, boy, Harry, or Scot, it's still heroin. And whether you call it snow, sugar, dust, coke, C, candy, girl, or Charlie, it's still cocaine. The Eight-O was ass-deep in both.

Heroin, an alkaloid derivative of morphine, is a white, or sometimes light brown powder, which closely resembles flour or talcum powder in appearance. Its chemical name is diacetylmorphine. It is taken by sniffing, or "snorting" as it is called in the street, and by injection into the veins. This sleep-inducive drug is classified as a depressive narcotic and is highly addictive with continued use, causing a deep physical and psychological dependence. The reaction on the user is a euphoric, drowsy state of well-being. It smothers feelings of anxiety, fear, or tension and transports the addict into a world of sluggishness and slow motion.

With the increase of body tolerance for the drug comes an increase in the dosage needed to "get off." As time goes on the addict's entire life is centered around the next fix. The usage contracts the pupils, slows the respiratory system and the pulse considerably, and swells the ankles and the wrists.

If he tries to stop, within hours the addict will be faced with severe sickness, characterized by perspiration, diarrhea, eye tearing, a rise in body temperature, shooting hot and cold sensations, headache, nausea, vomiting, shakes, aching bones, quickened breathing, muscle twitches, anxiety, and a strong desire for another "load."

Heroin, believe it or not, was developed as a cure for morphine addiction.

An overdose may easily lead to death.

Before the sellers put it on the market, they "cut," or dilute the heroin several times with quinine crystals, baking soda, or milk sugar. One kilo (kilogram: 2.2 pounds) of raw heroin when cut six times will have an approximate street value of a half-million dollars. It is easy to see why trafficking in it is called "big business." It is usually sold in three dollar and five dollar bags, or decks—glassine (frosty, cellophanelike) envelopes that contain approximately one grain of the powder.

The person who has a habit, a "thing" or a "jones," uses a set of "works" or "gimmicks" (hypodermic instruments) to "shoot up." A set of works consists of a bottle cap, known as the "cooker," an eyedropper, a piece of cotton, a hypodermic needle, or "spike," and sometimes a large bobby pin to hold the bottle cap. They fit nicely into an eyeglass case, a pencil case, or even an empty cigarette pack. It's a common practice among addicts to share the same set of works time and time again. With this comes the risk of easily spreading hepatitis and venereal diseases.

Heroin is placed in the cooker and mixed with water or spit. It is then heated with a match to dissolve the powder. The cotton is used as a filter as the liquid is drawn up into the eyedropper, and the spike is then attached to the end. A piece of rubber, cord, string, a belt, or anything available is tied tightly around the top of the arm to define the vein and the needle is injected. The liquid is then squeezed into the bloodstream and the needle is not removed until blood backs up into the eyedropper. The younger the addict, the harder it is to find the vein and often he must stick himself several times before he "connects."

Junkies will shoot up in an abandoned building, in a public bathroom, on a stairway, in a cellar, on a roof, just about anywhere; at any time of the day or night.

There are over one hundred thousand addicts in New York City and 1 percent of them die each year from an overdose. In fact, more New Yorkers between the ages of fifteen and thirty-five die each year as a result of addiction than from any other cause.

Cocaine, an extract from the coca (not to be confused with cocoa) bush leaf, is an odorless, white, sparkling powder that closely resembles sugar. Like heroin it is taken by sniffing and by injection into the veins. Unlike heroin, it is classified as a stimulant narcotic and is non-addictive, though it causes a heavy psychic and emotional dependence. The reaction on the user is an elevated euphoria, a feeling of excitement and exhilaration, often accompanied by a paranoid state and hallucinations.

The injection of a mixture of heroin and cocaine, called a "speedball," is a common practice among abusers of both drugs.

The body does not develop a tolerance level for cocaine, as it does for heroin, but a sudden increase in dosage can well lead to dangerous delusions of persecution, resulting in mixed feelings of anxiety and suspicion. The usage dilates the pupils, increases the heartbeat, and results in hyperactivity, muscle twitches, convulsions, loss of appetite, and hypertension. Repeated sniffing results in damage to the nasal membranes and repeated injection results in infections at the puncture sites.

There is no withdrawal syndrome with cocaine other than a psychic craving for the attached feeling of ecstasy.

Again, like heroin, an overdose may easily lead to death.

Cocaine is more expensive than heroin and accordingly the profits are greater. One kilo of raw cocaine when cut can sell on the street for close to eight hundred thousand dollars. It is usually sold in "spoons," one-gram packets of tinfoil, at a price of fifty dollars each, or smaller bags for ten dollars. Because it is so expensive, cocaine has been called the "drug of the rich," but there are plenty of poor people in Bedford-Stuyvesant using it every day.

Unlicensed possession and sale of narcotics in New York State are, of course, against the law, but the drug problem for the police is not as simply defined as that. There are also many crimes committed by addicts that are the result of their constant need for money. The generally accepted theory that heroin addiction is responsible for at least 50 percent of all burglaries in New York City underlines this problem. Burglary, larceny, robbery, and other related crimes are an everyday part of the addict's life. Even an addict with a relatively low-level habit needs $25 a day, seven days a week to support it. Because addicts are considered unreliable, it is difficult for them to get or hold a job and they are thus forced to turn to a life of crime for the necessary money. It must be remembered that what the addict gets when he fences the merchandise he steals is usually only one-fifth of the actual value. Therefore, in order to support a $25 daily habit, he must steal $125 worth of merchandise each day, $875 each week, $45,500 each year. Multiply that by the number of addicts you are dealing with and it is obvious why the Police Department is hard pressed to keep addiction at a minimum.

The first day I rode with Ray Manetta as my steady partner, we shook hands and started on the long road to friendship. For an hour or so we talked about our backgrounds and interests. And then about how we would take turns at making arrests. And then ...

"Do you have any pet peeves, Ed? Anything in particular bug you about this precinct?"

"I can't think of anything offhand," I said. "I'd rather work in a White precinct, I know that."

"Any arrest you like to make more than any others?"

"Not really. What're you driving at?"

"Well, for the past couple of months I've been gathering as much information as possible on the narcotics in this precinct. I've been trying to get some of the guys I've locked up to feed me information and so far I've been pretty lucky."

"What're you gonna fight a one-man war? There's junk running all over this place."

"No. I was hoping I could get you interested enough so we could fight a two-man war. There's just something about narcotics that bugs me and I'd like to do my share. You know what I mean?"

"Yeah! You aren't the only one on this job who hates drugs. But until you just mentioned it, I had never thought to specialize in it."

"Why not specialize? Look at Greg Mortin. He's made

more GLAs (Grand Larceny Auto) than anybody in the precinct. And Harry Barkley's got more intox drivers."

"Yeah, but Greg used to be a mechanic and he knows where to find the vehicle identification number on any American car. As for Barkley, he's got his own personal reasons."

"That's exactly it. Personal reasons. That's exactly why I'd like to break this precinct wide open with drug collars. I'd like to see at least one little section of this shithole they call Bedford-Stuyvesant cleaned up. Together we can do it."

He was really getting me hopped up about the idea. "You know, you've almost convinced me that it might be a good idea at that. But what about all the paperwork and the trips to the lab."

"Hey, I heard you were a pretty active guy, Ed. Don't tell me you'd let a little paperwork or a ride to Manhattan stand in your way. Besides, the captain has been looking to increase the drug collars and he's been giving days off for good ones as an incentive."

"OK, partner," I said, offering my hand for a shake. "I'm with you. Let's do our part to clean up the narcotics in the Eight-O."

And we did. Because of the extra work involved, most of the officers in the precinct avoided narcotics arrests, and therefore Ray and I, along with only four or five other men, made the bulk of them each month for the next year.

The first thing I did the next day was to grab a copy of the New York State Penal Law to see what it had to say about drugs and I learned a lot of things. There is a specific distinction between the terms narcotic drug and dangerous drug. Narcotic drugs are heroin, cocaine, opium and other opiates, morphine, marijuana. (Incidentally many of the younger officers feel marijuana is comparatively innocuous and is nowhere near the same league as heroin or cocaine. The fact that the penalties for its possession or sale are the same as for the latter is absolutely absurd.) The term "dangerous drugs" *includes* narcotic drugs, in addition to barbiturates (depressants), amphetamines (stimulants), and hallucinogenic drugs (LSD, mescaline, DMT, and the like).

There are six degrees of criminal possession of dangerous drugs and four degrees of criminal sale of dangerous drugs. Two factors are absolutely necessary for criminal possession: a person must possess the drug unlawfully and he must have full knowledge that it is in his possession. Along the same line, for criminal sale a person must knowingly sell the drug unlawfully. In other words you can't arrest a licensed researcher examining marijuana or a medical doctor legally administering morphine.

Criminal possession in the sixth degree is simply the possession of a dangerous drug. This is a misdemeanor. The fifth degree is the possession of the dangerous drug with the intent to sell. This is a class E felony (sentence not to exceed four years). The fourth degree is the possession of a narcotic drug with the intent to sell or, without the intent, simple possession of at least one-eighth of an ounce of heroin or cocaine (other weights for various drugs are included in the law, but because I was to concentrate mainly on heroin and cocaine abusers I was not interested and won't list them now). This is a D felony (sentence not to exceed seven years). The third degree is the possession of at least one ounce of heroin or cocaine and is a C felony (sentence not to exceed fifteen years). The second degree is the possession of at least eight ounces and is a B felony (sentence not to exceed twenty-five years). The first degree is the possession of at lease sixteen ounces and is an A felony (sentence is life imprisonment).

Criminal sale in the fourth degree is the sale of a dangerous drug (D felony). Sale in the third degree is the sale of a narcotic drug (C felony). The second degree is the sale of a narcotic drug to a person under twenty-one or at least eight ounces of heroin or cocaine to anyone (B felony). The first degree is the sale of at least sixteen ounces (A felony).

It must be pointed out that all amounts specified in the law (e.g., eight ounces of heroin necessary for criminal possession second degree) relate to aggregate weights seized. It makes no difference how much of the actual drug is in the mixture. For instance, someone who possesses or sells eight ounces of raw heroin is charged with a B felony, whereas someone who possesses or sells eighteen ounces of a mixture of milk sugar and heroin—even if the quantity of heroin contained therein is only one ounce—is charged with an A felony.

But reading the penal law wasn't all. I sent away for booklets, pamphlets, and any other material available on drugs. I visited a Phoenix House, a Methadone Center, and a New York State Narcotic Addiction Control Center, where I talked to many people and obtained more literature in a effort to better understand the problem. Ray and I read and studied as much as we could, as we simultaneously gathered information, on duty and off, from a network of informers.

Although the material stated why people become addicted and what they must do to stop, it made no mention of the filth and absolute sewerlike habitats of the drug users and pushers. I had thought I had seen the worst possible conditions in the precinct before I got my seat, but once I started making drug arrests I uncovered an even dirtier, slimier world.

After a while we discovered what buildings were the most active in drug traffic and we keyed on those locations. Each night we made the rounds, building to building, searching for violators. Entering the rat-infested, roach-ridden tenements made my flesh crawl but it was necessary if I wanted to make any collars.

One night we made a regular stop at a building on Grand Avenue. As we stepped through the door, the pervasive, nauseating stench of the ghetto increased. Hardened phlegm spotted the walls and glassine envelopes were scattered on the vomit-covered floor.

We climbed the stairs slowly and softly in case there was anyone shooting up in the halls. If not, we had intentions of checking out the roof before we went on to the next building. Ray was ahead of me and quietly advancing when suddenly he broke the silence in the air with a loud command and a simultaneous dart upward.

"Hey! Hold it right there," he yelled at someone I could not yet see. In a second, though, I had climbed enough stairs to see a dark figure turn from an open door and thrust a linoleum knife toward my partner's face.

"Watch it!" I screamed, and Ray stooped to the floor with suddenly weighted shoulders. Former boxer that he was, he sunk a right cross deep to the midsection of the assailant, causing him to cry out in pain. He withdrew it quickly and grabbed the attacker's right wrist with both hands, shoving his arm skyward. The limb was ripped from its socket with a gritting sound and the weapon fell harmlessly to the floor. Ray lifted his knee to his opponent's groin and slammed him against the wall. With lightning speed he clasped his hands behind the Negro's neck and with a downward jerk sent the front of his head smashing to the floor. He landed with all his weight as he fell on top of him.

"Here, Ed, cuff this guy," he said, offering me a rear mount on the man.

"I've got him," I said, clasping his limp right arm and bending his left one to the rear. I cuffed him mechanically. His eyes were closed and he was not stirring as bile spewed from the corner of his mouth.

"Open up ... you're under arrest," Ray shouted at the closed door, which appeared to be weak and rotted. "Open up."

"Did you see the sale?" I asked.

"I saw it." He was breathing heavily now from the workout. "He threw it over there ... see it?" He pointed about three feet down the hall, away from the motionless body. "A cunt inside sold it to him."

"I got it," I said, retrieving the barbiturate pill from the damp floor.

"Open up," Ray yelled again. "Open up or we'll break it in."

No answer.

"Let's break it in," he said.

Convinced the buyer was unconscious and not about to go anyplace for a while, we drew our guns, stepped back a pace, and kicked at the door, one high, one low. It was so decayed, it not only swung open but loosed from the hinge on top and fell sideways, hanging. A disgusting odor greeted us.

We crouched to both sides of the doorway, ready for anything, when, casually, as if we had only interrupted her interest in a TV program, a bony Negro woman stepped into view and barked: "Come on in, boys. Make yourselves at home." Her lips were gummy white and she wore a blond wig that was tilted askew.

We entered cautiously. The rancid smell was thick. The place looked as if it had just been hit with a tornado. Wrinkled clothes were everywhere. Papers, books, and garbage were strewn across the room. Two apparent junkies, one male, one female, nodded blissfully on a tattered sofa.

We brought "Sleeping Beauty" in from the hall and searched the apartment as best we could. Incredibly we came up with a vial of barbiturates and assorted hypodermic instruments spread loosely through the debris and about a dozen glassine envelopes of heroin in the bathroom. Heaven only knows how much we missed.

After the search, we herded the four prisoners outside and piled them into the back seat of the radio car. On the way to the station house the female pusher was furious.

"Here I am paying the district one hundred dollars a week for protection and I still get arrested. Ain't that a kick in the ass?"

I didn't believe her, but it wouldn't have made any difference if it were true. She wasn't paying me. In my best Stan Laurel, I took my hat off, scratched the top of my head, and said: "It most certainly is, Ollie." We all got a good laugh.

We charged her with "sale" and the next week she moved out of the apartment. I never saw her again.

That was the first of about one hundred arrests Ray and I either made or assisted in making over the next year, en route to making the Eight-O the number one precinct in the city in increased drug arrests. No arrest gave us more pleasure than "Tonka" from Pacific Street.

On information obtained from a few informants, we had learned that a Black man named Tonka was the main supplier of a notorious building. He was a real fancy dresser who drove around the precinct in a nice new Eldorado. By his overly careful actions whenever we were near, we knew he sensed we were on to him.

One day, quite by chance, Ray and I were turning the corner in the radio car and saw Tonka entering the building with a girl. We parked and ran in behind them.

Ray went up one stairway and I went up the other. By

the time I reached the second or third floor, Ray had already caught them cold with a bag of cocaine, which we later learned was valued at over two thousand dollars.

Not only was I happy that we had arrested one of the biggest pushers in Bedford-Stuyvesant, but also because I got to drive his Eldorado to the station house. That was the first time I ever drove one.

As time went on, Ray and I crawled on damp basement floors and soot-covered roofs in search of drug abusers. We had "meets" with informants in dimly lit, foul-smelling apartments, where it was impossible to sit or stand for more than five minutes without feeling a roach crawl up your leg, or a rat nibble at your shoe. We fought, arrested, and came in constant contact with diseased people whose skins were covered with scales and boils and whose bodies stunk of human waste.

Without realizing it at first, I developed a vehement animosity toward the Blacks I was arresting. I was sickened by the evil environment in which they lived and I held that against them. I blamed them for making my life miserable. In my quest to accomplish a goal, I had brought myself into touch with that ugly environment, but blamed the Negroes. All Negroes. I channeled all the unpleasant reactions I received from the constant sight of the disgusting surroundings and from the constant contact with the diseased people whom I encountered into a profound hatred for all Blacks.

I had developed prejudices before. I was definitely deserving of the title "bigot." But now I was a violent racist. I became short tempered and nasty in my words and actions. I began to slap people around. I thought nothing of calling a Black man "nigger" to his face, because that's what he was to me; that's what all Blacks were to me.

I took my short temper and my cruelty home to my family. I contaminated my wife and children with dirty, foul-mouthed talk against all Negroes. When I came home from work, I yelled incessantly and listened to no pleas or excuses. I was a madman at times, ranting and raving through the house, screaming at the most insignificant things and barking at my children for the little mistakes that children are supposed to make.

Then one day something happened that induced me to take a good, long look at myself.

My hate for Negroes had grown so intense that when I saw that I was scheduled to ride with a Black patrolman one night that Ray had taken off, I asked to be reassigned. Most Black and White patrolmen usually got along with each other pretty well in the Eight-O because they were united against a common foe—crime—and the danger in Bedford-Stuyvesant was so great that they couldn't afford to be anything but friendly. Even the most militant, biased men controlled their feelings when riding with a member of the other race and in the beginning so did I. But lately I had been so keyed up that I preferred a rookie's assignment to guard a prisoner at Brooklyn Jewish Hospital to riding with a Negro.

On my way there that night I passed Nate. He had been pointed out to me two years earlier by a patrolman who told me the fifteen-year-old was dealing narcotics. "He's making more than both of us together," he had said. "Not only that, but his family is getting over four hundred dollars a month from welfare, in addition to free rent. And this little hump is selling heroin, making a bundle. Where's the justice?"

Indeed, where is the justice? I kept my eye on him and sure enough one day a little over a year later he was arrested for possession of drugs. Because he was only sixteen (and looked even younger) and because his lawyer described him as "a poor underprivileged youngster," the judge saw fit to let him walk out of the courtroom. "The poor underprivileged youngster" spit at another officer when he attempted to straighten him out and set him on the right path. He went right back to selling heroin.

A little more than a month later, Ray and I caught Nate and another youth in a hallway with quite a large amount of narcotics. Enough to charge both with "intent to sell," a D felony. Again the judge was persuaded by his youthful appearance and his lawyer's pleas, and set a minimal bail.

Once more, a little over a month after that, Ray arrested him (I had taken the day off) for "intent to sell," and again he was out on the street in a short time selling junk.

Nate represented everything to which I was opposed. I was trying to clean up the drug problem; Nate was selling drugs. I was trying to persuade the judges to keep the pushers behind bars and force the addicts to seek help; Nate walked out of court a lot sooner than he should have, even after two felony and one misdemeanor drug arrests within a short period. And Nate was Black.

"Hey, you honky mother-fucker," he yelled, sitting on a stoop. I was stunned by the brazenness of this scrawny kid. He had to be high, I figured. "You ain't nothin' but a mother-fuckin' pig . . . oink, oink."

I approached him warily, without uttering a word, looking for signs of drug-induced euphoria. But there was none. Two albumenized globes contrasted with a dark Brillo head with sharp, defined features.

For some reason, I couldn't imagine what, he apparently thought he was immune to arrest. Or, perhaps because of the leniency of the courts, he just didn't care. If he knew how I felt about him, he would have shut up.

"Are you talking to me?" I asked, suppressing the temptation to add "boy."

"Ain't no other White mother-fuckers on the street, is there?" he snorted.

A crowd began to collect and he continued to taunt me, using abusive and obscene language, until at length I told him he was under arrest. When I tried to take him in, he resisted. He couldn't have made me any happier. With one swipe of my open hand, bursting with all my pent-up emotions, I smacked him on the side of the head and knocked him to the ground. I placed the cuffs on him and dragged him to the station house.

I sat him down in the back room and asked another officer to keep an eye on him, while I ran up to my locker. All I could think about was that maybe this time justice would triumph and the judge might see that Nate wasn't such a "poor underprivileged youngster" after all. But in order for that to be possible, he had to be charged with a narcotics violation.

In my locker, as is the case of many a policeman's locker, I had a deck of narcotics for just such an occasion. From an arrest that would not be affected by it, officers would take one or two decks to keep in their lockers.

Some men would want them to add to a misdemeanor arrest to make it a felony (for instance, if a man had fifty-three bags of heroin on him at the time of arrest he could only be charged with a misdemeanor, so they would add two bags making the total fifty-five, the necessary amount for a felony charge) and some men would want them to "flake" a prisoner, i.e., to place a bag or two on him if he was "clean."

When I conducted a search of Nate's personal belongings, I planted the deck. In my haste to balance the scales of justice it had never occurred to me that he might be "dirty" to begin with. He was. He had narcotics in his pocket all along and my plant was unnecessary. When I found his drugs, it dawned on me what I had become.

I had no right to wear the uniform, acting in the manner that I had. I had slipped into a life of decadence, corruption, and crime and I despised that kind of life. I had wanted a steady seat so badly the year before, when I got it, I found out it was "killing" me. Instead of looking forward to work each day, as I had done, I found myself utilizing all the time I had built up with my good arrest rewards to take off at every available chance. I got knots in my stomach the day I realized I had to get out of the job, before it was too late.

The first thing I did was ask the captain for a change in assignment. He was a bit puzzled, but consented. In December, 1970, I became the regular telephone-switchboard operator of the Eight-O precinct, where I stayed for over six months.

The next thing I did, after discussing it with my wife, was to apply to the University of Southern California. I would hope to get a leave of absence from the department, but if not I was prepared to resign.

The fact that I had decided to leave, giving up my duties in the street for a "teat job" in the station house, did not prevent me from functioning as a police officer. One afternoon, on my day off, I had driven my wife to a shopping center near our home with arrangements to pick her up in a half-hour, while I made a visit to the bank. I had to make a deposit and usually I parked the car and walked in. But this day there was no line at all at the drive-in teller's window so I made my deposit from the car. As I pulled away from the window and stopped in the driveway for oncoming traffic, I noticed an old, beat-up Chevy with three male Negroes, all in their twenties, pull up alongside the building. Reacting as a policeman, I was immediately suspicious. It was close to closing, a perfect time to hit the bank. Moreover, three Negroes in my all-White neighborhood stuck out like a sore thumb. I stared at them for a second and then at their license plate before I drove off.

Could they be planning to stick up the bank? Nah, it's probably just my imagination. Then again there aren't any stores nearby, so they're not out shopping. And I'm sure they don't live in the neighborhood, so they wouldn't be making a deposit. Maybe they're going to make a large withdrawal—of somebody else's money. I better go back just to be sure.

I circled back and drove slowly past the front entrance. One of the men was sitting behind the wheel of the car outside and the other two were just entering the bank door. I was holding up traffic and the guy behind me was blowing his horn, but I had to see what they were up to. The entire front of the bank was made of glass, so I could look right in. One stationed himself by the door while the other bypassed a long line and approached a woman teller at a "closed" window. It *was* a rip-off.

I stomped on the gas pedal and raced to the next corner where there was usually a patrolman assigned to direct traffic. He wasn't there. I made a U-turn through the red light and sped back to the bank. My heart was pounding heavily and beads of nervous perspiration formed on my brow. I pulled into the bank's parking lot, unholstered my off-duty revolver, placed it under my jacket, nestling it in my armpit, and headed toward the side entrance.

My one advantage, I figured, was that I knew who they were, and they didn't know who I was. The side of the building was not made of glass and I couldn't see inside, but as I was about to open the door I heard a woman scream. I rushed in just as the two men bolted through the front door into the street. I ran after them but by the time I reached the entrance I heard them slam their car doors and screech rubber at the curb. I ran back to the parking lot and jumped in my car. I screamed out of the driveway right behind a man in a station wagon, who I assumed was another off-duty patrolman picking up the chase. He told me later he was an electrician. (I don't know what the hell he was going to do if he caught up with them.) I couldn't see the trio's getaway car, but I figured the man in front of me could as we ran a dozen red lights and narrowly missed as many collisions barreling through the streets, so I stayed right on his tail. We lost them. I drove back to the bank and a radio car team was on the scene taking a report. I gave them a description of the three bandits and the license plate number of the car. While we were talking, a report of another bank holdup a few blocks away came over the air.

"Wouldn't it be something if it was the same trio," I said.

I found out later it was. In a little more than fifteen minutes, they had taken the two banks for over nine thousand dollars. With the aid of my descriptions and those of others at the scene of both holdups, I believe two of the three men were arrested a short time later by a joint force of New York City detectives and agents from the Federal Bureau of Investigation. The last I heard, the third was still being sought.

I often wonder what would have happened had I entered the bank a few seconds earlier. It is entirely possible I might have been killed. But I was still a police officer and instinctively reacted like one, even though I was getting out.

CHAPTER 17

Even before I joined the department I dreamed of becoming a detective. Not that a uniformed patrolman's duties are not exciting, but a detective's duties are primarily involved with investigation and present more of an opportunity to use your intelligence and show your worth. There is more prestige and professionalism as a detective. Moreover, a third-grade detective makes over one thousand dollars a year more than a patrolman, a second-grade detective makes close to sergeant's pay, and a first grader close to lieutenant's. There is no written test that has to be passed to become a detective. Hard work, a lot of activity, aggressiveness, and a reputation for being on the ball will give any patrolman a good crack at the promotion. Of course, a good hook wouldn't hurt any, either.

With the change of status there is a change of shields. The patrolman's, though metallic, is referred to as the white shield and the detective's, though blue and gold, is referred to simply as the gold shield. Throughout the department any shield, regardless of denoted rank, is referred to as "the tin." Before getting the gold shield, however, it is necessary to serve an apprenticeship of from two to five years in plainclothes duty. The plainclothes unit of the department is concerned mainly with violations related to the public moral aspects of society: gambling and prostitution. (There are many other areas in the department that necessitate working in plainclothes, for instance, the narcotics division and the bureau of special services.

Apprenticeships in any one of these units can lead to the gold shield.) An extensive course, the Criminal Investigation Course, covering all the laws in those moral areas, defining them, explaining them, having guest speakers talk about their practical use, is given to all candidates for plainclothes.

In order to attend the school you must first be nominated by your commanding officer. After that you must attend an interview with a sergeant or lieutenant from the plainclothes screening unit who pulls your personnel folder and scrutinizes every facet of your past performance from the day you were appointed. If you pass that interview, you must finally appear there before a board of three high-ranking officers who quiz you about conditions in your own command to see if you are up on all current vice activities and they must be certain that you are the cream of the crop before they recommend you. Accordingly, there is a high percentage of turndowns as a result of these two interviews.

The first contact I had with anyone in the department in regard to working in plainclothes was while I was still working in the telephone company. I had just met the written and physical requirements for the job when one evening at my home I received a telephone call from a lieutenant who asked me to report to the Police Academy the following night, but didn't tell me why. It was important, he said, and must be kept a secret. I was even not to tell my wife. I had just seen a James Bond movie the day before the phone call, so I was ripe for all the secrecy surrounding the meeting. I told my wife I was going to a telephone company union meeting and reported to the Police Academy as requested. For an hour or so the lieutenant and I sat in one of the classrooms and he asked me questions such as, "Why do you want to be a police officer?" "How did you find out about the Police Department recruitment tests?" "Do you have any relatives on the job?" "Any friends?" When he was finished he thanked me and said good-night. I asked him why he had called me down and he told me, rather unconvincingly, that he was researching the advertising policies of the department. I didn't buy it and he knew it, but I didn't press the issue.

Now a meeting of this nature is by no means a regular

procedure for a new man. In succeeding years I must have asked over a hundred men if they had attended such an interview and every answer was negative. One day in the Eight-O, however, I was on the switchboard and happened to mention it to the lieutenant on the desk, who, coincidentally, used to work in a unit where interviews like that were conducted for incoming recruits. He told me that it was a screening for a special assignment in plainclothes where nobody would have known I was a police officer. I would have told people that I had changed my mind about joining the force, I would have gone through private training by private instructors at the Police Academy, and in all likelihood I would not have carried a gun or ID most of the time. My main function would have been to try to penetrate and report on radical factions around the city, such as the Weathermen, SDS, and others. Black men, of course, were utilized for penetration into such militant organizations as the Black Panthers and Black Liberation Army. He speculated that I was not accepted because the men used in these positions are chosen primarily on the basis of having no friends or relatives on the job in order to lessen the chance of their true identity being uncovered. I had no relatives on the force but I had mentioned at the interview that I had many friends in the Police Department.

My next brush with a chance at plainclothes duty was while I was in the Police Academy. A high-ranking officer from the bureau of special services, BOSS (for some reason or another pronounced Bossey), an undercover unit with the purpose of keeping tabs on subversive groups, walked through the ranks of rookies singling out those who looked the most like they were not policemen. Now I was twenty-one and looked about sixteen. During my five years on the job (even though I had a moustache for my last four) I was constantly told by both outsiders and other police officers that I certainly didn't look like a patrolman. Most of the time I was told I looked like a high school senior. But luck wasn't with me that day because the big shot from BOSS never walked past me. He got halfway down my line and walked back again. I am certain that had he seen me he would have picked me as a likely candidate.

A little over two months after I was assigned to the Eight-O, I approached the captain and told him that I felt my youthful appearance would be beneficial to the department if I were assigned to plainclothes duty. He misunderstood and reluctantly forwarded my written request to the detective bureau. It was a little embarrassing reporting to the chief of detectives' office for an interview with only one year on the job and a total arrest record of three. I told the chief's right-hand man that a mistake had been made and that I was fully prepared to be rejected. He told me he wouldn't let me down and rejected me. Before I left though, he did say he liked my spirit and that if I were to become active in the near future I might stand a chance at another interview. As active as I was over the next two years, I felt that I was not active enough to deserve the gold shield without a stint in plainclothes first, so I never applied again.

On another occasion my guess that I was a good candidate for BOSS proved correct when a sergeant who was transferred from the Eight-O to that unit recommended me without my knowing it. When I went to that interview, the captain in charge told me that I was perfect, but that they were looking to recruit Blacks and there weren't enough openings for them to accept another White patrolman.

Finally, in the summer of 1970, on the basis of my activity, the captain of the Eight-O (a new one—the old one had retired) recommended me for the Criminal Investigation Course. I passed the two interviews at the screening unit with flying colors and it was just a matter of time before I was assigned to the class in the Police Academy.

The class was not formed until February, 1971, and by that time I had already made my decision to leave the job. However, I hadn't notified the department officially of my intentions; and I hadn't yet received a notice of acceptance or rejection from the University of Southern California, so I decided to attend the course and spend my last few months in "clothes."

For a short time I was drawn between which path to take: leave the job and go to school, or go to plainclothes, with a chance at becoming a detective. As much as I desired the gold shield and as certain as I was that I would attain it through plainclothes, I decided to stick with my original plan to leave the job. If granted a leave of absence, I figured, I could always come back if I felt I had made the wrong decision and again shoot for the promotion. If I stayed on and things got worse, if I got more involved with tainted activities, if my prejudices were intensified to a greater degree, I would probably forever regret not making the move when I had the chance.

There was good reason to suspect that if I stayed on, things would get worse and I would fall prey to further corruption. The general understanding throughout the force was that everybody in plainclothes was "on the pad" (i.e., wherever a pad existed). The term "pad" refers to a payoff system in which gamblers paid varying amounts to the plainclothes division within which they operated in return for protection against arrest. The total amount collected was then split among the plainclothesmen, bosses included, according to rank and risk involved in picking up the money. I had many conversations with former plainclothesmen and active plainclothesmen and the story was always the same: everybody's on the pad. If you don't take, the bosses arrange for your transfer out of the unit. Again the code of silence prevailed and there was little chance of anybody blowing the whistle. Of course, throughout the city the amount for each member varied from division to division. I had heard reports of from four hundred dollars per month to twelve hundred dollars per month, per patrolman, in different areas around town. The more gamblers paying, the bigger the pad, or kitty. And the bigger the pad, the bigger the cut per man. The only command where there was no pad supposedly was the public morals task force, where the quick turnover in personnel and the fact that the targets for arrest were street prostitutes and not gamblers made a pad unlikely.

I attended the Criminal Investigation Course for its entirety—a little over a month—and enjoyed the hell out of every minute. One of the instructors, a big, red-headed sergeant in his mid-thirties, the kind of guy you could look at a block away and know he was a police officer, was one of the funniest men I have ever had the pleasure of meeting. There were days when the class would be held up for fifteen to twenty minutes at a time until everyone got themselves back together after cracking up over something he had said or a face he had made. But, aside from his natural ability to make people laugh, the sergeant had a rare knack for making learning fun and he would have to rank in the top ten of my "All-Time Favorite Instructors" list (that goes for college, too).

He had been in plainclothes for many years, and had worked in many a division, and had arrested many a gambler, and had listened to many a wiretap, before he passed the sergeant's test and was reassigned to the Police Academy. He was a natural choice to teach the CIC course.

In the course we learned about the Italian lottery, the Chinese lottery, the Spanish lottery, the ins and outs of bookmaking and the numbers game, and just about every facet of gambling and betting that a police officer would ever be confronted with in the street. In addition, almost every day there was a guest speaker from either another unit in the New York City Police Department, a federal agency, another police department in the state, or a local agency, who emphasized the importance of the plainclothesman in modern times and who explained the functions of whatever outfit they represented, always adding that we were welcome to seek their assistance at any time. The course was so worthwhile and everybody who attended it got so much out of it, that I feel it should be given to all patrolmen, whether they are plainclothes candidates or not.

At that time, I became friendly with two patrolmen, Dave Greenberg and Bob Hantz, who worked in a precinct bordering the Eight-O. The two men had an astonishing arrest record as partners and had received numerous departmental recognitions for outstanding arrests. As a result of their daring exploits, they were nicknamed Batman and Robin, after another dynamic duo. Each had a little less time on the job than I. Their main concentration, too, was narcotics violators and from time to time I had heard rumors that they were involved in various shady deals. I found both of them to be quite congenial and disregarded the rumors, never delving into their private affairs. At the end of the course we shook hands and wished each other good luck. The next time I was to see them would be under strange circumstances.

I was reassigned to the Eight-O where I would wait until orders were issued assigning me to a plainclothes command.

By late March I still had not received a letter of acceptance or rejection from the University of Southern California, so I decided to kill two birds with one stone—vacation in California to take a badly needed rest and check out my chances of acceptance. I was sunning one day in the beautiful Los Angeles weather when I received word from New York that an inspector in the internal affairs division, which investigates allegations of corruption within the department, wanted to talk to me. I called long distance at my own expense, and when I reached him, he said there was nothing to worry about, there was no investigation or allegation concerning me, but that when I returned to New York he would like me to report to his office for a talk. He asked me not to mention it to anyone. I couldn't imagine what he wanted to talk about. I enjoyed the rest of my vacation, and when I returned to New York, I reported to his office on my own time.

"Sit down, Ed. Make yourself at home." He was near fifty with graying hair and he had bags under his eyes, probably from too much worry, too little sleep. He sat behind his desk the entire time, so it was impossible to tell how tall he was or how much he weighed.

"What is it you wanted to see me about, inspector?" I asked, taking a seat near the front of his desk.

"You, Ed. I want to talk to you about you."

"I don't get ya."

"Well, you're going to be going into plainclothes soon and I've had a look at your record. . . . I don't mind telling you it's rather impressive."

"Thank you, sir."

"Let me get to the point. Ed, we know that there's a pad in some divisions and we know how they work. We know that you won't get any money for the first few months until you're checked out, but that then you'll get your envelope. We know also, that there aren't just patrolmen on these pads. What we want you to do is go

THE PATROLMAN: A COP'S STORY 189

out to one of these divisions, whichever one we're most interested in, and gather specifics. We want you to take the money just like everybody else. We want to know who's on and who's not, if anybody. We want to know who gives you the envelope and how high the payoffs go. We want to know what gamblers are paying. We want you to file a report with us every week with as much information as you can compile."

"Boy, you sure don't beat around the bush."

"You can't in this business, Ed. It's a hard, fast job. A job where you won't have too many friends if you join up. It's completely voluntary, of course. Nobody's going to force you to do anything. You'll have to decide for yourself. If you don't accept, we won't hold it against you. You'll still go to clothes. But I feel it only fair to tell you that we've asked a few other men, in fact we've got a few men out in the field working for us right now, so you'll never really know for sure who's who. You've got a damn good record, Ed, and you're highly regarded by every boss you've worked for. We'd like to have you aboard."

There was a short pause and then I asked: "If you don't mind my asking, what's in it for me? A gold shield?"

"Unfortunately not. I can't promise you anything. Anything except you'll know that you're doing your part to make this a better Police Department. Listen, Ed, I've got my time in already. In a short while I'll be putting my papers in and heading South. You're a young guy. You've got a long way to go on this job, and judging from your past performance, you'll go far." If only he knew I was planning to leave. "Whether you accept or not is no skin off my nose. I'd like you to volunteer because it's my job to recruit men. It's a God damn tough job, too, not being able to offer any rewards, but I'm stuck with it for now. It's completely understandable if you turn it down, though, and again let me emphasize it won't be held against you. If it's against your nature or you think it's not for you, no matter what the reason, don't do it."

I stared at him for a second. "When do I have to let you know?"

"Take your time. There's no hurry. Next week sometime, or the week after."

"OK," I said, rising and walking toward the door. "I'll get back to you."

"Good enough. And no matter what you decide, good luck in clothes."

"Thanks." At the door I hesitated and turned for one final question. "By the way, what happens to the money I accept when I get on the pad?"

He laughed a little bit. "Sorry, Ed. You voucher it and turn it over to us."

I laughed a little, too. "Oh, well."

I thought about it for two weeks. I would be leaving in a few months, I figured, and because there was a waiting period before you got on the pad in a division—usually a few months—I probably wouldn't be able to supply any useful information. Moreover, the inspector had hit the nail right on the head when he suggested it might be against my nature. I couldn't bring myself to rat on brother officers. I called him up and turned it down. I felt good about being asked, though. It indicated that the department thought highly of me. They didn't ask everybody.

In the middle of May I received a letter of acceptance from USC and started making arrangements to sell my house.

For the next few months in the Eight-O, I alternated between the switchboard and a few special plainclothes assignments (it was hot shit trying to work undercover in an all-Black precinct), until on July 14 I received orders to report to the public morals task force (PMTF), a part of the 3rd division in midtown Manhattan. I was relieved about not being assigned to a command where there was a pad, even though I'd never have to decide whether to get on or not—I'd be long gone before I had to make that choice. I guess I just had had enough of that environment—and on a much smaller scale.

A few months earlier the department had yielded to the pressure of constant complaints about the mass of prostitutes that flooded the midtown area every night by concentrating a large number of uniformed men in that section between the hours of 6 P.M. and 2 A.M. Their main function was to harass the girls and so keep them off the street, especially around the Theater District. They also responded by doubling the number of plainclothesmen assigned to the public morals task force, whose primary function was to arrest the girls.

The amount of time that a patrolman could remain in the unit with any degree of effectiveness before most of the prostitutes in town got to know him was about three months. Therefore, every few months there was a turnover in the outfit and the men who left it were reassigned to divisions to work on gamblers.

Working plainclothes in Manhattan was a whole new world—a beautiful world compared to the conditions in the Black ghetto. First was the fact that you worked in a suit. Nobody said you had to, yet everybody did. Mainly, just because they wanted to. Besides, you had to look like you had some money in order to get a girl "to hit on you" (i.e., to make you an offer).

Next was the routine. A fantastic routine. The hours were from 10 P.M. one night to 2 P.M. the next afternoon—a double tour—but it wasn't as bad as it sounds. In fact it wasn't bad at all. At ten o'clock everyone would have his assignment and turn out of the office (a small room on the second floor of the 18th precinct). Everybody was assigned in pairs, or if a guy's partner was on vacation, teams of three; but you never worked alone. From the office, depending on what part of town you were working, everybody met in a certain bar in that area. You'd have a couple of drinks and shoot the breeze until about midnight, then set out to make two arrests. (A quota prevailed: two collars per man per night. There were constant threats by the bosses that if you failed to meet the quota consistently you would get "flopped back into the bag [uniform]," but there were men who ignored it and never got flopped.)

If you were lucky enough to bag four girls (i.e., two for you, two for your partner) right away and you were fast enough with the booking process, it was conceivable that you would have time for one more drink before the bars closed. At that time you proceeded to your favorite hotel where you were put up for the night at no charge. There is one hotel right in the center of midtown with a worldwide reputation for its exquisiteness, and for the longest time I had wanted to sleep there one night just to see what it was like. I was thrilled to find out they were "good" to the men from the unit and not only did I sleep there one night, but any night I was in the vicinity—for nothing.

In the morning, around nine o'clock, it was off to court. But Criminal Court for a plainclothesman in PMTF is not like Criminal Court for a uniformed man in the Eight-O. First of all, you type up your own affidavits at your own convenience and the DA initials them. There are no long lines to wait on. The only thing you have to wait for is the yellow sheet to come in from BCI (bureau of criminal investigation). Secondly, in Manhattan the court personnel take care of the probation interview and the photographing of the prisoner for you. As soon as you have your yellow sheets in hand, you add them to the mounds of court papers that you've filled out sometime at your leisure during the night, and you get the case docketed. From the docket room the papers are sent into the court.

For some reason or other the judges hear the prostitutes' cases first and nobody seems to mind. All the uniformed officers from the city, in court with their arrests, and all the civilian complainants, witnesses, and sex freaks, jockey for position to get a good look at the girls and to hear the charges as their cases are read aloud. A typical affidavit would read:

> Patrolman Edward F. Droge, Jr., Shield #26665, Public Morals Task Force, being duly sworn, says that on 8/10/71 at about 12:30 A.M. at 57th Street and 6th Avenue, New York County, City and State of New York, the defendant Jane Doe committed the offenses of: 1. Prostitution 230.00P.L. 2. Loitering 240.35.6P.L. in that: Deponent [officer] did observe the defendant approach a male and engage him in conversation, during which time deponent states he did overhear the defendant offer to commit an unlawful sexual act [whatever the term in street vernacular was] for the sum of $20.00. Said male refused and walked away.

The last line would not necessarily be true. "Said male" might have run away when he saw the officer approaching or heard him placing the female under arrest. (Collaring the "johns"—customers—was not the PMTF policy, however. Just the girls. There were policewomen assigned near the end of the summer though, whose job it was to look like prostitutes, try to get propositioned and collar the johns. I heard that the first few weeks most of the people getting arrested were lawyers, judges, and big businessmen. There are a lot of so-called respectable people running around midtown every night picking up hookers.)

The arrest described above would be that of an "overhear," as compared to a "direct" in which the officer is the recipient of the proposition. If you grabbed a batch of blank affidavits in court, you could take them home and prepare a few overhears and a few directs, just leaving the date, time, location, defendant, act, and amount spaces blank. It made life at court a little easier.

In PMTF you use your own car for transportation and spend a lot of your own money on expenses. There is an expense account with a maximum allowance of $98 per month, but the costs of gas for the car and treating the girls to a drink or a meal to provide the right atmosphere for the offer sometimes runs to double that amount. Moreover, the expense checks are always at least two months in arrears. My partner, Joe Reilly, a helluva nice guy, and I took turns using each other's car and loaning each other ten dollars until the checks came in, if we were caught short.

We pulled a weekend chart with a beautiful schedule that ran as follows: 10 P.M. Monday to 2 P.M. Tuesday, 10 P.M. Wednesday to 2 P.M. Thursday, 10 P.M. Friday to 2 P.M. Saturday, Sunday and Monday off, 10 P.M. Tuesday to 2 P.M. Wednesday, 10 P.M. Thursday to 2 P.M. Friday, Saturday and Sunday off, and so on. I thought it was great; especially since most days I was finished with court before lunch and was home by 2 P.M. That meant I had the rest of that day and night off, all the following day and part of the following night until I left my house about 9 P.M. (for you math buffs: thirty-two hour swing between each tour; eighty hour swing on each weekend). Everybody else in the unit worked the same type of chart, but with different days off. If you had any lost time coming to you (and I had plenty), you could put two days together and come up with a mini-vacation.

The bosses were pretty good. They never breathed down your neck out in the street and as long as you brought your two collars in every night, they were happy.

But to me, without a doubt, the things that made PMTF, plainclothes, and midtown Manhattan so exciting were the girls. Most of them, anyhow. I found a lot of them to be funny, clever, and surprisingly beautiful. They came in all shapes and sizes, Black, White, Yellow, and Red. As one guy put it when I brought a beauty in one night: "If I wasn't afraid my tongue might fall off, I'd eat her in a department store window."

In our outfit we were concerned only with street prostitutes, as opposed to "pross" who worked with madams out of plush pads all over town. Before I worked in PMTF, the "pussy posse," I had assumed that all the good-looking hookers were indoors, but with the range of beauties out on the street, I soon realized I was mistaken.

On some nights, especially the weekends, Lexington Avenue, Seventh Avenue, Eighth Avenue, and Broadway, from Fifty-seventh Street to Forty-second Street were overflowing with "girls of the night." But those are only the most active areas. I would venture a guess and say that you could not walk anywhere in midtown in a straight direction on any night for more than fifteen minutes without seeing a prostitute. I'd be willing to bet on it on a Saturday around 1 A.M.

After all the head knocking I had done in the Eight-O, it would follow that I would have been quite at ease locking up ladies of ill repute, but on the contrary I was quite nervous at first. There is something unnerving about a beautiful girl coming up to you and saying: "How would you like it if I sucked you dry?"—no matter who she is.

Most of the time the conversation would go like this:

Her: "Hi, honey. Wanna go out?"
Me: "Sure. What've you got in mind?"
Her: "How about a good old-fashioned fuck?"
Me: "How much?"
Her: "Twenty. Throw in another ten and I'll give you a nice trip around the world. What do you say?"
Me: "Sure."

With that I would take her hand as if I was about to dash off to either a hotel room or her apartment and once assured of a firm grip whisper in her ear: "You're under arrest."

Most of the time there was no trouble, but a few of the girls were locked up so often that the prospect of another night in the can made them bolt. If I was up to it, I'd chase them a block or so, otherwise I'd just let them go. There were plenty more where they came from.

Invariably on the way to the station house we would get some terribly tempting offers to let them go, but we never accepted. I liked to start up a conversation to keep their minds off the fact that they were being arrested and make the night go as peaceably and as quickly as possible. My favorite question was: "What was your most unique trick [customer]?" Not one girl got insulted. They loved to talk about their affairs. A cute redhead told me about a john who flew her to Cleveland one night to go down on a business associate and flew her back to New York the next afternoon. She got seven hundred dollars plus all expenses. One girl, a Black, told me of numerous tricks who paid varying amounts to let them perform cunnilingus on her. All she had to do was lie back and enjoy it. Another spoke of a rich attorney who paid one hundred dollars to have her watch him as he masturbated. She would encourage him with: "Oh I just love this—it really turns me on. Oooh it's so-o-o big." She didn't even have to get her clothes wrinkled. And so the stories went.

After Joe and I had rounded up four girls in the rear of the car, we'd head in to the task force office to process the arrests. That was a sight to behold. With from ten to twenty men working each night, and each with two collars, there was wall-to-wall prostitutes. None of them cared what was hanging out or showing, either. Most of them weren't wearing enough to cover their vital parts in the first place, and rarely anything underneath. In the beginning it was fun but after a while I got used to it. Many of the girls that looked pretty in the street were not so pretty in the light. Occasionally there was a fag or two spread around the room, also. They dress in padded women's clothes, get picked up in the street, get their rocks off with an act of fellatio on the john, and get paid for it. If there is no attempt at sexual intercourse, the john goes away with a smile on his face never knowing about the fag, and the fag departs not only with a smile but a fat wallet.

Prostitution is a misdemeanor in New York State and most of the girls I arrested pleaded guilty, receiving fines of from one to three hundred dollars. Rarely were they sentenced to jail. One girl I arrested had over forty busts in the past three years, but still managed to find her way back to the streets of Manhattan without too much trouble.

If a hooker was fined, she rarely had to wait longer than an hour before her pimp paid it, or waited not at all if she had the money with her. If the latter was the case the pimp reimbursed her. After all she's his bread and butter. (Most pimps are Black, by the way.) It works like this: the girl turns as many tricks as she can each night and then hands all the proceeds to her pimp. Not a part of the proceeds—all. In return he feeds her, clothes her, and puts her up in a nice apartment. She is either happy working with that arrangement or she doesn't work at all. A threat of a severe beating or even death usually persuades the girl to see it his way. They know the threat is not idle. The more girls in a pimp's stable, the more money he makes, of course. To show he's a good sport he takes the whole "family" out for dinner and a night on the town once a year, usually Thanksgiving Day. The profits are enormous as evidenced by the many "pimpmobiles" cruising around Manhattan: big, fancy luxury cars with hood and trunk scoops, green alligator roofs, purple grilles, wide-rimmed, white wall tires (the white walls sometimes made of patent leather), and other such features. Most of them cost well over twenty thousand dollars and are paid for in cash.

As in any phase of police work, locking up prostitutes wasn't without its hazards. One night I was trying to put the cuffs on a Black girl who had just given me a direct. She was resisting arrest vehemently. Out of the clear blue came her pimp who punched me in the mouth in an attempt to free her. Luckily Joe was close by, and when he saw what had happened, he pounced on the Black man. The girl got away, not before biting me first, but the guy didn't. He put up a rough battle all the way into the station house and up into the PMTF office. I handcuffed him to a chair while I went downstairs to retrieve some forms and when I came back he was uncuffed. I was furious. I found out that, of all people, the boss who was working that night, a lieutenant, had taken them off. I recuffed him and stormed into the lieutenant's office with daggers in my eyes. At the top of my lungs I told him he had no God damn right going near my prisoner. He was my responsibility. If he escaped, I'd have to pay the consequences. In the future he was to stay the hell away from my prisoners. And me. I walked out of the office, slamming the door behind me. A short time later I reported sick from the blows, kicks, and bites suffered in making the arrest and went home. The captain in charge of that unit backed me up, saying the lieutenant had been wrong to uncuff my prisoner, and he supposedly bawled him out.

All in all, I liked the public morals task force, but it wasn't enough to change my mind about leaving. On August 1, 1971, I submitted a request for a leave of absence. By Friday, August 27, I had heard no word on it so I called up headquarters to get a report on the progress. I was scheduled to leave on a plane to California on Wednesday, September 1. Nobody in headquarters knew anything about it. Somewhere along the chain of command it had been misplaced. So on August 27 I reported personally to headquarters to fill out the proper forms. By the time I left at the end of the day the only thing remaining before the leave became official was the police commissioner's signature. An inspector from the personnel bureau had said he'd call me as soon as the PC signed it. All day Monday there was no call. Tuesday morning I called him and he said, "You can't rush the boss on something like this." If he didn't sign it by Tuesday at 5 P.M., before he left his office, I would be flying to California the next day AWOL. At 4:58 P.M. I received word that my leave was official.

CHAPTER 18

"... Sir."

"Huh!"

"We'll be landing shortly, sir. Please fasten your seat belt."

"Oh, yes. I'm sorry. I must've been daydreaming." I blushed a little at the mini-skirted stewardess and strapped the belt across my lap.

The captain's southern-accented voice echoed over the intercom. "Good morning, ladies and gentlemen. We've just received clearance from the tower at Kennedy and we'll be on the ground in a few minutes. Please remain seated until the aircraft is completely stopped and the passenger ramp is attached to the terminal. That is an FAA regulation, provided for your safety. It is now 6:22 A.M. Eastern Standard Time, sixty degrees in the city and raining. It's been my pleasure to have you aboard this morning and I hope you all had a pleasant flight. Have a good time in New York, we're looking forward to seeing you again real soon. Thank you for flying American Airlines."

I looked out the window again and stared into the fog overhanging Jamaica Bay and the airport. It suddenly dawned on me that the men in suits who had come to the house looking for me the day I left for California must've been from the Knapp Commission. My wife wrote me saying that they had been carrying attaché cases and had said they were old friends of mine, but that they wouldn't leave their names. One guy was smiling all the time. I wrote back saying that I didn't have any friends like that. They were probably from the department; maybe I forgot to fill out a form when I turned my guns in, I said in a letter. But I'll bet it was two men from the commission. Well, I'll soon find out.

I wonder what they're going to want me to do. Tell them that policemen take money? They've been around for over a year now—I'm sure they know that. Finger some guys? I hope they don't ask me to do that. Oh, what the hell am I getting myself all worked up for? Another couple of hours and I'll know exactly what they want.

But I couldn't stop thinking about it.

The fuckin' Knapp Commission. Man, of all things to get jammed up in, I gotta get involved with the Knapp Commission. I don't think there's a police officer in the city with a good word for it. Their guys are everywhere, poking around, trying to grab some guy with his hand in the till. I'm surprised they haven't bagged anybody yet. Or, maybe they have and I just don't know about it. Christ, the way they insinuate that every cop is on the take, therefore they're all bad, dishonest people. That's just not so. They're God damn good men. Why, to be appointed you have to pass that extensive character background investigation. That's a proof right there that the majority of the men are basically honest. It's just that fuckin' system. That fuckin' tradition. And, besides, just because a guy takes what the people offer doesn't mean he's not a good police officer. It doesn't stop some guys from making three, four, five dollars a month. Or prevent them from getting shot at. Or taking sick or injured people to the hospital. Or ... aw, how can a guy like Whitman Knapp know that? Or that hump Armstrong. They know what it's like to be attorneys—they don't have the foggiest idea of what it's like to be a cop. Why don't they just leave Police Department business to the Police Department?

With a sudden feeling of speed and a screeching of rubber, we had landed. I walked slowly through the passenger terminal, into the baggage area to retrieve my suitcases, then made my way to a nearby coffee shop. I wasn't supposed to meet Armstrong until 8 A.M. After breakfast—toast and coffee—I grabbed a cab for the trip to Manhattan. It had been decided that the commission office was too risky, in that there were police brass walking in and out of the building all day. A few units in the department had their offices on the same floor. I wasn't too anxious to bump into anybody I knew on the job, so we agreed to meet downtown in the Financial District, in Armstrong's law firm office.

In the cab, riding along the VanWyck Expressway, the driver started up a conversation. I tried to cut him short as politely as I could, I just didn't feel like talking, but before he stopped he informed me he was an off-duty patrolman, moonlighting for a couple of extra bucks. I didn't dare tell him that I was on the job. "The Police Department says we're professionals," he said. "Then why don't they pay us professional wages? I gotta come out here and break my balls every day off just to make ends meet. Some professional." I could relate to that. I had hacked a cab part-time before, too, and had said the same thing. When he asked me what I did for a living, I told him I was a student. With the morning rush hour, we arrived at Pine Street at 7:55 P.M. The meter read eleven dollars and I gave him fifteen, telling him to keep it.

The building at 80 Pine Street is a towering skyscraper, one block from the East River, a few blocks from Wall Street. I took the elevator to the seventeenth floor and asked the receptionist for Michael Armstrong. He wasn't in yet. She told me to wait in the coffee hutch, a small room next to his office. Two cups of instant and four shortbread cookies later, he came in.

Mike Armstrong is a former football player for Yale, about six-one, one-ninety, late thirties, with forever tousled brown hair, light, almost blond eyebrows, masculine features, and an expensive wardrobe. He is soft-spoken, yet knowledgeable and convincing, bubbling with charisma.

"Ed?"

"Yes."

"I'm Mike Armstrong," he said, offering me his hand, and I shook it. His clothes were soaked from the rain. "Just let me get this raincoat off and we can grab a cup of coffee and sit in my office."

I poured out two cups for us while he was gone and in a minute when he returned he thanked me, added milk and sugar to his, and led the way to his office. I wasn't impressed; I had expected something much bigger, plusher. He explained quickly that he was only using this temporarily, while his regular office was being redone. The floors were carpeted, a bare wooden desk was positioned near the window to afford a towering view of the streets below, and three or four guest chairs were lined up along the wall.

"Pull up a chair, Ed. How was the flight?"

"Not bad," I said, selecting the only one with a cushion on it. At that moment we were joined by a fair-haired man, with glasses and a turned-up nose.

"This is John Sweeney, Ed," Armstrong said. "He's a federal agent on loan to the commission. He'll be sitting in with us today."

I shook his hand as he pulled up a chair on Armstrong's side of the desk, facing me. There was an embarrassing silence for a few seconds as both of them studied me, then the chief counsel settled back in his chair.

"As I said to you on the phone Wednesday, Ed, I'd like you to work with us. The mere fact that you've traveled back here shows me you've got a good head on your shoulders. Joe Foley said you seemed like a pretty bright guy, and I tend to believe him."

"If I was so smart, I wouldn't have been caught."

"Not necessarily. But that's neither here nor there. The fact remains we've got you. And we've got you pretty good."

"I'm listening."

"We've caught a lot more guys who don't suspect a thing. And they won't know anything until it's too late. But you've got a chance, Ed. You agree to help me and I'll promise to do all I can to help you ... providing I'm convinced you're giving it 100 percent. The more you help us, the more you help yourself."

"What exactly do you want?"

"Well, first I want you to tell me everything you know. I want you to start from the day you were appointed and go right through to the day you left for California. Believe me, when I tell you, Ed, you won't be the first one to talk to us so there will be a lot of incidents and setups that we're familiar with. But we want to hear them anyhow.

Our main objective is to see if there's a widespread pattern of corruption in the department. It's my contention that there is. I don't buy that 'few rotten apples in the barrel' theory. I think it's a deeper, more serious problem." It stuck me that he referred to it as a problem. Even the Police Academy instructors had not considered it that. Hey, maybe I'd misjudged this guy. "And we've got to get to the root of that problem if we ever expect to bring the department back the respect it deserves. Contrary to common belief, Ed, I don't hate cops. My whole life I've been pro-cop. But I think I can make the department a little better by cleaning it up a bit. It's tough to teach an old dog new tricks, so there'll be plenty of men who will never change. But I'm thinking of the rookies who'll be coming on in the future. What of them? Don't you think we can give them a better start right in the beginning by letting them know what's in store for them? Don't forget they're the old-timers of tomorrow. Don't you think this department could use an overhaul? It'll take a long time, but it'll be worth it in the end." He was beginning to make a lot of sense. "Now I don't know what kind of guy you are, Ed. Before today you were just a name on a piece of paper. For all I know you could have been the biggest thief in the department or on the other hand you could be somebody who got caught in the machine, but in either event whatever you have to tell us is important, no matter how insignificant it sounds to you. There's a good chance it will corroborate what we already know but it might very well be something we know nothing about."

"So suppose I tell you everything I know—then what?"

"Then you're going to have to wear a wire. You're going to have to have an incriminating conversation with somebody about a payoff or something, while we record it."

"A conversation with who?"

"First things first. We'll let you know."

"I don't think I can do something like that. That's a real scumbag move."

"You don't have too many good cards in your hand to play, Ed. I know how tough something like that can be, but it's gotta be done. We can't go into the hearings with just hearsay evidence. We've got to have some hard facts and be able to back them up."

"Hearings?"

"Yes, that's the third thing we want you to do. In a month we have our public hearings and we want you to be a witness."

"How public are they?"

"The press, radio, television."

"You've gotta be kidding me. You want me to appear at a public hearing and spill my guts?"

"That's right, Ed."

"And if I refuse?"

"Whatever deals we could have made will be off."

"You really kill me. 'Whatever deals we could have made.' It seems to me this deal is pretty lopsided. I tell you everything I know, I wear a wire for you, and I appear at your public hearings. All you do is say you'll do your best to help me. You offer no guarantee, no nothing."

"I can't guarantee you what the district attorney or the police comissioner is going to do, Ed. I'd only be lying if I said I could. But believe me, we're the best hope you've got right now if you want to stay out of jail."

"Fuck jail. I'm not worrying about jail. I'm thinking about my family. And school. Why the fuck do you think I left this God damn job."

"How would you support your family in jail, Ed?"

I paused for a minute and stared in his eyes. "I see what you mean." I looked at the floor and then out the window through the raindrops. It was a dismal day. I turned back to his face. "Listen. Forget the guarantees. If I do everything you ask, what're my chances for immunity?"

"Good."

"And the department? Would I be able to stay?"

"I don't know. We'll have to cross that bridge when we come to it. Do you want to stay?"

"I don't know."

For the first time Sweeney spoke up. "Are you with us?"

"I guess I don't have much choice."

"You're doing the right thing, Ed. I don't think you'll be

sorry," said Armstrong. "Do me a favor, John, get us all some coffee and ask Chicky to give you another yellow pad for me. This might be a long day."

And it was. I told him the whole story, from beginning to end. I talked in generalities most of the time, without mentioning any names, and the hours seemed like minutes.

When it was time for lunch, Armstrong offered to pay the tab for some sandwiches we had sent out for. I offered a dollar but he insisted on paying. I placed the money in his hand saying simply: "That's how it all starts—the free meal." He understood exactly and took the dollar.

In the middle of the afternoon, with our ties and jackets off and our sleeves rolled up, I was about halfway through when we were joined by two more agents. They were introduced only as Brian and Ralph.

Ralph was about my height, weighing ten or fifteen more pounds, had black wavy hair, and a dark complexion. Brian was on the heavy side. He was clean-cut, with short sideburns, full lips, a double chin, and a perpetual smile. He walked into the room laughing, and when I left him later that day, he was laughing. Everytime I saw him he was either grinning ear to ear, or laughing.

I was shocked to find out that these two men were, so to speak, the whole Knapp Commission investigative team. The policemen in the street had all thought that there were hundreds of agents combing the city, lurking in every doorway. But Brian and Ralph were it right now. A few months earlier there had been more men but they were all gone. Sweeney was relatively new and was helping out on the inside. Ralph was a private attorney and former FBI agent, Brian an undercover man for a federal agency, and together they worked on every lead that came into the office. Soon they would work with me. I found out later that Brian was one of the men with a suit and attaché case who had come looking for me at my house the day I left for California.

We sat in that room, Armstrong, Sweeney, Brian, Ralph, and I, until eight-thirty that night. At that time, after I had told them as much as I could remember, Brian offered to give me a ride home.

My wife still wasn't aware that I was back in New York. I planned on telling her everything that happened, the entire truth. But no one else. Absolute secrecy was imperative for what I was about to do, so I would lie to everyone and tell them I returned because I had not been prepared for the reactions of my family to my being away. People are less apt to delve deeply into someone else's private affairs and I was confident that most would accept that reason without asking too many questions. I hoped the department felt that same way and wouldn't hassle me too much when I asked for my gun and shield back.

When I arrived at my mother-in-law's, needless to say, my wife, my children, my mother-in-law, and my father-in-law were all surprised to see me. During a barrage of hugs and kisses, my wife asked: "What happened, Ed? Is something wrong?"

"No. Nothing's wrong." I'm not good at lying to my wife. "I just decided that I made an impulsive move. I didn't give it enough thought. I should be home here with you and the kids. So I figured I better withdraw and come back now before classes start so I wouldn't lose any money. Let's just chalk the airfare up to experience." Her eyes told me she didn't buy it. Her parents did, though, so we broke out a bottle and toasted a drink to my return. My kids didn't understand anything except their daddy was home and they couldn't have cared less why.

As we sat around the dining room table and compared California's weather to New York's, I kept glancing to my wife. I wanted to take her aside and tell her the truth, but I didn't want to be too obvious. I would have to wait until the time was right. There's not too much privacy for seven people in a five-room apartment. Then when the talk died down a bit she stood up and walked to the closet, returning with her coat.

"Let's go for a walk, Ed," she said, and her mother seconded it, adding that it was a good idea for us to be alone for a little while.

"Sure," I said, seeing an opportunity to let my wife know the real reason for my return. I put my jacket on and we started out for the park a few blocks away. It was drizzling, but the air was uncommonly clean smelling and refreshing. We walked very slowly, arm in arm.

"You're hiding something, Ed. You can't make me

believe you came back because you hadn't given the move enough thought. You gave it over a year's thought. And in two weeks you change your mind? That's not like you. I'm happy you're back and I really don't care why. But I know there's something else." My wife's powers of perception never cease to amaze me.

"Yes. There is something else. Something has happened that's going to affect us for the rest of our lives." I stopped and pulled her close to me. I stared straight in her eyes and my gut ached as I suppressed the tears in my eyes. I would not allow myself to cry in front of my wife. "I told you that one of the reasons I wanted to get off the force was because I was taking money. Well, I was caught taking money and I didn't know it. From who and how much aren't very important. The only thing that matters right now is what I do to make up for it. If I play my cards right, I stand a chance of maybe being able to go back to school someday. If I refuse to cooperate with the people who caught me, I'll probably wind up in jail."

"Who caught you?"

"The Knapp Commission. In a way, I'm lucky it was them. If it were the department, there wouldn't be any second chances."

"What can I do, Ed?"

"For the next few weeks I'll be doing some crazy things. Just bear with me. There's no need for you to know exactly what I'm doing or where I'm going, but one thing you must know. Sometime in the middle of October, at the Knapp Commission public hearings, I'll be telling everyone publicly, on television, that I took money while I was on the job. I'll admit to the world that I was a crooked cop." Again I felt I was about to cry, but savagely resisted.

"Oh, God, Eddie," she said as she hugged me. Passersby looked at us curiously, but we didn't care. "Do you have to?"

"Not really. I don't have to do anything they ask me to do, but I'm beginning to realize more and more that I can be an important key in ridding the department of an ugly sore that has been allowed to grow. Not only will I be helping myself, but I will be helping the department. If, in some small way, I can contribute my services to break the system of corruption and make being a police officer the kind of position I had thought it to be when I was growing up, I'm going to do it. I'm going to do what I have to to end the God damn tradition. It's too late to do anything about its ruining me, but it's not too late for the rookies of the future. I'm afraid there won't be too many people who will understand, though, honey, and we're going to lose most, if not all, our friends."

"Whatever you think is best, Ed. I'm with you all the way." She was whimpering now. She was hurt and afraid, but filled with strength and courage.

I kissed her. Her eyes were red and her cheeks were wet, not from the rain.

A feather in my throat made me cough and my eyes filled unexpectedly as I said what I had so often left unsaid: "I love you, Joanne."

We walked back to the house and I explained that the first thing I must try to do was to get back on the job.

I started making phone calls and filling out forms the next day. Aside from the usual red tape, I had comparatively few problems and on October 1 I was reinstated to the Police Department, reassigned to the public morals task force. Only now I was a double agent.

CHAPTER 19

Wearing a wire for the Knapp Commission made me feel terribly low, almost half a man, but I kept telling myself it was absolutely necessary for my good, my family's good, and the department's good. I also rationalized to myself that had the person whom I went after been in my shoes he would have gone after me the same way. But no matter what excuses I thought up, nothing made me feel anything but miserable about doing it. Thank God there were only two occasions.

My first target for recorded conversation was an officer named Bud Hunt who I had worked with in the Eight-O before he was transferred to another precinct. During my talks with Mike Armstrong and company, they were easily able to discern the fact that I didn't like this man. We never got along and we avoided each other as much as possible. Still, we were on speaking terms and after his transfer I ran into him at a few social functions where we chewed the fat without incident. It was obvious my heart wasn't in trying to set someone up, especially someone I liked, so to make things as easy as possible it was decided I would go after him.

The arrangement was for me to "happen by" his new command while he was working and engage him in an incriminating conversation about gamblers. The reason I was in the neighborhood, I would say, was because I was trying to set up some protection for a bookie who was interested in "action" in the area. In return I would receive one thousand dollars. I was to offer part of this money to Hunt if he could help me out.

At the last minute, however, because of my experience in the public morals task force, it was thought that a story of a madam looking to locate a brothel in the neighborhood would go over better, so it was changed. There was a particularly interesting result.

On the sunny afternoon of the setup I met with Brian and Ralph and we rode to the outskirts of Hunt's precinct, about fifteen to twenty miles away from the Eight-O. We parked on a deserted street and Brian and I remained inside while Ralph retrieved an attaché case from the trunk. When he brought it into the car and opened it up, I almost couldn't believe my eyes. I had imagined the transmitting equipment would be minuscule, sophisticated devices. On the contrary, what Ralph had in his case was enormous in comparison. It consisted of a dirty white girdle belt, about six inches wide, equipped with inside pouches in which you placed a battery pack, about the same size and shape as a carton of cigarettes, and a transmitting device, a little bit bigger than a paperbound book with five hundred pages. In addition there were sets of antenna wire and microphone wire that had to be taped to my body to insure a strong signal. Brian and Ralph would sit in the car within eyesight—just in case anything went wrong—and record the conversation.

"You've gotta be kidding," I said.

"What's wrong?" Brian was laughing.

"What's wrong? He'll fuckin' shoot me before he gets close to me with the bulges I'll have from that getup."

Brian was laughing uncontrollably now. I didn't think it was too funny. Ralph spoke. "You haven't got it on yet. Don't worry, he'll never notice it. We've used this personally a hundred times."

"You're lucky you're alive."

"Give it a chance. Try it on."

Brian pulled himself together long enough to help me stretch it around my waist, and with my pants half off, I hopped out of the front seat onto the sidewalk to slip in the battery pack and transmitter. I pulled my pants up and found it impossible to fasten them properly. Brian started laughing again.

"You'll have to pull it up higher," said Ralph. "Wear it inside your shirt, above your pants."

I pulled it higher and was able to zip my pants. I stuffed my shirt in and puffed it out a bit to try to conceal the bulges. The sun was too hot to wear a jacket without looking conspicuous. "How does it look?"

"Not bad. Walk a few feet and come back." I did and Ralph shook his head. "You can't even notice it. It probably feels funny to you 'cause you're conscious of it, but you can't even notice it."

"How about these?" I asked, pulling two long gray wires from inside my shirt. On the end of one was a small, clip-on microphone and on the other nothing. Brian got out of the car with a role of Scotch tape and told me to open my shirt. While he was taping the empty-ended antenna wire to my chest, an old woman walking her dog came down the street unobserved. I tried to cover up my bare chest so she wouldn't see the equipment and Brian fell back on the hood of the car laughing like a hyena. She looked at us with crossed eyes and kept walking. She probably thought we were perverts. With the microphone clipped to the front of my pants, behind my belt, I was all set. I took a walk halfway down the block with Brian so Ralph could see if everything was working properly. He signaled us to come back and we were off.

They both kept giving me last-minute advice on what to do and what not to do, but I was too nervous to hear anything. As I left the car a block from the station house Ralph said: "You can't even notice it. Don't worry."

My watch had stopped, but I knew it was around four o'clock. I was hoping to catch Hunt before he turned out for a four to twelve. There was a patrolman standing right by the front door, so I walked up to him and flashed my shield.

"Hi, I'm on the job. Is Bud Hunt around?"

"Just a second, I'll see if he's inside." It didn't appear that he had noticed any bulges. In a minute he returned.

"He's already out in a car, but I gave him a 10-2. He'll be in in a minute."

"Thanks." I stood on the front steps just looking around and the other patrolman walked inside again. A man came out of the station house with work clothes on and walked over to a power lawn mower sitting in the patch of grass that surrounded the building. Don't tell me he's going to start this thing up and cut the grass now. Sure enough. It was inordinately noisy.

I walked inside and after showing my shield to the desk officer I asked him if I could take a leak. He pointed out the bathroom in the rear. It wasn't until I got in there that I realized the contraption I was wearing could only transmit; I couldn't receive anything. I had wanted to know if Brian and Ralph could hear me talking outside over the lawn mower. I was alone in the bathroom so while I urinated I said in a tone loud enough to be picked up on the mike: "Nothing I can do about that lawn mower. I'll try to move as far away from it as I can." I finished up, left the bathroom, thanked the desk officer as I passed him, and went outside to the front steps.

Pulling up in his radio car, with another man driving, was Bud Hunt. He exited and walked toward me. I was waiting for his eyes to dart to my waist, but they didn't. My knees started shaking. I tried to act as cool as possible. Over Hunt's shoulder I could see Brian and Ralph passing by, glancing over nonchalantly. I hoped they could hear me. The man with the lawn mower was around back.

"Ed Droge. What the fuck are you doing here?"

"How ya doin', Bud. Long time no see."

"Yeah. What brings you into this neck of the woods?"

"Listen. Can we get away from the front door here? It's kinda important."

"Sure." With that he walked to the side of the station house and I followed. The mower was still blaring away. "What's on your mind?" he said, taking up a spot by a high wire fence.

"I wanted to ask you to do me a favor."

"Yeah."

"I guess you know I've been over in the 3rd division task force."

"Yeah, you lucky stiff."

"Well, I've got a deal brewin'. I'm trying to set up some protection for a madam."

Right away he took a wary attitude. "Hey, whatever you do, don't get involved with them women, Ed. Something goes wrong and they turn on you like that," he said, snapping his fingers.

"Yeah, but I got a good deal going."

"I don't care what kind of deal you've got. I'm telling you that's bad business." I had positioned my back to the fence to give him less of a chance to put his hands on me as soon as I remembered Bud Hunt is the type of guy that has a habit of touching you when he talks to you. He's always using his hands to emphasize things. "I wish it was something I could help you with, Ed." Like gamblers, I wondered? Too late to change stories now.

I could tell he wasn't going to bite and I figured right then and there that he had something against making deals with women.

As we both walked toward the front of the building, he came perilously close. I was thinking of giving it one more try, but my heart pounded heavily as he put his arm around my shoulder. I couldn't pull away without tipping my hand. He was saying something about the guys from the Eight-O I think, but I couldn't concentrate on anything but his hand. As we reached the front of the building, he slid his hand down the small of my back and his eyes opened wide. My knees trembled terribly and sweat poured from my brow. I'm sure he could hear my heart thumping. He didn't say anything for a second; he just stared at me. Then as he turned and walked quickly to the radio car he said: "Take it easy, Ed."

That was it. Did he feel it? I'm sure he must have ... almost sure. I wasn't about to stick around to find out so I just said, "So long, Bud," and walked away. A couple of blocks away Brian and Ralph picked me up.

"You're as white as a ghost," Ralph said.

"He touched the equipment."

"Naw," said Brian, "he would have said something."

"He didn't have to. I could see it in his eyes."

"Really?" said Ralph.

"Fuck this. I'm not doing this shit anymore. I must've lost five years off my life back there."

Brian started laughing.

Ralph was serious. "Well, at least you tried. But you didn't mention anything about the money. You shoulda hit him with the one thousand dollars."

"I couldn't think of anything but getting out of there as fast as I could."

Brian cut in. "We should have went after him with the gambler story."

Ralph pulled the car to the side of a deserted road and we listened to the last part of the tape. The mower notwithstanding it was pretty clear. Brian clumsily climbed into the back seat.

"We don't have him on anything here," Brian said. "Unless he doesn't report it. Even then it's only departmental charges." (As of this writing his actions are still being investigated.)

"Let's go," I said.

"Wait a minute," said Brian with a big grin. "Listen to this." He pushed the "rewind" button on the recorder and in a second hit the "stop." Then "play." It was the conversation between me and the patrolman in the front of the station house. We listened for a few minutes until the part came where I went into the bathroom to relieve myself. Brian burst out laughing as the distinct sound of my urine flowing into the bowl played loud and clear. He was holding his stomach in pain as he managed to belt out: "That's the best part." He laughed all the way home.

When I got out of the car in front of my house, I turned to him. "Well, I'm glad I brightened up your day," I said and slammed the door.

Even though Hunt never spread the word that I had tried to set him up, which probably meant he hadn't felt the equipment, I hoped the commission wouldn't want me to wear a wire again. But they did.

Apparently I wasn't the only one who had heard bad rumors about Dave Greenberg and Bob Hantz, Batman and Robin, the pair I had met in the Criminal Investigation Course. When Mike Armstrong asked me if I knew them and I told him yes, as casual acquaintances in the academy plainclothes school, he was pleased. So, too, were Brian and Ralph when they found out. No one would tell me what they knew about the duo that I didn't know, but it resulted in their being chosen my next target.

"Hello."

"Bob?"

"Yeah. Who's this?"

"Ed Droge."

"Ed who?"

"Ed Droge from the CIC course. From the Eight-O."

"Oh, yeah. How are you, Ed? I haven't seen you since the course. I heard you went to the posse, you hump. How do you like it over there?"

"It's pretty good."

"Well, what's on your mind?"

"I'd like to talk to you, but not while you're on the station house phone. I don't trust it. Can you call me back."

"Sure. I'm just getting off. I'll call you about six. I oughta be home by then."

"Great." I gave him my number and waited patiently by the phone, rehearsing my story and checking out my recording equipment. I knew what squad he was in. I had called him at 4 P.M. because I knew he'd be signing out by the switchboard. The bit about the station house phone was merely a ploy.

At six o'clock the phone rang and it was Bob.

"Are you home?" I asked.

"No. I stopped off at a little restaurant for something to eat. This is a pay phone. It's safe."

"Good. Listen, I've got a deal going that you might be interested in. If not, fine. Just tell me when to stop and we'll hang up good friends. OK?"

"Sure. Go ahead."

"Well, when I was in the Eight-O, I had a contract with this guy for a little while."

"What was he into?"

"Narcotics."

"Go ahead."

"I ran into him down in court yesterday and he tells me his spot in the Eight-O is too hot, he's gonna move. It winds up he's picked a place in your precinct and he wants me to help him get some protection. Are you interested?"

"Uniform protection?"

"Yeah, the sector. A monthly contract for the eight guys. In return, me and you get five hundred off the top."

"Sounds good. When can I meet him?"

"How about tomorrow night?"

"Great. Where?"

"I'll call you at the precinct at four again. I'll tell you where then."

"Good enough. Talk to you tomorrow." He hung up.

I quickly called Mike Armstrong and Brian and told them what had happened. I played the tape for them over the phone. They were thrilled. Brian said he'd call me in the morning.

When Brian called, he told me to meet him, Ralph, and another commission member named Julius at 1 P.M. at Sixty-fifth Street and Eighth Avenue, Brooklyn, a few blocks from my home. On three of the corners at that intersection are gas stations. On the other is a ball field; that was the corner I was to meet them. I arrived early and waited about twenty minutes before they came. I piled into the back seat of Brian's car next to Julius and was introduced.

Julius is also an attorney. In his mid-forties with olive skin, gray-streaked hair, three expensive-looking rings, and a well-cut, pinstriped suit, he has the air of a Mafia chieftain—until he opens his mouth.

They couldn't get a Negro on such short notice, so Julius was supposed to be "my man" for the meeting, and he had even brought an Italian stogie for the occasion. But it was too easy to tell he knew little about narcotics and I was certain Hantz would pick it up. Aside from that, whenever he cursed he sounded like he had never uttered a four-letter word before. He said "Furk you," instead of "Fuck you." And in a trial run at what he was to say at the meeting he said in an Edward G. Robinson voice: "Listen you furkin' mug, I want you to furkin' keep your furkin' part of the furkin' bargain, yeah." He was trying too hard. Even I had to laugh along with Brian. He just didn't fit. So, I was to go it alone.

At 4 P.M., while the three waited outside, I went into my house and called Bob.

"He can't make it," I said, "but I'll meet you anyhow and we can talk everything over."

"OK, good. I hope he gave you some money, man. I'm hurtin'." That sounded a little bit too carefree. Bob wasn't the type of guy to say something that obvious over the phone.

"Yeah ... we'll talk about that later."

"Where do you want to meet?"

"There's a little luncheonette on Eighty-sixth Street between Fourth and Fifth avenues out here in Bay Ridge. Do you know where I mean?"

"I don't know the place but I'll find it."

"I'll meet you there about seven o'clock."

"OK. Hey, how about if I bring Dave along? We're partners in everything, you know."

"Sure."

"Good. See you at seven. And don't forget the money."

When he hung up, I had a strange feeling he was on to me. I brought the cassette tape and my portable recorder mainly because it was in my neighborhood. Julius, Brian, Ralph, and Julius to get their opinions. Brian just laughed, Ralph said he didn't think so, and Julius said: "Not a furkin' chance." I dismissed it as my imagination.

We rode to the restaurant to get a good look at the layout. I had picked the spot off the top of my head, mainly because it was in my neighborhood. Julius, Brian, and I went in for a cup of coffee and Ralph called the office from a pay phone in the street. As you walk in the front door of the luncheonette there are booths, about ten in all, lined up the length of the left-side wall. On the right side there's a counter in the front and a kitchen in the rear. I figured if I were there before they were that evening, I could sit at a booth in the rear, on the outside of the seat, so that both of them would sit together opposite me. That would present less of a risk of their accidentally touching the equipment.

When we were together again in the car, Ralph said that there was no sense in Julius hanging around, so he took off for the commission office.

Brian, Ralph, and I rode around Bay Ridge for an hour or so, shooting the breeze and trying to get our strategy straight for the meeting. Brian and Ralph would both stay outside the luncheonette. They gave me two hundred dollars, federally vouchered money, and when I handed it to Hantz and Greenberg I was to plainly say: "Here's the two hundred dollars." If anything went wrong I was simply to call their names and they'd come running.

At six-thirty I wired up with considerably less hassle near a park a few blocks from the luncheonette. It was breezy so I was able to wear a light jacket to cover up any bulges from the equipment.

At six-fifty I entered the restaurant. The first thing I noticed was a man at the counter to the right and two immediately to my left in a booth, all of whom looked like police officers. I don't know exactly why, but it's relatively easy for one policeman to spot another. There's just something about the way a man looks, or carries himself.

A waving hand in a rear booth distracted my thoughts. It was Dave Greenberg. Shit. They were here already and sitting across from each other at the table. I'd have to sit next to one of them. I hoped I picked the one that wasn't too frisky with his hands. I felt my nervous syndrome coming on, but forced a smile and walked to the back. I wished I wasn't there.

We said our hellos and I sat next to Dave Greenberg, facing Hantz, the man at the counter, and the front of the restaurant. A waitress came over immediately and we all ordered hamburgers, french fries, and Cokes. When she walked away, Bob asked me how I liked working in PMTF and for the next ten minutes we discussed plainclothes duty in Manhattan and speculated on why they hadn't been called yet. Probably just didn't get to them on the list yet, we concluded. Dave kept looking me over: glancing at my arms, then to my lap. I was sure he was looking to see if I was wired. When he put his arm up behind me, resting it on the booth, my stomach drew tense. Was it so obvious? Were the bulges that noticeable? Were the wires sticking out? In a second, though, he withdrew his arm from behind me and placed both elbows on the table.

I was about to bring up the deal and the money when a handsome man with white hair, dressed in a green suit, approached the table. He bent down toward us and in a whisper said: "Terminate the meeting. We're all working on the same side." He turned and tapped the man I had pinned as a cop at the counter and walked toward the front of the luncheonette. On the way out he signaled to the two other men in the booth and they followed.

We all stared at each other for a second, then Bob said: "I don't believe this. Are you wired?" I nodded.

"You, too?" I asked. They both nodded.

It was embarrassing. Hantz and Greenberg had turned me in—as they were supposed to—but I had no excuse. I was shocked at their unconcern. Obviously they blamed the whole thing on a typical Police Department mix-up. The man with the white hair, they told me, was a sergeant from the internal affairs division.

"Who you working with?" Bob asked. "PMAD?"

"Yes." I lied because I figured it would look better for me if I was working for a unit within the department, like the public morals administrative division, which sometimes handled complaints of crooked cops. Anything but the Knapp Commission.

"Wow," said Dave Greenberg.

There was another pause, then Bob broke the silence again. "To tell you the truth, I'm kinda glad it worked out this way. My heart wasn't really in this."

Mine was in my mouth.

"Friends?" Dave said, offering me his hand.

"You bet." I was eager to be friends. I shook his, then Bob's, just as our hamburgers arrived. We ate rather silently and I blushed a few times, but by the time we finished I didn't feel half as bad as when we had begun. I paid the check with the commission's money and we walked outside. Two men from the internal affairs division met them and hustled them away, but not before we all shook hands again and exchanged a few pleasantries. Brian and Ralph appeared from nowhere and Brian related the story. He had walked past the luncheonette to look in the window and on his way back to the car he spotted a sergeant from IAD with whom he had worked a case on the weekend prior. On some cases the commission and the department worked hand in hand, he said. As usual Brian was laughing. He and the sergeant said hello and almost simultaneously they asked each other why they were in the neighborhood. It didn't take long to figure out. Thus the termination. Brian remarked that the department had dispatched between ten and fifteen men to the area. "... as compared to only two from the Commission," he beamed.

"Three," I said.

Everyone piled into cars and headed for the internal

affairs division, a maze of offices on Poplar Street in the
Brooklyn Heights section of Brooklyn. When I arrived
people were running all over the place. Mike Armstrong
was there, Chief Sidney Cooper, the head of the division,
was there, Batman and Robin were there, dozens of bosses
ranging from sergeant to inspector were there, and of
course Brian, Ralph, and I were there. After hours of explanations and formal interviews, everything was straightened out. But my cover was blown. At least I wouldn't have
to wear a wire again.

For the third time that night, I shook hands with Hantz
and Greenberg before they left. And before I left, I saw a
good friend of mine, Ben Bronson, the new PBA delegate
for Brooklyn North, whose friendship I had valued dearly
in the Eight-O. He didn't say anything; he just shook his
head in disgust at me from the end of a long corridor.
When I walked toward him, he turned quickly out the
door. With him went many friendships, for his first stop
was the Eight-O. By the next afternoon, almost every man
I knew on the job was aware of what I had done. Only
one close friend, Bill Marso, called to see if there was any
truth to the rumor. I told him that it was unfortunately
true, but that I was not at liberty to tell the whole story
yet. It wouldn't be long, though, I said, before everyone
would know. We hung up friends—for the last time. I was
disappointed that Ray Manetta didn't call, but I didn't
blame him.

There were two theories about Bob Hantz and Dave
Greenberg. One was that they were indeed bad apples, but
had been waiting for a setup of this nature. The second
was that they were truly honest, upstanding patrolmen. I
believe the latter. Apparently, so did the police commissioner, for a few months later he made them detectives. I
was tempted to send them a telegram of congratulations,
but didn't want to take a chance on my sincerity being
misconstrued.

The unveiling of my involvement with the Knapp
Commission was followed by my temporary assignment to
the internal affairs division the next day, October 6, 1971.

CHAPTER 20

Having been assigned to the internal affairs division, I reported to the Poplar Street office every day for over two weeks. With typewriters constantly clicking, phones constantly ringing, tape recorders constantly whirring, and people constantly hustling about, it's a busy place. It was extremely monotonous for me, however, sitting on a bench in the waiting room, alone all day, reading the same newspaper three times. And that was only for two weeks; I would soon realize that this lesson in monotony was a brief interlude.

The only breaks came when I was given the third degree twice: once by IAD and once by the district attorney's office. Naturally, representatives from those two quarters were eager to hear what I had to say.

The Knapp Commission public hearings opened Monday, October 18, at the Bar Association Building on West Forty-fourth Street in Manhattan. They were carried live on television in the New York area and I was able to secure a seat in front of the only TV in the IAD office. One man from that command was assigned to watch and take notes, though at one time or other everybody on the floor paused for a moment, watching Mike Armstrong tease the public with films of a payoff to a patrolman in the New York City Police Department, identified only as a Mr. P. The exchange of money took place on a street in mid-Manhattan, a payment to protect a madam and her "house" from exposure and arrest, and was filmed from an office building nearby. The agent for the madam was in reality a myopic mercenary, recruited by the Knapp Commission.

It was made clear to the public that some policemen would testify during the hearings, the first the next day, but their identities were not revealed. However, no one was quite prepared for the shock of the first witness, Patrolman William Phillips, a fourteen-year veteran of the force and the previous day's mysterious Mr. P. His statement, "Every plainclothesman in the city is on the pad," shocked not only the public, but also the thirty-two thousand members of the department. The fact came as no surprise to most police officers—they knew—rather they were surprised at the spotlighted revelation by another police officer, a break in the code of silence, the strength of which had been heretofore likened to that of the Sicilian *omertà*. He admitted to having participated in venal arrangements throughout the city, asserting he was typical of the department, and went on to detail payoffs from gamblers that he and other policemen, bosses included, had contracted and accepted while he was secretly working with the Knapp Commission. Taped conversations between him and some of those other police officers were played intermittently as the vile story of decay in the ranks began to unfold. The momentary stops in front of the IAD television to catch what was going on now became long, silent vigils as the men tried to take in what was going on—the apparently complete sellout of this "brother in blue." I sat silently, knowing that Friday it would be me on the screen, telling my story.

I knew that my wife, my parents, my brother, my two sisters, and my in-laws were watching, too. It was difficult telling them the truth, but I had to prepare them for my appearance. My mother and father were especially affected. It pained them deeply to hear what I had to say, but I felt it was my place to tell them personally what I had done in the past. It wasn't easy telling them I had taken money. My father was always boasting to neighbors, relatives, and friends about how proud he was to be the father of an honest cop. And my mother had been so happy when I told her of my plans to be a lawyer. She had always wanted me to be a lawyer and was disappointed when I chose to be a police officer. She had been afraid for me constantly since I was assigned to such a rough precinct. She was heartbroken when I told her that what I had done would probably prevent me from staying a police officer or ever becoming an attorney. Though disappointed, they didn't hesitate an instant in offering me whatever help they could.

It seemed the majority of the news outlets in New York had prejudged the outcome and were content to allocate little, if any, time to hearings, which were expected to be typical of many investigations into police corruption. So at first the hearings received relatively little coverage. When Patrolman Phillips testified on Tuesday morning he sat at a table adorned with few microphones. However, as the day wore on and his testimony revealed a fantastic graft system in the department, substantiated with films and tapes, every TV and radio station in New York and surrounding states dispatched men to the scene until, at day's end, the table was covered with broadcasting equipment. From then on not only were the proceedings carried live each day, but they were also recapped on the six and eleven o'clock network news and rerun in entirety every evening on the local PBS channel. Each day the size of the gallery of curious citizens, police brass, reporters, and newscasters grew considerably, until Thursday, and every day thereafter, the main room of the Bar Association was crammed—standing room only—with onlookers.

Patrolman Phillips was labeled a bad apple in the barrel, a rogue cop, atypical of the department, by the PC, the press, radio, and TV broadcasters and, of course, the Patrolman's Benevolent Association. With every new day and every new revelation the Knapp Commission was ridiculed as a circus and Phillips branded an outright thief and liar. He was only one man, skeptics said. They claimed the stories he related concerning and implicating other police officers were outrageous; corruption was not widespread in the New York City Police Department.

Then on Friday afternoon, October 22, it was my turn to testify.

"Where are you supposed to meet him?" my father asked as he pulled to the curb across the street from the Bar Association Building. He was referring to a commission agent named Warren, who had told me to meet him outside so I wouldn't have any trouble getting into the building or finding the room to which I was to report.

"Right here. I'm a little early, though. I sure hope nobody I know happens by."

At that precise time a uniformed patrolman appeared by the curb door and motioned at my father to move his car. Thank God I didn't know him. The sign read: "No Standing Anytime." I reached for my shield as my father opened the window.

"I'm on the job, officer," I said. "We'll only be a few minutes and we won't leave the car unattended. Is that all right?"

"Sure," he said and he walked on, a courtesy from one police officer to another.

It would be the last time I could ever expect that courtesy. In a few hours if I asked a patrolman that same question, the answer would certainly be negative, to say the least.

"Listen, Ed. Are you sure you don't want me to come in?"

"No, pop. Thanks a lot, anyhow. Joanne wanted to come, too, but I told her no. I know how you both want to be with me when I'm in trouble, but this is something I've just got to do on my own."

About fifteen minutes passed and I grew increasingly nervous, thinking about what I was about to do. Presently I noticed the agent approaching.

"There he is," I said, opening the door. "Here goes."

The pain in my father's face was obvious. He was always so proud of me, no matter what I did: in schoolwork, playing baseball or football, umpiring in the Little League, and as a police officer. But today I was offering him little for which to be proud. He knew it took a lot of courage for what I was about to do, but he didn't think it was the right thing. I had failed to make him understand. But no matter how he felt, he would never stand in my way while I did something that *I* thought was right. We shook hands.

"Good luck, son."

"Thanks, pop."

Warren saw me as I exited the car and motioned me to

follow him into a coffee shop. After getting two containers to go, we walked toward the Bar Building.

"All ready?" he asked.

"As I'll ever be."

There was an official standing at the front door and he immediately recognized Warren. I passed unquestioned as the agent signaled that I was with him. Dozens of men, some of whom I recognized as TV newscasters, were milling about, smoking and conversing in the ground floor lobby. I walked through the middle of them and up the stairs to the right, virtually unobserved. No one knew who I was or what I was about to do. On the second floor we turned right and walked down a stately corridor toward what I later found out was the hearing room. About ten feet shy of it we turned left into a narrow, winding corridor that led us to a side office, adjoining the hearing room. Mike Armstrong was there along with Whitman Knapp and the other commission members.

"Hi, Ed. How do you feel?" asked Mike, offering me a hand for a shake.

"Nervous. Very nervous."

"Don't worry. Just relax. Once you're out there, you'll forget all about the cameras and the microphones."

"Listen, Mike. I want you to tell Brian not to sit behind you. I was watching him on television when Phillips was testifying and he was smiling all the time. This isn't a funny matter, Mike. And I don't want to risk giving anyone the impression that I'm anything but dead serious."

"Sure, Ed. I'll tell him."

In a few minutes everyone but me entered the adjoining room and the fifth day of the Knapp Commission public hearings had begun. I was scheduled to go on after a short break, an hour or so into the session. Ralph was to testify ahead of me, relating his experiences and findings as a commission agent.

As I sat waiting I grew extremely nervous. My hands trembled and I had butterflies in my stomach. When I got up occasionally, I stood on wobbly knees. There was too much time to think about what I was about to do. I hoped and hoped that some men in the department would understand, but I came to the conclusion that it would be too much to expect. I contemplated my own likely reactions to someone testifying openly had I not been involved with the commission. I knew no policeman would think I was doing the right thing. I resigned myself to that fact.

Finally the door to the hearing room opened and Mike Armstrong walked through, followed by Ralph, a few agents, and a couple of bosses from the internal affairs division.

"OK, Ed. You're next. Still nervous?" Mike said.

"A little," I lied.

"Try to relax."

"That's easy for you to say. You're asking the questions. I'm answering them."

"I know it's hard, Ed."

"I wonder," I said. "I really wonder." With that he turned and walked back toward the hearing room door, everyone following him back inside except Ralph. He put his arm around me and led me over to the door.

"Good luck, Ed," he said.

"Thanks, Ralph." I stood at the entrance to the hearing room as order was restored inside and Ralph entered, staying in sight so he could signal me when I was called. I realized then that I wasn't only nervous, I was scared. This was the most important step in my life. I prayed I wouldn't regret it.

I kept thinking how much I had wanted to get away from the gamblers and the bribes and the system and the tradition and the narcotics and the pushers and the junkies and the depravity and the dirt and the crime and the ghetto; how much I wanted to go to school, study hard, get my law degree, find a new career, be somebody respectable, an attorney, a good attorney, one of the best attorneys in the country. I realized that in just a few moments when I told the world what I had done as a police officer, I would forfeit my chances at those ideals.

When my name was called, I walked mechanically toward Ralph. The people in the overpacked room buzzed and the cameras whirred. Because the doors were kept closed to keep out the overflow of the crowd, it was hot and sticky. My palms were sweaty; as was my brow. The room smelled like a gymnasium. Just as I reached Ralph a dozen flashbulbs popped and a row of floodlights blinded me, adding also to the intense heat. I couldn't see where I was going. I just walked toward the lights until I saw Mike Armstrong sitting at a table. Opposite him was the table where I was to sit, every inch covered with microphones. Above us sat Whitman Knapp and the other commission members, most notably Cyrus Vance, the former assistant to the United States Secretary of State and former representative to the Paris peace talks. I was sworn in by the commission chairman and sat down. I rested my elbows on the arms of the chair and grasped my left hand with my right in front of me. It was the only way to keep them from shaking. The camera bulbs kept popping and at least two dozen pictures were snapped in a thirty-second span while Mike Armstrong readied his notes. After clearing the photographers and reporters from between him and me, he glanced up.

"Will you give your name to the recorder, please."

My mouth and throat went dry and my first attempt to speak was thwarted by a high, cracking voice, noticeably quivering in anticipation. I cleared my throat. "Edward F. Droge, Jr."

"And what is your occupation?"

"I'm a patrolman in the New York City Police Department." The crowd hummed.

"Are you married, Officer Droge?"

"Yes, sir, I am."

"Do you have any children?"

"Yes, sir, three."

After a quick rundown on my past commands, my activity, my concentration in narcotics, and my eleven departmental recognitions in a question/answer format—Armstrong asking me questions he had asked me many times in the past month—I was led in detail through all my corrupt experiences in the department. It started when he said: "Officer Droge, I'd like you to go back to the beginning of your career." It wasn't over for another two and one-half hours.

During that time, my voice remained steady and people told me later that I appeared calm, but I couldn't stop shaking. At one point I reached for a glass of water on the table, but when I picked it up, my unsteady hand was so obvious that I set it right down without taking a drink.

My heart wasn't in it, but I settled down after a while

and relaxed as best I could. I mentioned no one by name. I told of my experiences in corruption to the best of my recollection. I talked of the drunken driver in the Nine-O, the free meals, and the factories. I spoke of the Cavallero brothers, Vito the runner, Jimmy "the Screw," Tony Passera, Tommy "Bones" Zekia, the Ziganette game, the dice game, the poker game, the tow truck money, the "after hours" clubs, the "juice joints," check cashers, supermarkets, city marshals, "scores" from lawyers, the night I "flaked" Nate, and the deal I had with Lou Daniels not to show up in court, which was witnessed by the commission.

"Following that you carried out your plans to attend college in California?"

"Yes, sir, I did."

"And your family was here."

"That's correct."

"And you planned on going out there, start your education, and join them when you could."

"Yes, sir."

"Then on September 15 you were contacted by telephone by us ... and you agreed to come back."

"That's correct."

During a long pause in which Mike Armstrong seemed to be gathering his thoughts, I took a deep breath. Then he continued.

"Officer Droge, do you realize now what you stand to lose for doing what you've admitted to today?"

My gut ached and again my throat grew dry. I thought of my wife. My children. My parents. For the third time in less than a month I was on the verge of tears. "Yes, I do, sir."

Another long pause and very seriously through a silence so thick you could cut it with a knife, Mike Armstrong stared into my eyes and said: "Do you think it was worth it?"

I lowered my head, looking into my lap, and suppressed an involuntary urge to break down. My eyes welled with tears as I raised my head and stared back. Solemnly I answered, "No way in the world."

"I have no further questions."

I was hustled by police brass and commission personnel

into an office adjoining the hearing room. Reporters flocked to the door asking for interviews, but I refused. I had done enough talking for one day. I was patted on the back and congratulated by everyone except those with badges in their pockets. Whitman Knapp, Mike Armstrong, and the other commission members shook my hand and commended me on a fine deed. I didn't know what to think. On the other hand I had betrayed my fellow officers by openly revealing the corruption on the job, dealing a severe blow to their already waning morale and exposing them to ridicule and abuse. But on the other hand I had done a great service for the department in the long run by letting people know there was a problem and perhaps igniting a spark to rid the force of corruption.

The degree to which the department expected favorable reactions, especially from members of the force, was evidenced by the fact that two sergeants were assigned to guard me twenty-four hours a day (and the detail was to last four months). Thankfully, their services were never needed for I received no serious threats to my life though I lived in fear for many weeks, wondering what was around every corner, wary of everyone I passed. Some of the sergeants on the detail obviously resented their assignment and made no bones about letting me know. In a way I couldn't blame them, but at the same time I made no bones about letting them know they weren't to treat me as a prisoner or a criminal. Most of them were quiet when they were with me, speaking only when spoken to, but there were a few who understood my predicament, even if they didn't agree that I had done the right thing. I didn't mind discussing my actions with them, for often it was my only conversation with someone outside of my family the entire day.

My testimony corroborated most of the basic information divulged by Patrolman Phillips, who, incidentally, I had never met. I didn't lie; and no one accused me of lying. I didn't tell anybody anything that they hadn't already known or suspected; but I did own up to things in public that no police officer before in the history of the United States had ever admitted. No one called me a rogue cop. On the contrary, because of my arrest record and eleven departmental recognitions I was hailed a "hero cop," who had fallen in with the wrong company. As nice as that title is, I must say that I was no more a hero than thousands of other men who were loyal to their work on a very dangerous job. But I had served to stem the tide of bad ink against the commission and made people stop to think that maybe there was a serious problem of corruption on the force.

For a week or so after my appearance at the hearings I stayed home as the department, more specifically the internal affairs division, prepared for an extensive investigation regarding my testimony. I watched the rest of the hearings on television as a former police officer added further corroboration to the previous testimony and numerous other witnesses, a tow truck driver, a known gambler, representatives of the hotel and construction industries, and Knapp investigators related evidence of corruption on the job. A detective, Frank Serpico, and a sergeant, David Durk, related their stories on how they approached City Hall with information concerning corruption, but were given the runaround. Many city officials and higher-ups in the department also appeared and refuted their allegations. It was the printing in the New York *Times* of Serpico's and Durk's claims of widespread corruption on the job that prompted the mayor to organize the commission in the first place.

Again, at home, I was faced with the monotony of nothing to do. I had no friends. There was no place to go, no one to go with and, aside from my wife and family, no one even to talk to.

I was then called into IAD every day where I was interrogated thoroughly on my testimony. As grueling as the sessions were—bare light shining above, tape recorder going, questions fired from all directions in a small room—I was relieved to be doing something instead of wasting my life doing nothing.

On November 1 I was suspended from the force, but because I was still to report to IAD to aid in their investigation and because the United States attorney and the Manhattan and Kings County district attorneys exerted actual or implied pressure on the police commissioner, I was kept on the payroll. That was the first time someone had been suspended with pay in the history of the New York City Police Department.

After hours and hours of questioning, when it was believed I was drained dry of any information, I began a God-awful stretch sitting on a bench in the IAD waiting room, again, doing nothing. The longest time in my life before this experience that I had been idle was for two weeks in 1965 when I was confined to bed after suffering a leg injury in a softball game. It was murder then; it was worse now. I was to sit and rot, alone, staring at four walls eight hours a day for four months.

At first I read everything I could get my hands on: newspapers, magazines, books. There was plenty of time to think and I mulled over my past five years on the job, constantly dwelling on my racism, an attitude that had truly bothered me. If nothing else, during those miserable months of solitude, I was able to place things in their proper perspective and return to normalcy in regard to the Blacks and their plight.

Few men chose to talk to me and those who did were too busy to devote more than five minutes of their time. I craved conversation and companionship, but there was none. Long days of loneliness and ennui can easily drive a man to the brink of insanity. The men on the job, who a short time before had made me wealthy with friends, no longer wanted anything to do with me. Instead of warm hellos and enjoyable hours of shooting the shit, I was met with snide remarks and obscene language whenever I was recognized by another officer. My ease of mind at the sight of another patrolman, a brother in blue, especially in a tight fix, and my assurance of a friend, even if I did not know him, turned to paranoia and the feeling of a potential enemy. I was ostracized not because I was guilty of lying, but because I had dared to tell the truth. Yet, I blamed no one for their reactions, for most probably I would have reacted the same, had I been on the outside looking in.

The hours in "my room" also provided me with ample time to contemplate my future. I had still not received any guarantees of immunity from the district attorney or leniency from the police commissioner. I could only hope that they were able to appreciate the difficulty and value of what I had done. From day to day I had to wonder if I was to be arrested. Heaven knows there were many who would have been delighted to see just that happen. One in particular, a lieutenant in the internal affairs division, kept telling me how he was oiling up his handcuffs every night, just waiting to slap them on my wrists. He said that if I were not arrested and dismissed from the force, which he was doing everything in his power to bring about, he would put his retirement papers in as a demonstration of protest. He tormented me every day in an effort to provoke me into an act I would regret. I had seriously contemplated breaking his nose with a swift right, but understood fully that an act of that nature would surely destroy any hope that I had of being restored to duty.

There was, however, another lieutenant who gave me needed confidence that everything would work out in the end. He suggested I use my eight hours a day studying for the upcoming sergeant's exam. In addition, I am quite certain that the head of the division, Chief Sidney Cooper, was in my corner. They were probably the only two and I thank them sincerely for understanding. It was a pleasant thought that the police commissioner would lift my suspension. If I was dismissed, I would have to take whatever work was available to an admitted thief, regardless of the circumstances, fired from the Police Department. I wanted reinstatement very much. But, then, where would I work? And with whom? I no longer had a place in the department.

Then, one day in February, I picked up the newspaper and gasped at the headline: "Knapp Cop Indicted." I ripped the page in half in my effort to get to the story. It was only in the second paragraph that I realized it referred to Patrolman Phillips. The Manhattan district attorney's office had indicted him for murder, alleging that he was responsible for the shooting of a Manhattan pimp and one of his girls around Christmastime a few years before. I was reassured that day by Chief Cooper that actions taken against Phillips had no bearing whatsoever on me and I breathed a sigh of relief. That case on Phillips is still pending. I have no way in the world of knowing whether he is guilty or not, but I must say the charge was rather convenient for those who would like to see the commission discredited.

Finally, the waiting, the worrying, the pain of not knowing, and the period of idleness and waste was over. At noon on March 8, 1972, I was reinstated as a patrolman. A police officer once more. And now much wiser, much more mature. The police commissioner had shown me that he was able to discern the value of my course and I was truly grateful.

But, as big as the New York City Police Department is, I felt there was no room for me and at 2 P.M., the same date, I elected to resign.

—*June, 1972*

Epilogue

At summer's end, 1972, the Knapp Commission released to the public an initial report of its findings and principal recommendations for combatting police corruption in the future. After lengthy discussions with Mike Armstrong, chief counsel, and the other report writers, and having read the findings as objectively as possible, I felt it appropriate to report my reactions.

Though windy and rhetorical in spots, on the whole the report is constructive and worthy of due consideration by the Police Department and both the city and state administrations. Many good points are raised and the majority of suggestions are valid. However, there are more than a few instances where I disagree with the commission's outlook or where I find their recommendations lacking.

To start, the report does include what I believe should be the main theory on which to base their uphill battle—the pride of the policeman—yet, judging by the brief mention of it, the commission almost missed its significance. "We believe," they state, "that, given proper leadership and support, many police who have slipped into corruption would exchange their illicit income for the satisfaction of belonging to a corruption-free department in which they could take genuine pride." Moreover, I believe that the force that unites police officers in venality, if channeled correctly, can be used to combat corruption. Often a policeman feels that pride and loyalty to the group are his most prized possessions. Which leads me to the next point.

Contrary to the commission's belief that the department's official acknowledgment of the extent to which corruption actually exists in the city "can hardly damage its image," I feel its image would indeed be tarnished. By the same token, their contention that a policeman whose commander denies the existence of widespread corruption can only conclude that he is either "hopelessly naïve or content to let the corruption continue" is not entirely true. There are various reasons for a commander to deny the existence of corruption. I think it is obvious to many men that a commander cannot admit to widespread corruption without irreparably hurting his rank-and-file and, it seems plain to me, admitting his own ineptitude. It is one of his duties to stick up for his men and his department. I shudder to think of the detrimental effect an outright admission of guilt would have on an already demoralized force. And let us not forget this country is built on the notion of being innocent until proven guilty. However, I do agree that the best course for the department is to temporarily swallow its pride, as painful as that might be, and admit to its shortcomings, with the knowledge that ultimately the members will benefit by it. It hurts a bit to think of the respect the men of other police departments across the country enjoy —men no farther afield than the troopers on the New York State Thruway, for example—while the men of the New York City Police Department are subject to constant ridicule. Yet, the only way to attain that respect and create that desired image is to root out the corrupt tradition inlaid in the department now and join forces to keep it out forever.

I support the recent appointment of the special deputy attorney general as overseer, so to speak, whose job is "to investigate and prosecute all crimes involving corruption in the criminal process"—if for no other reason than because there *is* a corruption problem in the city and it's serious enough to warrant a separate and distinct office, with no ties to the department, to keep it in check.

I also agree with the suggestion to reorganize the department's Inspectional Services Bureau, in which the anti-corruption forces are housed, along the lines of the Inspections Office of the Internal Revenue Service, in an effort to concentrate a bit more on the *problem* at hand; under the proposed plan, the agents of this office can expect to spend their careers there and thus never need worry about serving with or being commanded by a person they have investigated. As much as I favor the periodic rotation of policemen to give them a feel of every aspect of the department—not suggested by the commission, incidentally—I do feel that the corruption unit is one that should recruit dedicated men who would not move once they are accepted.

It's about time somebody brought the anachronistic Sabbath laws to the public's attention. The idea that certain stores should not sell specific goods on Sunday went out with the custom of washing your weary houseguest's feet. The recommendation that the gambling laws be relaxed is another step in the right direction. Only the members of organized crime syndicates stand to suffer when the state takes off-track betting to the next level, which includes legalizing policy bets and sports bets. In the same vein, a careful study and revision of the laws pertaining to the construction, liquor, bar, and restaurant industries are in order, as well as a reconsideration and definition of responsibilities. As stated in the commission's report: "It is ridiculous to have an armed police officer wasting his time (and that of his partner and supervising sergeant) checking restaurant washrooms to find out whether they are properly supplied with soap."

I must confess, however, that I did not find very constructive the commission's proposal for a blanket transfer of responsibility wherever a regulatory agency has jurisdiction, regardless of the truism that policemen are apt to "pursue vigorously a corrupt public official who is not one of their own" (if for no other reason in the current climate than to shift the spotlight). The commission assumes that "corruption in other agencies—undesirable as it is—has far less impact upon the body politic than corruption among the police," and recognizes that the redelegation of power will not eliminate corruption but merely transfer it to other agencies. This leaves a great deal to be desired and is not an adequate foundation on which to base their proposal.

I am in full accord with the suggestion to arrest any and all bribers and to make public such arrests as an additional deterrent.

I concur, too, with the advice that the department establish a central personnel file to facilitate investigations and furnish replies to legitimate inquiries. The commission suggests also that the internal affairs division maintain a confidential dossier containing "all facts and allegations concerning a police employee's career." I conditionally agree. Contrary to the view of the commission, I think the member of the force under investigation should be told of the existence of this file upon completion of a fruitless investigation on an unfounded charge or upon acquittal. He would then have the right—as does any unconvicted civilian in a criminal court—to have all traces of that case destroyed and stricken from the record. It should only be maintained during an investigation and kept after a conviction. At one time the simple fact that a man had been arrested —regardless of the disposition—was enough to keep him off the job. We have progressed to a point where now each case is individually reviewed and even a misdemeanor conviction might be overlooked for an applicant if circumstances are extenuating. In line with this, I feel that any record of unproven allegations held against a man would be a regression on the part of the department.

I understand the importance and the emphasis that the commission places on the strict enforcement of the departmental regulation that all meetings with gamblers, criminals, or persons involved in illegal activities be recorded, but I can personally attest to the impossibility of making such a report at a spontaneous meeting without defeating the purpose of the department. Therefore, I must obviously disagree with the strong language of the commission in stating that "Departmental charges be brought against violators in *all* instances. The validity of the excuse for such meetings should bear only upon the penalties imposed." If that suggestion is followed to the letter it would be unfair to many an innocent policeman who might suffer as a result of his zeal to do his job and aid both the department and the public. Is he expected to say, "Wait a minute while I report this meeting," to a gambler or informant when bumping into him by chance in the street, where an opportunity of obtaining useful information is a distinct possibility?

The recommendation that the Administrative Code be revised to broaden certain powers of the police commissioner is long overdue. At present, when disciplining a police officer convicted in departmental proceedings, the police commissioner's only alternative for punishment more severe than a 30-day loss of pay or vacation is dismissal. This is a sizable gap that should be filled. In addition, I believe the police commissioner should have the power to demote a man one rank lower than his present civil service rank when the gravity of the offense calls for it. For example, a captain could be broken to lieutenant, a lieutenant to sergeant, and a sergeant to patrolman. It may come as a surprise to many a reader that this alternative is not presently available to the commissioner.

The way it stands now, if a man is dismissed from the force he automatically forfeits his pension. There are no exceptions to this rule and there is no consideration of his prior record, the reason for his dismissal, or the number of years served. A dismissed member's only recourse is the Court of Appeals. I think the commission captures my sentiments adequately when it states: "Although a police commissioner should be able to dismiss any policeman found to be corrupt, it by no means follows that a single act of corruption justifies what may amount to a fine of several hundred thousand dollars, the commuted value of many officers' vested pension rights. No civilian would be subjected to a comparable penalty." The commission's solution of separating pension proceedings and departmental proceedings is simple enough and likewise commendable.

On one hand, the commission recognizes the problem of excessive red tape involved when handling property or evidence, yet they turn around and suggest that a daily report, in duplicate "at least," reporting the officer's every move, be submitted after every tour because they found the memo books, which are retained by the officers, often "uniformly useless." Please, no more forms. The idea of a daily report is sound, but the method sour. I like the memo books, with perhaps a bit more scrutiny. The policeman is inundated with so many forms and reports, I think the department should be striving to decrease, rather than increase, them. The less red tape the better, and, as a result, the less chance of breaking departmental rules and procedures aimed at professionalism.

The commission recommends that informants be paid by the department. As an ex-police officer with an above-average share of activity, I know full well how big a role informants play in criminal arrests and I wholeheartedly agree.

I firmly believe all uniformed officers should wear name tags, as the commission suggests. I must go one step further in quest of professionalism and better public relations by recommending that uniformed policemen "quick salute" a civilian who addresses them in the street. It would be difficult not to be impressed by a police officer who salutes you when you approach him for directions. It should not be necessary to stand erect, chest out, gut in, and so on. A simple hand-to-cap gesture would suffice and certainly go a long way in projecting a good image.

It is hard to imagine how anyone could have let the contrary happen, but I agree with the commission on "an absolute ban against the swearing in of police officers until their background investigations have been finished and reviewed."

The concept of a National Police Academy for sincere applicants seeking a police career is not only intriguing and challenging, but downright good sense. Setting it up on a plane with the service academies across the country, with a three- or four-year obligation upon graduation, is the best idea.

In regard to present members of the force, it would not be too farfetched to have all police officers attend college on city time. As long as the men were being paid while attending, I'm sure there wouldn't be too many beefs from their line organizations, and the department would be investing in a better educated force.

The commission closes their report with a recommendation that "general information concerning corruption should be prepared and made available to all communications media showing the changes and dispositions of all departmental actions against corrupt officers by rank and command." They even go so far as to imply that publishing the names of the accused officers is a good idea. I feel that an attack against corruption can be waged effectively without subjecting the department to wide-scale exposure of disciplinary charges. This tactic, moreover, would give anti-police forces ammunition to fire at the police and in the long run would damage the image of the department. Moreover, innocent men would be implicated. Publishing names is ridiculous and should be forgotten immediately. Disciplinary action against the offender is punishment enough, and the department has no right to subject his family to unnecessary ridicule. *I know.*

The other recommendations of the report can generally be considered to be in accord with my thoughts, but not worth going into.

There are, however, some points to be made that the commission either ignored or failed to uncover. It is apparent to me that the police commissioner is fully aware of the existing conditions of corruption in the department. It would be paradoxical for him to wage such a large-scale war if he himself didn't think corruption was widespread.

I deem it a good idea to introduce business-minded people into the department who would be concerned with production and efficiency, as the police commissioner has done. The department has been for years a very good example of the poor business management typical of a municipal organization. The simple fact that payroll can't get an overtime check to a policeman until two or three months after it's due, when private industry—in corporations with a lot more employees—can have it for their workers the following week, is very disconcerting and an obvious sign of the need for improvement.

I feel there should be more incentives and rewards for good work on the job. The practice of policemen being permitted to accept unsolicited Christmas gifts should be investigated thoroughly and not thought to be completely out of the question. In addition, there should be more promotion incentives, including the possibility of two new ranks—one stripe and two—between patrolman and sergeant. As it stands now, the general idea most men have is that if you don't pass the sergeant's exam or have a "hook" to help you become a detective, you are doomed to the position of career patrolman and are therefore very unenthusiastic about excessive activity. If merit and production played a more important role in promotion, I feel there would be a new wave of positive thinking in the department.

Finally, I must place emphasis on the point that I feel certainly demanded more attention than it received from the commission report writers. It is imperative that the anti-corruption campaign be concentrated in the Police Academy. The rookies are the key to future success and if they can be made to see and understand the *problem* of corruption, then maybe one day police officers in New York City will be able to enjoy a reputation as men of unquestioned integrity whose positions are among the most respectable and prestigious in the world. The pride of New York would have no one to thank but themselves.

Afterword

As an afterthought I would like to say that I feel I did the right thing when I came back from California and agreed to work for the Knapp Commission. It was a chance to square myself. When I learned of the public hearings I saw a chance to show the rest of the men on the job what it might cost if they were caught. I saw a turnaround in the department where in the future a police officer would be able to testify that all of the men he worked with were *honest*, and I hoped that perhaps my testimony would contribute to that change. I saw an end to the system, the tradition, the *problem*.

If, by testifying, I have convinced just one patrolman that instead of accepting a bribe, he should arrest, without exception, the person offering the money, then I have done my job. I have cooperated 100 percent with the commission and the department since coming back, and I would like to think I have accomplished a lot more.

I will miss being a police officer. I will miss the uniform. I will miss the exhilarating feeling and excitement of riding through the streets on patrol. Despite the current low morale, I will miss the pride. I will miss the search for true police professionalism; I will be unable to strive for that goal effectively as a civilian. But, above all, I will miss the friends. None more so than my partner. There are no better men in this world. There is no more difficult kind of work.

As for my apparent escape from prosecution, I still have no guarantees of immunity. I will simply state that my family and I have suffered immeasurably and irreparably—more than anyone will ever know—and I fear it is not over. I've paid for my mistake many times.